GIRLS CAN BE COWBOYS TOO!
VOLUME I

SNAKES IN THE ATTIC, WILDFIRE, AND
"IF YOU DON'T HAVE A DOG, USE A CAT!"

A tribute to today's Western Woman

By Rose Miller

OTHER BOOKS BY ROSE MILLER

Girls Can Be Cowboys Too! Volume II

The Horse That Wouldn't Trot

Mules, Mules and More Mules

Dogs, Dogs and More Dogs

The Gospel of Visitation (mostly by husband, Hal Miller)

Schnauzer Territory (coming)

www.rosemiller.net

IN APPRECIATION

A very special thank you to my very dear friend, Nadine Nel. She graciously drove main roads and some not-so-main roads as together we traipsed the Arizona countryside meeting with many of these special women. Her companionship and driving skills made the writing of this book even more of a delight.

And huge thanks to the awesome gals who shared their charming and inspiring stories. I feel very honored to have met you and written this book.

Also thanks to Bob Whitney for all his support.

TABLE OF CONTENTS

Introduction

When we first moved from Indiana to Arizona, I endeavored to meet my local ranch women neighbors. The first one, Kim McElroy was a hoot to talk with and soon we both were laughing our heads off as we shared animal escapades, and how we survived them. Not long after that I put the finishing touches on my Dog memoir: *Dogs, Dogs and More Dogs* and wondered if I was going to stop writing, or if just maybe another book was waiting to be written—a book about wonderfully strong, funny and hard-working ranch women. I was going to call it *Ranch Wives* but I ran out of bona fide ranch wives (although they were much *more* than wives— more like ranch partners). When I asked for referrals, I began to receive the names of an eclectic group of ladies, but all had two things in common: the love of animals and land.

Then a problem occurred. I had so many wonderful stories, I decided not to cut any out, but the book became 523 pages long. After it was first printed in 2018, I made the decision in 2019, to split the book into Volume I and Volume II.

Read slowly and savor each unique tale!

KIM McELROY
Broken Horn D Ranch

I met Kim in 2012 shortly after my retired chiropractor husband, Hal, and our son, Bob, moved to Prescott, Arizona from Indiana. To meet new friends and neighbors, I relied on introductions from others and "cold calling" to see if I could come visit. It was lonely for me, as we had moved from a close knit family community on our horse farm to the "wilderness" of Las Vegas Ranch Estates, about 25 miles north of town. Several of the old time ranches had been broken up into lots for homes. We were fortunate to now live on one, but neighbors were not close by.

Mom, Dad, my sister Linda, and her family of husband and seven children and my own family (with four children) lived in homes on five acres set aside from our 140 acre horse farm in Indiana. Ever since I was a four-year-old child, I had wanted to move to a farm and *raise horses*. Eventually, I got that chance in Goshen, Indiana where I raised, trained, showed and judged Tennessee Walking horses. That breed was required because my back shuddered at the thought of riding a trot. It was a family affair and my family neighbors were only yards from my home. We were ready for a change when Hal retired; we fell in love with Prescott, the Arizona weather, and our new home. What I wasn't ready for was not knowing anyone. With horses, mules, dogs and cats, I missed my old support system of close family and the ladies who boarded their horses at the New Acre Farm.

Kim was the first ranch lady I phoned to see if I could visit. One of my new doctors, the late Dr. Heidi Hartman-Taylor, upon hearing I had horses and mules said, "You have to meet Kim, you will love her," and gave me Kim's business card. (They sell organic grass-fed beef.) It

2

took a few weeks before we got connected, but finally the day arrived.

Kim was easy to talk to, and soon we were talking our heads off—and laughing. It helped that she had come from her own training barn in Ohio, as that gave us a connection and background that I could relate to. She trained "English style": hunter jumper, dressage, combined training (jumping, dressage and cross country), and was actually very happy with what she was doing—except for the stinky weather—I also could relate to that! Northern Indiana and northern Ohio surely did have that in common.

She and husband Dave Pawel came to the Phoenix area to visit family one Christmas about 19 years ago. Leaving Ohio in 22 below zero weather and coming to the sunshine in Arizona eventually persuaded them to move here. Yep, us too! Another interesting thing to me was what I call her "God experience." Deciding to move is one thing, but there is a lot involved, most importantly, selling one's existing residence and sometimes a business. Kim told me, "I put my training establishment on the market, thinking, I will see what happens, and in a few months, it had sold!" So many other "imported" gals I have chatted with tell the same story: something happened and it all worked out. Same thing happened with us. One could only surmise we are supposed to be here in this lovely God-given country. Their first ranch was in New River, Arizona, where Kim again trained horses. But this time it was western training: cutting, roping, western pleasure. To train horses to work cows, they got some cows—and buffalo! "You used buffalo to rope?" I asked, stunned.

"No, used them for cutting, and cows for roping. We bought two cows, Number One and Number Two. After they got too large for roping, we bred them."

"What breed were they?"

"Corriente."

Kyle, my farrier in Indiana, had raised this breed, so I was somewhat familiar with it. The Corriente descended from Spanish animals brought to the Americas in the late 15th century by Columbus. Kyle was into rodeo, and this breed is used for sport events as they are tough, quick and have horns (useful for roping and bulldogging). As Kim explained, "They will work for you, they don't quit on you. After you have worked a Hereford for a few minutes, they just stop and look at you." Maybe the Hereford is smarter, I wondered. Kim laughed. "No, they are just bred for beef with short legs and a stocky body."

When we moved to Arizona, I began seeing herds of Corriente, including Kim and Dave's. They are a smaller cow, with long horns, are easy keepers, require less water and can live well on sparse open range. They have become popular for their meat which is leaner than most modern beef cattle. I had wondered how Kim and Dave had decided on the Corriente. I was beginning to see. First two cows, then calves, and later a bull named Foghorn...

Typically, the Broken Horn D ranch keeps their cows in small groups, each with a bull. The bulls keep their ladies together and look out for them, but whenever they meet each other the bulls are civil. No fighting. Another thing the Corriente bulls are valued for is their virility. One of their bulls is 10 years old and still has a 100 percent calf crop with 25 cows.

****

June 18, 2013 dawned just like any other day until around 11:30 a.m. Kim who was working in the yard saw a plume of smoke in the area of Granite Mountain about eight miles southeast of them. As she watched it got bigger and bigger. Fire! Pre-monsoon and so, so dry. Kim called the local fire station and was told the fire was in the Prescott Forest and supposedly under control. "He sounded a little irritated," she said.

"At you?"

"No, I think he was irritated at the Forest Service because they had refused help from Prescott." Turned out he was certainly right to be irritated!

As the day went on the Doce fire, as it was named, got larger and larger, soon to encompass 5,000 acres and getting close to a herd of their cows that was pastured in the area.

Toward afternoon, Dave called some of his cowboy buddies, and they assured him they were available to help evacuate if needed. The fire was crazy. It burned hot and fast and the wind was fickle. Arizona had been particularly dry the last few seasons and the Manzanita and other brush were extremely flammable. The air temperature was hot with very low humidity.

The American Ranch development was in the fire's path and the people were told to evacuate. Should they evacuate the herd? Their Dove

Tail pasture was close to American Ranch. Even if the herd was safe from fire, later when the monsoon rains came, all the ash from the hill side could be washed into the stream where they drank, and that would be a problem. So, Dave decided to go ahead with getting the herd out.

Hooking up all their trailers, loading their horses and joining with friends with their stock trailers, five of them headed to the herd of 20 cows, their calves, plus one bull. But where would they find the cattle? It was late in the afternoon by now and if they had to round them up from the *really* rough and hilly 900-acre pasture, time might not be on their side. But Kim had a thought.

"You know," she told Dave, "I bet they are going to be right down in the creek. They always are this time of the afternoon, it is cool, and they want water and the green grass." But Dave wanted to sweep the pasture to be sure there were no stragglers. It was steep, straight up, straight down and rocky. Fortunately, the men knew the pasture as they had worked it before.

Kim rode up to the top of a close ridge and could see, yes indeed, the cows were right there by the stream. She called and told Dave they were here, but she couldn't count them because of the bends in the creek. He wanted to continue to check, and it was a good thing too because there was a cow way up on the ridge with a tiny baby calf lying under a large oak bush. Secluding herself to calve is normal behavior for a cow. They will normally keep away from the herd until the baby is about three days old, but this one was about two and a half miles from the corrals.

Kim said, "It was obvious that the cow and the day-old calf were not going to go all the way down the steep rocky hillside to the corral and trailers, and since the fire didn't seem to be an immediate threat, Dave decided to leave them there and go back later for them."

"Why didn't you put the calf over the saddle and have the cow follow?" I asked. "There are many paintings of cowboys doing that."

"First, I don't think any of *our* horses would be agreeable, and actually, it is seldom done—it makes a better painting than reality. Second, I doubt that cow would follow. When you pick the baby calves up, the mothers lose the scent, and cannot find them. In an emergency, it would be worth trying, but here Dave thought the pair was safe enough."

All the other cows, the bull, and the babies were herded into the permanent corral with a cattle chute; the cows and the bull were loaded into trailers with the babies in separate trailers. There were 20 cows with their calves so the trailers were pretty stuffed. You didn't want to leave anyone behind as you might separate a cow from her calf. Plus it was getting late. The idea was to keep the bovine stress to a minimum. It was also safer to separate the momma cows from the calves and put them in separate trailers because if you put wrong family members together it would be dangerous for the calves. The horses had to have a ride home too, so it was quite a caravan. By now it was 6 p.m., and fortunately, it was only a short ten miles to the Crossroads pasture where they would be unloaded.

To unload, they backed all the trailers up to the holding pen beside each other, removed a few of the metal pen panels to enlarge the opening and let them all out together. They held the cattle in the pens until the cows and calves found each other and had settled down. By this time, it was dark and as they drove back home they could see the ominous, horrible blaze of the fire coming down Granite Mountain, getting closer and closer to the American Ranch development. It was chilling.

The Crossroad pasture already had a herd, complete with bull, and the two bulls had a few words and snorts for each other and then the new bull took his ladies to another part of the grazing land and they stayed that way until weaning time in the fall.

The next day Dave took the trailer to that upper area, using a different route to get the errant cow and her calf. He roped the cow and was able to haul her into the trailer.

This, Kim explained, was a system. You tied the cow in the trailer with the rope that was around her horns. Then you put on another rope, run it through the front of the trailer, and using your horse to pull, you encouraged her into the trailer. It was much easier if you had another person to persuade the rear end of the cow, but Dave got her in. This was one of their older cows and in the past had experience with being "helped" in other situations. So she wasn't too shocked at the whole affair.

Next he went for the calf, thinking he could rope its hind feet, catch it and take to trailer. However, the calf didn't respond to Dave's presence. Kim explained, "When the mommas leave their very young babies, they tell them, 'stay here until I return.' When you come across them, they hunker down and stretch out their necks and look up at you through their eyelashes, but don't move. They think you are a predator. I have even almost stepped on some when I was on horseback scouting for babies. Of course, if you aren't careful and get really close, they likely will jump up and run, which you don't want because at least half the time they will run in the wrong direction—*away* from mom.

"But this baby wasn't even getting up, so Dave got off his horse…"

"Hey," I interrupted, "Do you ground tie your horses like we see in the movies when you get off for something like this?" I had really wondered about that. I had trained my show horses that competed in Trail Obstacle classes to ground tie, but I sure would never want to count on them in an open 900 acres.

"No! We hang on to them, or maybe hobble the horses if we are working, like fixing a fence. You sure don't want to be without a horse out here! So Dave walked up to the baby, but still the calf stayed put. Now Dave is thinking that there is something wrong with the calf. He decided that it couldn't see—he was blind. He picked him up—not too hard as it was only two days old—and with his trusty cow horse in hand, put the tiny baby in the back seat of the four-door dually truck. With momma and his cow horse in separate sections of the trailer and the calf riding shotgun, they headed back to headquarters. We named him Doce after the fire. He lived there with the cow all summer.

"Later that season we had a doggie calf, his mom had died from hardware disease. So sad that with all the grazing available, the cows can still pick up pieces of metal, wire, or trash and eventually will die. When we bought our ranch, it was covered in junk and as much as we clean it up, now and then a cow will still find a piece of 'death.' Cows are indiscriminate grazers, grabbing with their tongues and whatever happens to be there goes down the gullet.

"We named that calf Munchkin and the calves lived together. So Doce had his own 'seeing eye' buddy growing up."

"You said you had 'terrorized' Doce's momma before, as she was one of your older cows. What happened?

"Well," Kim explained, "soon after we bought her, we had a big coyote problem, and Dave was worried they might get the calf, so we decided to bring her into headquarters. She wasn't that far away from the ranch corrals, but the cow had other thoughts and didn't want to leave. Dave picked up the calf, thinking the cow would surely follow him, but the momma lost the scent of her calf after a few steps, so he had to keep going back to let her smell her calf and try again. It took two hours to get them over here to the pens! She was used to us intervening in her life. We still have 'Number 37' and she is a good mother."

The fire never got to the Dove Tail area, but debris from the fire did wash into the creek, along with slurry that was used to put out the fire. It would take months for the pasture to be useful again. The Doce fire was man-started, burned 6,767 acres, and was essentially out on June 23, having burned for six days. Although a moderately large fire fought with more than 500 firefighters, heavy air tankers and numerous large helicopters, it burned more or less true to a wildfire. No fire-crew person was injured, which was absolutely amazing and miraculous, considering how close to the fire many of them came in protecting the American Ranch development. No structures were lost either. It was an incredible outcome.

But soon to follow the Doce fire would be a monster fire, not so much in actual size but horrifying; one that did not burn in a predicted or hoped for pattern—one that would have disastrous and dreadful results.

Toward the end of June, the weather patterns over Arizona shift. Moist air from Mexico flows in from the south, and thunderstorms are born. This is the "monsoon" season. As the storms build in the higher elevations along the Mogollon Rim (an approximate 200-mile-long escarpment running east to west that divides the upper from the lower elevations of Arizona), they suck in desert heat with the moist air from Mexico, then move to lower areas and dump their welcome moisture.

On Friday, June 28, just ten days after the Doce fire started, a series of dry lightning strikes hit the rocky and extremely dry brush of the Yarnell Hill area. Perhaps if this had happened a few weeks later, rain would more likely have accompanied that lightning. Then the story could have been quite different. By mid-morning on Sunday, the fire was traveling northeast on a mile-wide front. And then it happened…

A big storm front, advancing *from* the north, bringing exceptionally high winds and no rain, changed the direction and increased the ferocity of the inferno on Yarnell Hill. It was later determined that winds in excess of 50 miles per hour, with flame lengths estimated at 70 feet, tilted to near horizontal as the fire rapidly exploded through the area, trapped and enveloped 19 of the 20 Prescott-based Granite Mountain Hotshots. Their protective shields were no match for the estimated 2,000-degree heat. Only their lookout was spared.

These were among the same brave and courageous firefighters who had so valiantly fought and conquered the Doce fire. It was the worst national wildfire disaster since the South Canyon fire near Glenwood Springs, Colorado, where 14 firefighters had perished in

1994.

Prescott still mourns this horrendous loss.

Our family is from the Midwest, and much too familiar with tornados. In 1965, we lost everything but our lives to one of those monsters. We lived with tornado watches, warnings and area tornadoes for nearly 50 years until we moved to Arizona. I had worried, watched and prayed for my human and animal family in Indiana. What had I gotten into now? My appreciation and even awe for the ranchers and others who live in this beautiful, but sometimes dangerous area, increased after hearing of Kim and Dave's evacuation. It is good to have amazing friends.

****

"Kim, tell me the story about Dave, the yearling steer, and the Baltimore Northern & Santa Fe railroad tracks."

"Well, it happened last year on the K8, which is part of the forest service lease the Camp Wood Cattle Company uses. The CCC raises cattle, but also buys additional yearlings in the fall and puts them there over the winter. Typically these are Black Angus. Yearlings are probably the worst—like a group of teenagers—to deal with. Part is their age and part is their life experience. With our cows, they know when they see someone on horseback, they are going to be gathered up, they know where the water is—they get used to the routine, and the calves get that education also. When you buy a group of "outside" steers, they don't know where they are.

"When you dump a bunch of cows into a strange area, they *have* to walk the perimeter, whether it is two or two thousand acres. And yearlings do the same thing. I have seen them get into a corner of a pasture and especially if it is less than ninety degrees, they get stuck. The leaders get in the corner and say, 'Yup, can't go any farther,' and the ones in the back keep coming. Next thing you know there are 50 of them stuck in the corner. Then they push the leaders *through* the fence, and now they are out.

"It is very common for a group to get 'blowed up' in a corner, maybe during a storm, and they will just stand there. And so on a good yearling operation, someone is out there all the time on horseback—getting them out of the corner, being sure they get to water, making sure they are 'using the country', not just eating in one small area and then wondering where the food has gone. This is another good thing about our

9

Corriente cattle. They will 'use the country' on their own, traveling all over their pastures."

"I know I am not a rancher," I said grinning, "but why don't they just put an old cow in with them to show them how to live? Keep them out of the corners?"

"Some do, but they don't always stay together. We put some older steers in one of our pastures with the younger ones, hoping that might happen, but they don't really hang out together. I wonder if the older steers look at the younger ones and think, '*really—why would you do that?*'

"So, Dave is over at the K8 making sure the yearlings are OK—walking around, moving them a little, gathering up stragglers, looking for sickness—all this keeps the cattle sort of gentle too, so when it comes time to gather them in the fall, they aren't quite as wild. Anyway, he realizes he is missing three. Cattle sometimes lean through the wire fencing for a blade of grass—which is always greener on the other side—and then 'fall through.' Especially if they are in the forest service leases you really want to keep a close eye on them. There is a railroad that runs through there and Dave could tell by the cow tracks that they had gotten through the fence onto the railroad right-of-way. Luckily there are gates along the right of way, so Dave could get through. He was able to chase two yearlings back through the gate, but one escaped.

"The lone steer ended being out there for two days, and Dave had to get it back really soon, as it had no water. Finally, Dave finds the steer, and the chase and challenge is on. First of all, these are not horned cattle, they are big, stocky Angus, so you have to rope them around the neck. If you can do it, you rope them around the neck and get a front leg too, that way you don't choke them and shut off their oxygen. Then they are *really* stupid! Also, roping in an arena for sport or practice is nothing like roping along a railroad right-of-way. It is a 'forever straight' run, with rocks and holes in your path.

"Dave ropes it—around the neck—gets it dallied to his saddle horn, and then he hears a train coming."

The BNSF train only runs about four times a day, so this is just plain bad luck.

"Dave is on Badger, who could buck if he cared to," Kim continued. "He wouldn't have been the first choice for this situation. Dave is thinking, 'I am going to die here...' He wasn't about to let the steer go as it took days to find him, the steer really did need water, and if he let him lose, being a yearling, he probably would run right in front of the big scary locomotive, so Dave dallies the steer on as short a rope as he can around the saddle horn, and backs up close to the right-of-way fence and just prays that all goes well. As the train roars past, Dave nods to the engineer; old Badger stands still, the yearling stands, and the train charges on."

All in a cowboy's day's work!

Kim's comment: Sometimes it is better to hear about things *after* they happen.

"So, I take it you like a cow and calf operation better than buying and finishing steers?"

"Yes," Kim answered, "but there can be situations with them too. One spring we were watching the cows at headquarters that were soon to calve. We had a first-calf heifer (one having her first baby) and had been watching her closely as first-time mommas can have more problems than an older cow. She was big bellied, looked like she had swallowed a 50-gallon drum, and then one day, the belly was gone, her milk bag was full of milk, but she had no baby—and she was *totally* unconcerned. Dave got his horse and went looking, but couldn't find it. Baby calves (as well as all babies) need the first milk—the colostrum—which is full of antibodies from the momma cow soon after birth. There is a small window where the baby can utilize those antibodies and it was getting to be past that point for this calf.

"We got a search group, some on horses, some on quads, and the dogs, and fanned out to search. The cow was still in the area and *still* totally indifferent. Usually if a cow has hidden her calf, she would get nervous or be in attack mode seeing a bunch of invaders about. One of the dogs finally found the calf. It was a tiny little thing, maybe only weighed 30 pounds (normal calves weigh around 60 pounds). Dave picked it up and carried it to the momma, thinking our problems were over, but no, the cow took one look at the calf and said, 'Nope, not mine.' This is very unusual for our Corriente cows. They generally are superior mommas.

"So we took it to the house along with the reluctant cow. We put the cow in the cattle chute we use for doctoring, and milked her. Then I had to run to the store and buy a lamb nipple that was small enough for the tiny calf's mouth. I did this a couple times a day for about a month. When the calf would get hungry it would go stand beside the chute. Eventually, the young cow took the calf and became a good momma

11

cow."

****

Kim lives close enough to me that I can visit now and then. Every time I go, I am surrounded by many dogs.

"How do you get your dogs?" I asked. "Any special ones that stand out?"

"Many are dogs that just wander in, I don't know where they come from. We surely are not close to a busy road. Some are rescued from other circumstances. For instance, this is Tres that you are petting. He has a story. About eight years ago, Dave was driving to Bagdad (Arizona) every day building a house on Wild Horse Ranch. Along the back-country road through the National Forest that he had to take to get there, he saw three puppies all alone along the road. Dave thought that was strange, so when he saw them again the next day, he decided to rescue them.

"He stopped on his way home and tried to get them, but they were really skittish and ran off. He left an uneaten sandwich for them. The next day as he was driving, he saw them from a distance, curled up in some leaves in the sun. I remember it was December 17 and it was cold. So he parked his truck a ways a way and *crawled* up real slow on his hands and knees so they didn't see him coming. From past experience seeing them, he figured out that the tri colored one (Tres) was the most timid. He thought if he could get that one, he would be in good shape. He managed to grab the puppy and put him in his shirt and got him in the truck. Then he went back and got the black and white one, and the white one followed him to the truck.

"Then he calls me and tells me he is bringing home three puppies. I think it will be hard to find homes for them as it is right before Christmas—and we do not need anything more to do, but of course we keep them. We put them in an empty horse stall with food and water and sat with them now and then to get them gentled, but my goodness, they were so timid. After several days they got less afraid and we let them out into the barn after we closed the doors. I had several old hounds at the time; Slick was a black female, arthritic, and nearly deaf. She would just stand there and let the puppies sniff and look at her.

"Dave does these animal narrations: 'What is that? Is it alive? I don't know, she looks like she is dead, she isn't even moving. Let's get up a little closer.' All the while Old Slick is standing totally oblivious to

12

the pups.

"We named them Zip, Whitey and Tres. They became the most loyal dogs, and then they got sick. I think it was parvo; Zip passed away, but we had Whitey and Tres for a long time, and as you see Tres is still here. At the same time we had these two, I took a puppy from a litter a friend had. The momma dog was a Chow and had wandered in ready to give birth, so my friend had puppies to find homes for. She thought I had to have one. What are friends for, right?

"Three of the pups were similar looking, but the fourth one was big, leggy and looked like a sheepdog. Obviously, they had different fathers, which isn't all that uncommon when dogs are running lose. I took that one and named her Pooh Bear. She was a sight hound and would lie and watch for things to chase. One day I was riding my horse checking cattle and Pooh Bear was following along. All of a sudden, she sees a coyote in the distance. She takes off just loping along on her long legs and she could run easy. I called her, but she wouldn't come back. I was worried that the coyote would hurt or kill her, but she paid me no mind, just kept running. I could see the coyote turn his head a couple of times and look at my crazy dog. Pooh was getting closer and closer. If I hadn't seen it with my own eyes, I wouldn't have believed it, but Pooh got right up to the coyote and poked him right in the butt with her nose, turned and gleefully ran back to me. She had just wanted to tag him!"

Kim and Dave's cow operation is rather unique in that they raise the calf from new-born to market ready. Selling their organic grass-fed beef is done by finishing the calves on the ranch only on grass, then selling the animal to private buyers as a whole, half or quarter of beef. They transport the animal to the local processing plant themselves. Kim explained that since their calves and cows are transported from various pastures, going to the plant is not the first time they have ever been in a trailer, thus they are not as frightened with a new experience. She said the plant manager says her steers get off the trailer and look around like it is nothing out of the ordinary. This is important because when an animal is frightened and adrenalin is released, that has a deleterious effect on the meat, making it tougher. Kim also mentioned that the person at the processing plant really knows his business and the animals are treated humanely.

I remember when our family lost everything to an Indiana tornado and I had to sell my cow, the buyer said that he wasn't sure he would be able to use the meat. Many animals that met with the same end were unusable. Their meat was actually dark. As meat producers, it behooves one to be considerate of their animals, not just for a moral reason, but also for practicality and good business. Kim and Dave are good examples of this.

"Kim, what is your typical system of 'fall works'? What happens with the cows, bulls and calves?"

"Well, we gather them all in pens, and then sort off the bulls. Some of them are none too happy to leave the ladies. Next, we sort off the calves to be weaned, and they are *really* unhappy to leave the momma cow. Then we run the cows through a chute system so we can give them their vaccinations, one in each side of the neck. One is for Black Leg (a clostridia infection that is deadly) and the other is Vibrio/lepto (venereal diseases that cause abortion). And yes, even organically raised animals can be vaccinated."

"The cows stay in their current pasture, the bulls go into a bull pasture until spring, and the calves we haul to headquarters to finish weaning. There I can see that they eat OK and do not get sick. They bawl their heads off for about three days, and then give it up. We feed nice green alfalfa hay, and soon they are spoiled and looking for the next meal. We also vaccinate the calves now in the fall, as we did in the spring.

"We will keep them in the pens for a couple of weeks. I ride through them for a couple of hours each day, gradually moving them into larger and more pens as I get a handle on them. I also just move them around, split them up, put them back together, and hold them up so they will respect a horse and a person on foot. After a while I will let them drift out into the small two-acre pasture adjacent to the pens. We will continue to feed the alfalfa so they learn to come when we call. Even after they are finally out into the large thirty-acre pasture, I ride through them every day, otherwise they get wild and hard to handle."

One day in our new-found friendship, Kim called and asked if I wanted to go to the Phippen Museum to hear a group of ranch ladies give a talk about their experiences. *Would I?* That sounded fantastic, I was excited and plans were made. About an hour before we were to meet Kim called, "Rose, I am so sorry, I cannot go. Dave has broken down in his truck and I have to go rescue him."

And so it goes in the life of a ranch woman, you have to be prepared for anything…

Kim and Remy, one of her favorite horses
Now retired and living the good life!
Photo by Lorrie Lott

KIMBERLEY KNIGHT
Date Creek Ranch

One of the things that caused me stress when we moved from our horse farm in Indiana was finding veterinarians and a good farrier. Starting all over in new, albeit wonderful Arizona, was hard. Since I no longer showed my horses, they didn't need shoes, but the hot and dry climate of Arizona caused stress on the horses' hooves. I had cracks, abscesses, and sore soles. Riding in Indiana on frequently rained-on soil was easier on their bare feet.

When I discovered Amanda, I not only found an intuitive horse foot trimmer who just seemed to know what to do with a particular animal's hoof (she said she "listens" to the horse), but I also found a friend. When I shared my new book idea with her, she said, "You just *have* to meet Kimberley!" On a later visit Amanda came with her boyfriend and both of them reiterated that I would love Kimberley. "You are like two peas in a pod." After meeting Kimberley, I had to agree!

A problem with interviewing Kimberley was that she was two hours away, and I am an unhappy traveler. So far I had lucked out with my other ranch gals. They lived close by. Enlisting my friend, Nadine Nel, to accompany me and do the driving, we set out. Date Creek Ranch was 2,000 feet lower in elevation from Prescott, at a 3,000-foot elevation, and the temperature and flora changed as we went down. Her ranch was near Congress, Arizona, for anyone who is a map buff.

When we pulled off Highway 93 onto Date Creek Ranch Road and saw the sign saying that the road was "not maintained," I quickly became uncomfortable with having Nadine drive her vehicle over the rocky terrain, rutted from a recent rain. It always seems longer when you travel an unknown path, and this was no exception. We kept going and going, and both of us—in unspoken thoughts—wondered if we had missed a turn. Kimberley had said to call when we were in Congress and she would meet us at her ranch gate entrance. When we got there ahead of her, I tried to call. I could hear her, but she couldn't hear me. Couldn't text either. Hmm yes, somewhat "off the grid!" That would also explain all the solar panels we saw. When we finally saw Kimberley coming down the path on a four-wheeler to the gate, we breathed a sigh of relief.

We followed Kimberley to her house, used the potty, got water and got down to business.

One of my first questions is "How long have you been in Arizona?" because some gals have been born here, and some are transplanted.

"My family settled here in Arizona in the 1870s in the Miami/Globe area (east of Phoenix) and had an apple orchard and lived there for nearly 100 years. My mom was the ranch girl and my dad was a city boy, but he decided he wanted to be a rancher, and bought the present ranch in 1966."

"Why is it called Date Creek Ranch? I don't see any dates."

"There was a military camp close to here called Date Creek in the 1800s and it is thought maybe it got the name because of the Joshua Trees which gets this fruit on them that almost looks like a big date."

We had driven by many beautiful Joshua Trees on the way into the ranch. According to Wikipedia, the name "Joshua Tree" was given by a group of Mormon settlers who crossed the Mojave Desert in the mid-19th century. The tree's unique shape reminded them of a Biblical story in which Joshua reaches his hands up to the sky in prayer. These trees are fast growers for the desert. The trunk is made of thousands of small fibers and lacks annual growth rings. It has a top-heavy branch system, but also has what has been described as a deep and extensive root system, with roots possibly reaching up to 36 feet away. If it survives the rigors of the desert, it can live for hundreds of years with some specimens surviving up to a *thousand* years. The tallest trees reach about 49 feet.

"So, tell me more about your terrain. I heard you telling Nadine that this area is unique in that it has both Joshua trees and saguaro cactus."

"We are right on the border of the Mohave and Sonora Deserts. The Joshua tree only grows in the Mohave Desert and the saguaro cactus is from the Sonora. It is a peculiar mix."

Saguaro cactus is the largest cactus in the United States and will normally reach 40 feet tall. The tallest ever measured was over 78 feet. By 200 years old, the cactus has reached its full height. It is a master at desert survival. The cactus has a five-foot-deep tap root with many shallow roots extending around it only about three inches deep to trap the infrequent desert rains. Very little water is instantly used, but rather is stored in the fleshy sponge-like interior of the cactus for drought times. Some have several "arms" and some have none at all. This cactus is a symbol of the west as so many western movies, books, and pictures feature the saguaro cactus.

About two and half miles of Date Creek runs year around, and another mile or so runs eight months out of the year. By the house it wasn't flowing at present, but Kimberly said in October it probably would start again. The water-ways in Arizona fascinate me, even the drainage arroyos. In some parts the water flows like crazy on top of the grasses, then just like magic, it starts to dig a deep ravine for many feet, maybe miles, and then it stops and once more flows along the top of the ground. Strange to Indiana eyes. When I asked a cowboy about it he just grinned and said, "That is Arizona!" It actually is because part of the ground is clay, but when the water hits a sandy part, it begins digging the ravines. Arizona is a strange mix of the two, side by side.

"So," I asked Kimberley, "how long have *you* been doing this?"

"I grew up on the ranch, later went away to the University of Arizona to study animal science. Then I got a job in Texas working on a ranch for a while, moved back to Phoenix and lived there for ten years. I was a stay at home mom, but when I got divorced I moved back here in 1997."

"I saw from your ranch website that you raise naturally grown meat: grass fed beef and lamb, natural pork and pastured chickens. I am guessing that is your business—how you support yourself. How do people get your meat—you are in the middle of *nowhere!*"

"We go regularly to Phoenix, and the meat is processed in Chino Valley…"

"Yes, I know," I interrupted, "I just saw Kim McElroy and she said she saw you there, and this was the first time you gals had met. She is a fun lady and nice that you are both doing the same thing: good meat for the public."

Kimberley laughed. "Kim said, 'I hear Rose is going to interview you.' Then I put it together that you had sent me her story, so I read it—

finally—and got to know her through your words."

"I actually met you through Amanda and she told me that your ranch horses were barefooted. I thought that was interesting, but hard to believe. How does that work?"

"I met her when she came down to interview me for Western Horseman and we got to talking about barefoot trimming. I said that would never work down here with all the rocks and rough ground, but she thought it would, so we decided to give it a try. Now I really like it, but when we are gathering cattle they can't go barefoot, so we use horse boots, but I can turn the horses out in the rock pastures in their bare feet, and they get tough, hard as nails. Our horses are out 24/7 year around. It took some adjustment. At first when we removed the shoes the feet cracked and broke off, but in a relatively short time they got strong. It is so much better for a horse to be barefoot than have to wear metal shoes."

I agreed as that is what I was able to do after my show horses retired, and the feet definitely were healthier. My mules never wore shoes, but if an animal is ridden down the Grand Canyon for instance, they would need metal shoes. Barefoot is good, but cannot always be used, and you have to be committed to go through some rough patches and, as Kimberley said, use hoof boots where needed.

"The boots are really not made for people like us who work cattle in rough country; they are more for folks like you who trail ride. We have had to totally change our boots so they last."

"So then do you have to put the shoes back on when you do the roundups?"

"No, we use the boots, because if you put the shoes back on, it messes up their feet again, so we use the boots even though they are less than perfect. They are the weak link in our set up."

I wondered if she lost boots while working. I have had them come off now and then while I am riding on the relatively smooth trails. She said they did, and they must check frequently to be sure the boots are on. They are expensive, so it pays to be vigilant. Still, Kimberley agreed that it was worth it. "Now they have these big beautiful feet. They are gorgeous! I love them."

It could sound strange to non-horse people to hear someone go on and on about nice big beautiful feet on their horses, but on a working cow horse, you have to have strong feet. No foot—no horse.

"What kind of horses do you have? Quarter horses no doubt?"

"Well, you know, I laugh and say my best horses are a cross of

Quarter horse and something else. I swear that every registered horse I have has issues usually with their feet or legs."

My own experience with Quarter horses was only what I saw in the show ring when I lived in Indiana. They were not ranch horses. I was captivated by a pasture of mares and babies when we first moved to our new home in Arizona. Our show horses were born in the barn, pampered and trained from day-old babies to be friendly and learn to tie up and be led. These Arizona babies were born in the field and had to withstand cold rains, hot sun, cactus and rough terrain.

I had mentioned this herd to Kim McElroy. She explained that this particular herd was made up of old time Quarter horse mares that had strong bones and feet, not the "show models" that were all muscle and beautiful but perhaps weak in legs and feet. The stallion was a more refined show type cutting horse, and the cross made wonderful "ranch horses." Kim had shown me one of hers. He was beautiful, but sturdy in all ways that I could see.

By having the babies live in the open, they became strong, used to all weather and wildlife, the rocks and yes, the cactus, which they learn to avoid, not run into one like my mule had done while I was trail riding her. As a ranch horse chasing a cow, they can't trip over the rocks or run into a cactus. They must take care of themselves and the rider. As Kimberley says, "A horse that doesn't pay attention out here can easily hurt you."

She continued, "We don't raise our own horses; I like to find a yearling or two-year-old, and then turn them out in the rocks for a couple of years. I joke that we don't have Quarter horses, we have Rock horses! Also by turning them out, they learn to find their own food on the sparse range lands.

"But our emphasis is something else: raising beef. Every extra animal that we have here takes away food for a cow and that is how we make our money. I do love horses and appreciate ours, and actually would enjoy raising a few, but I cannot justify it on this land where we need all the grass for the cattle."

I wondered if they irrigated any of the land. Nadine and I had seen a patch of nice green as we came into the ranch.

Kimberley explained that they do irrigate a small area as the cattle are finished for eight weeks on green grass instead of grain as feedlot cattle are. They also grow trays of barley grass in a special incubator for additional nutrition. Grass fed beef without any grain has become very popular.

"How many do you sell, how big is your operation?"

"We sell about seven a month, and we could sell more, but in 2011 we had a serious drought and we had to get rid of some of our cattle. This cut down on the breeding animals; we are slowly building up our herd again, but this takes time. So, the question is: sell this heifer for beef, or keep her for the herd? It is a balancing act. Also, I wouldn't want to keep growing bigger and bigger. At the moment our operation is my husband, Stefan Wolf, and I, perhaps with our children getting involved later."

I understood that. This operation is a family affair without a lot of outside help. Staying small makes sense.

"What kind of cattle do you raise?"

"We have a Brahma cross. And the reason we use the Brahma is they do much better in this rough country with the hills, rocks and scanty grasses. The Angus and Hereford cows seem to be a little lazier, not so inclined to get out there and hunt for food. They are better suited to an area with irrigation or more natural grazing. Our Brahmas are good mothers and do a good job at taking care of the babies."

"Do you have much of a predator problem?"

"Some ranchers have problems with coyotes; we don't, but we have an issue with mountain lions. We go through spells where we have problems and usually it is our newborns. It isn't the bigger ones even though a lion could take those. What I think happens is when the mother has her baby, she puts it under a bush while she grazes and the lion finds it, because the rest of the time they are not going to mess with that mother!"

"Since yours are cross-bred with the Brahma and other beef types, do they have horns?"

"Yes, many do and the replacement heifers that we keep do have horns. They come in handy for protection."

Our conversation was abruptly interrupted by some serious cat squalling. Sitting on the porch step was a black cat making his wants known.

"This is our old cat; he wants back in the house. As he has gotten older, he expects us to cater to his every whim—and we do. We love our cats, and our dogs and horses and cows!"

She laughed and continued. "So anyway, we are experimenting with crossing the Brahma with the Gelbvieh cattle."

"Kimberley, I think maybe you should tell us about the two breeds you have. They both are a little unusual. For instance, the Brahma has that big hump in their necks. Do your crosses have that also?"

"Yes, most do, but they are a smaller hump. The things we like about them are that they can handle humidity, insects and the heat of the desert—they are the only cow that has sweat glands—they have smaller calves when born, so that is easy on the mothers, but the calves grow fast after they are born. They also have plenty of milk for the babies. They do have horns which stick out to the side, and sometimes curve to the back. Probably many people are introduced to them through bucking bulls in the rodeo. Many buckers are Brahma or crosses.

"Our Brahmas are gentle, but their dispositions respond to the treatment they receive. Well-bred and properly treated, they are easily handled, but still they can be a handful at times.

"The Gelbvieh are something new for us. We had been using the Brahma-Hereford cross, but the man we got our bulls from suggested we try the Gelbvieh, which are also good mothers, have smaller calves at birth and produce a good market product, and their temperament is a little bit better. We shall see how that works for us. I am open to new things. Some work, some do not."

"My friend Kim has the Corriente cows, have you ever thought about them? They are smaller though, but I guess you could have more of them."

"I know nothing about them, but have liked what I have heard. I do not think smaller is a bad thing, especially for our terrain. The industry pushes 'bigger is better' but that isn't necessarily true for our particular Arizona land."

As we chatted, one dog lay by the door and another inside the kitchen. I asked her about using the dogs on the cows. Did they train them?

"Yes, we do use them. They have a very strong instinct. The male is a Border collie; the female is a Border Collie-Blue Heeler cross. They are good dogs; they could be better; I could be a better trainer because having a good dog takes the place of two or three other people.

"We were just in New Zealand in February for a month and they have the most amazing stock dogs there. They can send their dogs out to gather a whole pasture! They can't ride horses in their mountain environment, some are so steep—it would be horrible on horses and the riders. Everyone over there knows what they are doing with the dogs—

and I *want* one, in fact I am thinking of asking someone to help me train mine.

"As you see, our area has some really steep places. It would be lovely to be able to send up a dog instead of tying my horse and walking up there myself."

I said, "I hear you about a good trained dog. Early in our Indiana farm life, I thought I would like to have a cow dog, so I got a Blue Heeler puppy. I had no idea how to train one; consequently, she chased everything she could: airplanes in the sky, cars in the driveway and eventually a horse into a tree branch. That was when I realized she wasn't for me. But she found a super home in Texas and became renowned in those parts for her prowess in handling tough livestock. A dog should be able to do what it is bred to do."

Kimberley said their philosophy on handling their cows is to keep stress to the minimum—so even though they have Brahmas, their cattle handle very easily. They rotate their pastures frequently to also avoid stress on the land, and the cows learn if they see her go to a gate and open it, they are to move on.

"The other day two adults and one ten-year-old kid moved our herd of 350 by ourselves with no fence to help us. Our cattle are so gentle that I got my lead cow out there and she asked, 'where do you want me to go?' I got her headed in the direction and she knew exactly which pasture we were heading to, and off she goes taking the herd with her. Our dogs are gentle but good enough to get them out of the brush if needed without scaring them.

"Something I have learned when you are moving a herd of cows is that if you watch, there will be a cow that goes off to the side away from the moving herd, and everybody says, 'that stupid cow, why isn't she staying with the herd?' Well, it is because one of the riders has stepped even just one step too far into her 'zone' and when they back off, she will come back in line.

"I don't care what anyone says, cows are *not* stupid. They are very intelligent and do the most amazing things. I just love cows. I have always been a dog, cat and horse lover, but the older I get the more I really love my cows. The more gently the cattle are handled, the better the meat is too. A frightened cow has high adrenalin and that can make the meat tougher.

"When we get in new cattle that are not very gentle, we have a game that we play with them. We put them in a relatively narrow lane between some corral fences and put a person at each end. Then one walks slowly into the cows and gently pushes them toward the other person."

"You are on a horse?" I asked.

"No, we do it on foot. You could do it on a horse, but we want them to get used to us on foot too. So, you gently push them back and forth, being careful not to get too close and frighten them. We call it 'Pitch and Catch' and it basically desensitizes them."

"You do this with the cattle you bring in, not your calves?"

"Sometimes we have to do it with ours. One of the things with Brahmas is you can have really gentle ones and some that are just goofy. I say that the calves have one personality when with their mother and another when we wean them."

I asked her about the size and weight of their cows. Brahma cattle are really big.

"Some are large, but as we grow our own, they are getting smaller. The country just doesn't sustain large, so the cattle are adapting genetically."

I found that to be fascinating. Nature at work.

"Where do they calve? Out in the middle of nowhere?"

"Yes, they gotta make it on their own. We lease about 38,000 acres and own about 640 acres around our headquarters. We have more than 50 pastures and we plan our grazing. Our cows are pretty much all in one herd, which is not the usual way of doing things. We wean the calves in the fall, but here is where it gets different. We put a nose ring in the calves and turn them back out with the cows. The ring prevents them from nursing, but they can stay with the herd."

"How often do you move the cows?"

"It depends on the pasture, how large, and what the grazing is like, but it can be from two months to one day. You can grow some amazing grass, even in Arizona, but you *must* give it time to recover."

I remember reading a book by Alan Day, brother to Sandra Day-O'Connor, the Supreme Court Justice. He told about having a wild horse sanctuary and how much it helped the grass grow and recover if the animals were moved frequently—more frequently than one would guess. That book is an excellent and enjoyable read: *The Horse Lover: a Cowboy's Quest to Save the Wild Mustangs.* It is an eye opener to the ways of the west—some good and some not so much, especially when the government gets involved. "OK, I am having a problem figuring out your cow herd because you have about 350 animals, but you only sell around seven beef a month. How does that happen?"

"It takes about two to three years to finish an animal. Because we do not push them on grain to make fat but only use grass, it takes longer to get to a finish weight for market."

"Tell me about your 'Fall Works,' a term I have learned that means rounding up cows and taking the calves away. How do you do it? You have these cows on all these acres—what is the process?"

"Well, we do things a little differently. One of our key goals is low stress and to make our animals lives as good as possible. I love taking good care of my cows. We have this sort of unwritten contract: we take the finest care of the cows to the best of our ability and on their last day, they take care of us.

"We wean differently, using something called 'blabs', which you put on their nose which keeps them from nursing, and you can turn them back out with the cows. It isn't 100 percent; sometimes they fall out too early and if they are good at it, they can turn their heads just so, and still nurse. The blabs stay in for two to three months and then we take them out. A lot of the time the calves continue to hang out with their mothers for the rest of their lives in a family group."

"But," I said, "You have to catch them to do this."

"Yes, we round up the cattle, sort them in those sorting pens, separate the calves, put them in the cattle chute and put in the nose blabs and then release them again.

"Another interesting and innovative thing we do with our young heifers that we plan to market so they can stay with the herd, is insert intrauterine devices in their uterus. This is an effective contraceptive so they can run with the bulls and the other cows but not get pregnant. We have the vet do this, but it is easy. Before we used the IUDs, we had to have a vet spay them, which is surgery.

"My husband is really good at getting on the internet and looking for new ways of doing things. He couldn't find any in the United States, but found a veterinarian in Argentina who had been using these successfully for a number of years. We had some shipped; they are very easy to use and so far we are very happy with the results. It has copper in it, so no hormones, which we wouldn't want to use with our natural beef. So far as I know we are the only ones that use them here in the U.S."

"Do you vaccinate?"

"Yes, in the spring when we brand, but only for blackleg which is a highly fatal infectious disease that affects the young animals. The acute nature of blackleg makes it hard to treat successfully and the animals are usually dead in 12 to 48 hours, but it is almost entirely preventable with the vaccine. The question in my mind is whether it actually is a problem for *us*. We challenge a lot of things, but I haven't yet done the research to justify not doing it. I have friends who do not vaccinate and have not had any problems."

"Here is a story about Kim at the Broken Horn D," I said. "I saw her the other day and between her finger and thumb was a black bruise. I asked her what happened, and she said they were vaccinating their weaned calves and she stuck herself with a needle. 'Ouch' I said. 'Oh well, she responded, at least now I know I am vaccinated against blackleg and abortion!'"

Vaccinations are again in the news with folks for and some against. My opinion is that we should have the right to choose for our human family. When we lived in Indiana, we vaccinated the horses for almost everything as we hauled them to shows, had outside mares coming in to be bred to our stallions, and had a lot of bugs. When I moved to more arid Arizona, kept the animals at home, I stopped vaccinating them. I hate to think how many vaccinations my 27-year-old horse has had in his life. The controversy as to whether it helps or in the long run causes problems will always be debated, I guess, but I do enjoy talking with others who believe as I do: Do what is absolutely necessary when necessary, space them out and do single vaccinations when possible.

"Speaking of vaccinations, what do you do with the dogs?" I asked.

"I do the distemper and parvo, but I use a moderate protocol. I do distemper, wait four weeks and then give the booster shot. Then four weeks later they get the parvo, and four weeks after that, the booster. I had a long battle saving our female dog after she contracted parvo so I do that vaccine.

"When Kit was about eight months old, she contracted parvo and was very sick. I took her to my vet who knew me quite well and knew there wasn't a lot they could do for her at the clinic that I couldn't do at home. Parvo is hard to treat and is expensive, so she sent me home with some medications. The usual treatment happens in the vet clinic, of course, but costs a lot. I have had a lot of experience treating animals, but this isn't anything I would recommend anyone take on themselves!"

Parvo is a nasty dog disease. I believe in vaccinating for it also. It is highly contagious virus which attacks the intestinal tract in particular, causing severe vomiting, loss of appetite and bloody, bad smelling diarrhea which can lead to life-threatening dehydration. The virus is also highly resistant and can live in the environment for months. So once you do have a case, then you would be more likely to have more issues without vaccinations. If treated quickly with IV fluids and certain medications, the dog has an 80 percent chance of surviving.

"I see Kit survived as she is lying in front of the door. What happened?" I asked.

"The vet put an IV catheter in a front leg; I brought her home and moved her into our walk-in tiled shower and hung her IV bag on a hook. She was pretty sick, bleeding from both ends, and wasn't going anywhere. I also looked into alternative treatments for Parvo that would help with the vomiting and diarrhea, and ordered some of those too.

"I moved into the bathroom with her and for four days, every *fifteen minutes*, I administered fluids and medications to her. It was quite an ordeal. I set my phone to wake me up to Johnny Cash's 'I'll Walk the Line,' got up, doctored her and went back to sleep. The funny part of this story is that about a year later I was out in the pasture in the quad with Kit checking cows. I got sleepy and thought I would stop and take a quick nap under a tree. I set my phone to wake me in thirty minutes. When 'I'll Walk the Line' came on, Kit jumped up and trotted off away from me and the tree! She had had enough of Johnny Cash and my treatments.

"I am not a big fan of human vaccines either, again unless it is really warranted," Kimberley added.

"I am not either," I said. "I was raised in northern Pennsylvania in the hills and unless we were dying, we didn't go to the doctor. Forget about vaccinations. However, I did get a smallpox vaccination. Guess that was the thing of the day 75 years ago! Mom had her home remedies and we braved many health issues. Mom and Dad did take me to the doctor to get my head stitched up when I was about 16. I had a horse accident which ended up with a cut scalp and lots of blood. It took about 45 minutes to get to the doctor. My biggest fear was that my parents would blame the 'innocent' horse, when in actuality, it was my fault."

Kimberley laughed. "It was sort of the same way here when I was growing up. If I fell off my horse, my dad would say, 'If you can still walk, get back up on your horse.' The unspoken rule was: we don't have time for that, we have work to do! My dad raised us much differently than I raised my kids.

"Here is a story about when I was a kid. My dad would put us kids on horses I would *never* put my children on. We didn't have a lot of money to buy great horses, in fact it was a challenge trying to hold on to this ranch. So, as Dad said, 'This is a horse we have, Kim, and this is what you are going to ride.' It didn't matter that she was blind in one eye and she had a really hard mouth. It didn't matter what bit you put in her mouth, she was impossible to stop. Dad said, 'Don't worry about it, just run her into a fence and she will stop.'

"One day I was riding her home and broke the cardinal rule that you never run or hurry your horse back home, because it will become barn sour and just want to hurry home no matter where you are. I was trotting along and she broke into a canter, then a gallop, and I was wondering how I was going to stop her. There was a gate at the front of the headquarters and I figured she would surely stop—like Dad said. But she didn't and jumped right over it."

"How old were you at this time?" I asked.

"Oh, about twelve. After that incident I decided I would buy my own horse. We kids got paid a little to help with the ranch, and my grandma helped me. Mom knew someone who sold horses in Wickenburg and I got my own horse that I could train and use as I wanted. Even at a young age, I didn't always agree with my dad's training."

Before I came to visit Kimberley, I had asked her to try and remember interesting stories.

"I have another story, but it is when I was young too. I was taking riding lessons in Wickenburg when I was about nine years old because I was in 4-H and doing horse shows. I was using one of the ranch horses that was a pretty good horse, but not in show ways. We didn't have a horse trailer, so we got her to jump up into the bed of our pickup truck—which did have board sides—and off we went.

"One day when we got home, Mom said to wait with the truck and horse, and she would be right back. Well, I thought I would be helpful and unload the mare by myself, but I couldn't remember if you had to untie her first, or open the back of the truck first. I told my younger brother to just hold her rope, don't untie, just hold while I opened the back. Well, as soon as the mare heard the back of the truck open, she started to back up and caught my brother's finger in the rope.

He screamed into the horse's ear, and she reared up and sent him flying through the air, and then she fell over backwards out of the truck, shearing the pipe rails which then fell over her like a cage."

Noticing my face turn pale, Kimberley smiled. "This story has a good ending. About now I am thinking about the big mess I have just caused, and there is my little brother who had just lost the end of his little finger. He is screaming and blood is going everywhere.

"My mom comes out and says, 'Kim take your brother in and run cold water over his hand,' and she takes the pipe sides off the mare and the horse pops up off the ground just fine, and surprisingly she was always good at getting in and out of the truck after that. It didn't ruin her mind. Like I said, she was a good horse!

"Another time we went to a show—me with my ranch horse riding in the back of the pickup and the other kids with show horses and trailers. When it was time to come home, my mom had picked up a roll of poly pipe to take home, but it took up half of the pickup bed. Folks gathered around, some shaking their heads and saying, 'She will never get in that truck.' Mom said, 'Sure she will,' and she did. She knew it was time to go home, poly pipe or not!

I said, "Your mom sounds like a really great ranch woman in her own right. She was actually the rancher and your dad was a city guy who married the ranch woman, right?"

"Right and that is how I have done it too. My husband is a city boy and he is from Germany. I am the one who runs the cows, plans the grazing and all that, and he keeps the equipment working, runs the office and talks to all the customers."

I laughed. "That is how it worked in my life too. My husband was a chiropractor in a one-man-office, and while he loved the land—he was born and raised in Kansas on a farmstead—he pretty much left me to my own devices on our Indiana New Acre Farm. I got to do things the way I wanted with the cows, horses, and various feathered creatures. I really was very lucky at times, as I could have been hurt doing some of the things I did, and I know that wouldn't have gone over well!"

Kimberley nodded. "I know, I think a lot of us look back and think how lucky we haven't been hurt."

I said, "Mary Matli, who is also in this book, is a poet and also a ranch gal. She invited me to go with her to one of the day-time sessions of the last Cowboy Poet's Gathering in Prescott this year. There were several gals reading their poetry, singing songs they had written and telling stories. One of the gals was older and after the program I stopped her and asked, 'Don't you worry about going out in the back country all by yourself?' She said, 'You cannot think about that.'"

"No, you can't," Kimberley acknowledged. "And lately I know so many people who have been hurt on horses that I have been thinking about it more, but you can't dwell on it, you just can't. However, the older I get, the more careful I am becoming. I don't really want to ride a colt anymore and if I get in a situation where I am not sure—like a *really* rocky area—I just get off and lead the horse through. I don't rope, so I don't have that possible wreck. The way I figure, I want to ride until the day I *decide* I don't want to. I don't want to be afraid. I know ranchers—cowboys—who when something happens and they get scared, they never ride again."

"I understand. You want to be able to 'hang it up' on your own terms. You said you don't rope your calves, so how do you brand, castrate and vaccinate them?"

"We use a calf table. It is like a little squeeze chute that they go into, and then it turns the calf on its side and we can do what we have to. It is a lot more gentle and easy on the calf than roping, we think. We are not the typical cowboy-type ranch. I like to think we are really progressive in many ways. I am always trying to find ways to minimize stress."

"OK, but how do you get them *into* the chute? Those calves have got to be rather feisty!"

"Well, you pretty much have to man-handle them. We get my son Ryan or one of his friends who don't mind getting stepped on or kicked—and we try to do them when they only weigh about 250 pounds, but a little baby calf can still hurt you! I would love to not have to brand, but it is required by law, or castrate, but living with a bunch of young bulls until they are two to three years old and ready to market, wouldn't be a good thing."

"Yeah, the visual of that scenario is alarming!" I said. I asked Kimberly how they managed the business of selling meat to customers.

"All the meat is sold before it is processed. We take several animals at a time to Chino Valley to Perkinsville Processing. We want the cattle to be processed immediately, not wait in pens. (The usual process is to pen them over night) My husband hauls them, he doesn't mind, but I don't want to take them on their last journey. He stays while each animal is humanely dispatched. We feel there is less stress on them that way, and the person at the plant doing this is very, *very* good at his job."

I had an acquaintance tell me that saying our own cattle were "humanely" processed was an oxymoron. It wasn't possible. I disagreed, as in Indiana I also had a local person very good at his job and a short distance from the farm. It is possible to honor the lives of those we eat; it just has to be *done* and the prospective meat buyers have to *find* it. It made me happy to hear both Kimberley and Kim tell me that same story about their market animals.

"Kim started taking her meat to the local Prescott Farmer's Market and sells out quickly. That proves people are willing to pay for good meat. How do you get the word out for your meats?"

"My dad started back in the '90s selling beef to his apple customers. We have an orchard and people bought apples and peaches. Then they asked about getting some of our beef, and that is how it started. We have never had to go to a farmer's market, plus now we do have a website where there is a lot of info about the ranch and the meat: https://datecreekranch.com/

I wondered about the other animals, for instance the hogs.

"We buy the baby piglets from a friend. We used to raise our own, but that is a lot of work, and actually harder than raising cattle, so now we buy the weaned babies."

"Do you turn the pigs loose on the ranch? They are 'free range' hogs?"

"I actually tried that, but pigs are just too hard on this environment. Pigs don't eat the top of the plant; they want to eat the *roots*! They go out there and dig up this plant—oh my gosh—it might take years to replace this plant—and off they go again. That doesn't work. So we keep them in a pasture that is irrigated and regenerated under the apple trees. They love that, they can eat the old apples, and if they dig holes, that is OK. They are happy pigs."

"What about the free-range chickens?"

"We buy chicks and they are in a brooder room for a couple of weeks then they go out to pasture, but they are in big movable pens that have a shelter to protect them from predators and the weather. Every day they get moved to a fresh spot. There is something magical about having chickens on grass. It makes the most amazing meat. Plus our chickens are not the Cornish cross which are bred for their exceptionally large breasts. Most people use these as they grow really, really fast, but they are very weak. They have bad legs, and if you walk up to them and say, 'boo' several might just die from a heart attack. This is an example of selective breeding that does not help the animal."

"Do you have a chicken for sale?" I asked, anticipating a lovely chicken dinner.

"You know, I am all sold out. I am raising 630 chickens right now and don't have my second batch of chicks in yet."

Nadine inquired about ordering one and was told she should order on-line and when they went to Prescott on business, they would let her know and take it up. Not only super meat, but customer service as well!

As we chatted, I realized that I had spoken to Kimberley before we had even moved to Arizona. I had found her website as I was looking for a source of raw meat for our dogs. It turned out that I was able to find a source for chicken backs in Prescott, and we had brought some of our own beef with us when we moved, so the dogs were well fed. But having a small herd of beef cows presented stories as well.

I thought Kimberley and Nadine would appreciate one of mine. Cows are really wonderful creatures and going along with what Kimberley had said: they are *not* stupid. Ours were Red Angus and one summer I borrowed a neighbor's bull for the ladies. He was a humongous Black Angus, relatively tame as he had been shown in 4-H for several years. I worried that he wouldn't be happy with me, but the man said not to worry, "As long as he has a cow, he will be happy."

It was September and we were celebrating my husband's birthday at our daughter's place which was about fifteen minutes away from home. As we were eating, I got a call from another neighbor wondering if we had Black Angus. I replied, not, and then remembered the bull. Oh gosh, he was loose.

All the cows were in a back pasture away from the barn with a gate that led into a corn field. Apparently someone (I figured it was the bull), worried at the gate until he opened it, and he headed in the direction of his home. Our cows stayed in the corn field. The bull got as far as the neighbor's fence, but he was headed in the right direction!

Eventually we got him back home and double chained the gate. When he had done his duty with the cows, I was ready to return him. I did worry that this big beast would be a challenge to load into the stock trailer. "Not to worry," the farmer said, "He will be fine." I figured he would come himself, and was disappointed to see he had sent some helpers who had *NO* idea how to load him. I had locked him in a pen by the barn which had a gate to the driveway. I told the guys to back the trailer into the pen just far enough, open the back gate, and we would try to tease Rock Hound into the trailer with some hay. No sooner had the trailer gate opened than the bull ran to it and jumped in. He was finally *going home*. They are not dumb beasts, not at all!

"OK," Kim said, "I have a story for you. Jake, one of my registered Quarter Horses, has ringbone (an arthritic condition of the ankle area). I thought I should find him a new home where he didn't have to work so hard, maybe just be a trail horse on more gentle paths. I found this really nice lady about an hour and a half from here, who really wanted him and I felt comfortable that she would take good care of him. I hauled him down to her house and spent several hours with her.

"Eventually I am ready to go home, get in the truck, and pull out onto the driveway which goes along the long arena that Jake is in, eating grass. He hears me leave and runs along the road whinnying the whole way. I turned the corner and looked back and he was still looking down the road, whinnying. I feel like this really bad person, like I am abandoning my horse.

"I kept in touch with the lady and one day she said, Jake is doing OK, but every time a horse trailer goes by, he runs to the fence and whinnies. A few weeks later she calls and says, 'You have to come get this horse; he just isn't happy here. I went to get him and said, 'See, Jake, this is what happens when you are lame. You go to a new home. Now if you promise not to be lame anymore, we will keep you at home.' So, I swear he is better than he used to be. He is still a little lame, but not like he used to be. You figure it out!"

I said, "I have a lady friend who is an animal communicator. I have talked with her to my animals for over twenty years. I sincerely believe that they hear us, and I think Jake said, 'Dang, I am going to *die* before I go to another home again.'"

As we had been chatting, a black cat jumped into my lap, earlier another had vehemently expressed his desire to be let into the house. "Tell me about your cats. I think this is the fourth black cat I have seen."

"Three. There is a cat door in the house that lets them out, but they cannot get back in. We have one who loves to hunt, carry her catch into the house and let it loose, so we fixed the door to open only one way."

"So why are they all black?"

"It just is a coincidence. Bonny and Clyde, a brother and sister, were tiny orphans, so for Mother's Day, my kids gave me these two kittens to raise on a bottle. We had just moved here and I thought, 'Oh my gosh, I just don't have time for this,' but we had so much fun bottle feeding and loving these kittens."

"How old are they now?"

"Probably seventeen. The one you are holding is Bonnie. The third cat is seven. We were in California, stopped at a gas station on our way home, and here comes a little kitty, meow, meow so plaintively, you know how they can pull on your heart. We asked the attendant if it belonged to anyone, and it didn't, so we took it home. I have to be careful as I would like to bring them all home..."

Kimberley & Stefan

"Tell me a little about your family, your children."

"My son and daughter were born while I was living in Phoenix. They were four and eight when I moved here.""

"Are they interested in ranching? Do you think they will want to inherit what you have?"

"Ryan lives here, but right now he is traveling in South America with his girlfriend. One side of my family are travelers, but I am not. Ryan is one of the travelers. All his life he has saved his money so he can travel. I wouldn't say he is passionate about the ranch though. His girlfriend is a city girl, but she *is* passionate about the environment and loves animals. So I told her, I want to train you to be a rancher! She said, 'Are you serious?' But I am. I need someone in my life that is as passionate as I am. When they get back, we will see if she really does like being a ranch gal."

If I were a younger woman, I would love to live the ranch life that Kimberley does. Amanda was right—we are two peas in a pod.

BONNIE EBSEN JACKSON
T.H.E. Ranch
(Teaching Humans with Equine) ™

I met Bonnie through Christy Garavetto who is our mutual horses' "body worker." Christy has an intuitive talent for finding out just "where it hurts" on a horse and doing a bang-up job of fixing it. Bonnie was open to an interview so, again in the company of my awesome friend, Nadine, I went to see her at her ranch. She lives in Skull Valley, a town a little south of Prescott, Arizona with a slightly lower elevation.

When I first heard Bonnie's name, my very next question was: Is she Buddy Ebsen's daughter? And yes, she is. Buddy Ebsen started his career as a dancer, was a writer, an avid sailor, and of course most of us know him as an actor. My favorites were the television shows, *The Beverley Hillbillies* and *Barnaby Jones.*

The lane to Bonnie's ranch is lined with ancient huge cottonwoods, which Bonnie later said were likely 300 years old. The water is good in that area and they have thrived. Bonnie invited us to sit in the gazebo where we could look down on the horses as they wandered in the arena.

"So," I asked, "how long have you been here and do you have any fun stories from your youth? What was it like living with a famous dad?"

"My husband and I have been here 24 years, and yes, of course, from my childhood here is one of my favorites. I am all about safety. I teach and facilitate safety around the horses. That is my job—to keep people safe while they are either learning to ride, or are in the T.H.E. equine-assisted therapy program. I am telling you this because the root of my safety comes from my father.

36

"I can remember being led around the backyard, holding my father's hand. He said, 'See that?' And he pointed to a red berry. 'Don't eat that. It'll kill ya! See that? (Pointing to an empty light socket.) That has electricity; don't put your finger in it, it'll kill ya!' That made a big impression on me."

"How old were you then?"

"Oh, around three to five, you know, that really impressionable age and when everything that comes out of your parent is truth! Eventually he got us some horses and we did some showing. One morning we came down to eat breakfast and he showed my sister and me a newspaper clipping of a horrible horse accident…in essence, 'It'll kill ya.' So I took that all in and it built a foundation of 'safety first' especially around horses because as we all three know, horses *can* kill ya!"

"Please explain more about your program. What do you do with horses and people?"

"Well, let's go back further to start with. When we moved from California, we knew we weren't going to make a living with what we had been doing. I was an actress and my husband, Bruce, was a musician."

"Wait, you weren't raised in Arizona? How did you get to Prescott?"

"When my mom was young, she was able to spend time in Arizona on a cattle ranch and had all these wonderful experiences. She made some lifelong friends with Navaho and Hopi code talkers during World War II. When we were young, she used to take us on trips to Arizona and I just loved it, especially the weather, which was monsoon season when we went. So, when I got older, I decided to go to school there.

"My mom said, 'Why don't you go to Vassar like I did?'

"'But,' I said, 'I cannot take my horse and it is *cold* there!'

"My mother found out about Prescott College, which had only been there a couple of years. And I could take my horse, so I was all set. Also, it was relatively small, which suited me; I did not want to go to a big university. I went for a year and studied anthropology, which I decided I didn't want to go into.

"I went off in another direction, actually going into my parents' business. My mother had graduated from Vassar with a theater degree and my dad was, among other things, a dancer, so it made sense that I would become a performer. And that is how I got started in acting. I acted professionally for 20 years, but when we moved here, I had no idea what I would do. "One day I was looking at the *Prescott Courier* and saw an ad for a part-time editor for a horse magazine. Are you familiar with Professional Choice Sport Medicine boots?"

"Yes, yes, I am," I said. Most horse owners are aware of one type of protective boots or another, since Murphy's Law works overtime if you own horses.

"Well, I had entered a contest when I first got here. I had this crazy Arabian gelding that I would ride with those protective boots on his legs. For the contest I wrote about how one time I was riding him to the Post Office, and he had gotten tangled up in a barbed wire fence right next to the railroad. A train was roaring toward us and I could see his whole short life flash before my eyes. I got him untangled in time and all was OK, but it would have been awful without those boots to protect his legs.

"I had written that up in the style of an old-time movie melodrama, won second place and got $400.00 worth of Professional Choice products. I submitted that to the horse magazine publisher, and he said, 'OK, you start on Monday!' I worked there for three years. The magazine was *The Western Horse*. When that magazine was sold, I got a job at *Trail Blazer* magazine as Associate Editor, eventually moving up to Managing Editor. Eventually that job was over too, and I asked myself exactly what did I want to do with my life? I decided to go back to school, finish the degree in Psychology that I had started many years ago, and work with people and horses in a healing environment.

"Through a friend I became involved with equine-assisted psychotherapy (EAP) and began providing horses for counseling sessions. The thing about EAP is you need instincts; you can't have just been in horses for a day. You need to be able to sense 'what happens before the thing that happens, happens,' and then what to do about it. You are working with people who can be quite anxious and they are not mindful of what a horse can do. You learn to call their attention to a possible problem in a way that doesn't heighten anxiety. I also got training in the 'Horse Boy Method.' Have you ever heard of that?"

Well no, neither Nadine nor I had. It was started by Rupert Isaacson whose son has autism. He wrote a book and was featured in a documentary—both called The Horse Boy—that was made about his son, Rowan, and how a relationship with horses seemed to aid in lessening the symptoms of autism. The Horse Boy Method addresses autism as both a skill set and a series of gifts, rather than a problem to be fixed. The Method helps people bridge the communication gap and connect more with the external world. It can also benefit neuro-psychiatric conditions such as ADD and ADHD.

Bonnie continued, "Rupert was a horseman, but didn't have horses at the time his son was young. One day the boy wandered off to a neighbor, who did have horses. Rupert frantically searched for him and found Rowan in a field, hugging a mare around the leg. When he caught up with his son, he noticed Rowan was calmer and had more language. Being in contact with a horse had soothed his nervous system.

"Rupert began to really research that and came up with a whole method of helping autistic people specifically, using the horses for somatic work (sensory, touch, smell, sight) but also for cognitive work.

"In equine-assisted activities, what we are trying to create is a symbiotic relationship between the horse and the human, often without using ropes or halters. But we need the clients to stay safe, and that is where I come in. In several of the programs, the person never gets on the back of the horse. They mingle with the horses, or may lead them around. I am also credentialed to teach horseback riding and I do have a few students. Pretty much this is a one-woman horse operation. I do have some volunteers and working students, but no paid staff.

I asked if she could walk us through a new person coming to the program and how she would work with them and what kind of people would they be. What would be their issues?

"Some people have heard of using horses for enrichment or coaching, and they want to experience that. These are not people with issues, except perhaps mild stress or anxiety—what we refer to as 'the worried well.' Those with a mental health diagnosis, needing a specialized kind of therapy, are referred to me by other mental health organizations. I have a mental health counselor or therapist accompany those people. It is important to make that distinction so I am never looked upon as the therapist."

I asked, "Do you ever work with persons with PTSD?"

"I do not have any soldiers right now. There is a place called Bethany's Gait in Prescott that specializes in helping military veterans and their families. What is important in working with veterans is that you have people on staff that can identify as veterans because their issues are so unique. People who have actually been where bullets are flying and bombs are exploding. Non-military people really cannot identify with that. We can have empathy, but we really cannot truly understand.

"We are, however, doing a lot of work with young men. There is a huge opiate epidemic in this country. It is shocking. Opiates have taken the place of casual drug use, such as marijuana, mostly because they've been so easy to get. If you overdose on marijuana, you fall asleep; if you do so on an opiate product, you die. So those I can work with. When they fill out their exit comments, they many times say something like, 'I really enjoyed Bonnie—she was just like my fun aunt who has horses.' And I like that."

"OK, so now we have a client's first visit that most likely has a trauma from some emotional issue. What do you do?"

"The sessions last about forty minutes. We go out and greet the horses in the large pen. I like the horses to have enough space around them so as we come around, they are the only horse in that energy field. I have them pick a horse that seems to be most like them. It can be the look or the 'feel' of the horse, or the energy level of the animal. I try not to guide them too much.

"Once they have picked a horse, I go catch it for them. Later on they will be tasked with catching their own horse. We bring that horse back and start grooming. There is something about grooming—the smell, feel, rhythm of brush strokes, and the closeness of a horse—that really brings a person into the present. My horses are mostly older and quiet. Some people use younger horses and believe it or not, those work out well with teenage boys!

"Catching and grooming might be all we do that first session, or I might encourage them to take the horse for a walk. They are holding the horse's rope and I say to just take your horse for a walk. Usually, they take a few steps, feel the horse resisting, and turn to look back at him. I tell them to pick a spot, focus on it, keep their eyes on it, walk to it and take the horse with them. And that is the first step in self-leadership. Learning to focus, go toward a goal and bring your charge with you. The difference between focused and unfocused energy is huge in leading a horse successfully. In fact, horses can teach us one of two things everybody needs: leadership or sensitivity.

"If the person comes in and he or she is all about dominance, thinking they will *make* the horse do such and such, the horse says, 'you better ask permission.' That is the step of sensitivity.

"Another person comes and is in awe of the horse and says, 'Oh great horse' and the horse says, 'OK, let me drag your around for a bit.' So, *they* need to learn leadership.

"I have worked with some young people from Juvenile Detention/Probation and Arizona's Children, an advocacy group for foster children. What was fascinating about the kids was that I was getting two stories. One was, 'Yeah, my dad worked on a ranch for a while and it was really cool for us.' It was a time of wonderful family memories when the family was together. Or their grandmother had horses and those were wonderful memories. The other story was, 'Yeah, I got bucked off a horse once or I got kicked by a horse. I'm not going near them!'

"Of the latter, I would I tell them, 'I am giving you permission to only get as close to a horse as your inner voice tells you.' I honor their feelings of self-preservation. I *have* to; remember my story—I am all about the safety. If they want to stay on the outside of the arena, that is perfectly fine. What I want to do is validate the honest feeling that comes up to them, not tell them to shake it off and disregard it.

"As you know, what horses hate is the incongruity of 'I am scared, but I am going to be brave.' They don't get that! They don't act that way. So invariably when I tell the client to practice self-care, the next time I see them, they are leading the horse. They have gotten the opportunity to reassess their feelings without the external pressure from me. They see their friends having fun and they realize no one is going to force them to do it.

"Just this last week I had a guy who said 'I got bucked off a horse...' and I said, 'You know what? I don't let anyone on my horses' backs unless they beg me—and not just once but numerous times.' And he immediately relaxed.

"Some do relapse and I feel so bad about that, but I have to hold on to the thought that one does what they can. Remember the starfish story?"

Yes, I did, I had used it at the ending of my dog book: *Dogs, Dogs and More Dogs*. As the story goes, a young man was walking the beach throwing starfish that had been washed up back into the ocean. An old man saw him and asked what he was doing. The young man said he was throwing back into the ocean the starfish that would die if left there. The old man said there were so many miles of beach and thousands of starfish that he could not possibly make a difference. As the young man threw another starfish back into the ocean, he said, "I made a difference to *that* one."

The starfish story has many applications, but in the case of my dog book, it was that even though you cannot save all the dogs needing homes, for the ones you do save it *does* "make a difference." And it would be the same with Bonnie and her clients.

Bonnie and Oz

I asked Bonnie if she had any especially interesting or rewarding stories of working with people.

"I have one that is definitely one of the most profound experiences that I ever had, especially facilitating with children. I work with a therapist, Tony Himes, who called me one day saying that he had an eight-year-old boy who was having trouble adjusting to the death of his mother. His dad was in jail and he was living with an uncle, and was getting into trouble in school. Tony brought him to the ranch and he was just adorable. I am drawn to children, especially those who seem to be in distress. Tony had a phone call, and asked me to take the youngster down to see the horses.

"He was fascinated by the horses, who were wandering around

the pasture, grazing. We weren't saying very much, I was just letting him take in the whole atmosphere. After a few minutes he said, 'Do horses die?' and I said, 'Yeah. Yeah, they do.' And we talked about how they might pass on, under what circumstances and so forth. I remember it was a very practical discussion. As we talked, I realized he was starting to process this thing that had happened to his mother, and which he had not been able to do anywhere else. Later Tony told me it had been a real breakthrough for the child; he was able to talk about his loss with feeling."

I asked Bonnie if she had other human or horse interest stories she would share.

"Well, here is a story about myself. I grew up showing horses and then I went off to college. After the year when I had taken my horse to college in Arizona, I took a break from horses. For more than a decade, I was focused on my career, then got married and had a child. All of a sudden, I was approaching forty and realized I was really, really missing horses. I looked around for a horse I could get. My sister said her boss had a coming three-year-old that he wanted to get rid of—cheap—and I went, 'I'm in!'"

About now Nadine and I are looking at each other and going "oh, oh." Nadine said, "This should be a good story!" Anyone with horse knowledge would know a coming three-year-old horse that someone wanted to *give away* could spell trouble.

"I bought him sight unseen," Bonnie continued. "I was that stupid. I thought to myself, I am a horse person, I grew up around them, showed them, what could go wrong?

"Well, he arrives—a sixteen-hand chestnut gelding with a flaxen mane and tail—and attitude. I am pretty sure he also had a sore back because the first time I got in the saddle he went from slow walking a few steps to rodeo time—big bucks."

"Did he buck you off?"

"He got me off a few times, but you know what? I learned to ride better! You *really* learn to ride when you are riding 'rough stock.' The difference between that horse and the well-trained, older show horses of my youth was night and day. My parents weren't stupid after all.

"His registered name was Badger's Commission. I believe changing a horse's attitude begins with their name."

"Oh, I believe that too. I would never name a horse 'Devil.'"

"Well, every time you say Badger, you are saying 'bad.' So I was wondering what would be a 'good' name for the horse, and came up with Goodman."

"So how did you and Goodman get along?"

"Great. I bought him for two hundred and fifty dollars. On his vet records when I got him, was scrawled in very angry handwriting: *This horse is crazy!* But I ignored that, and just thought, hmm, he is up on all his vaccines…

"Eventually we got along well. I learned to tell when something was going to happen because he would hunch up and get taller. But he learned that when I pulled on one rein, he was going to turn around and around and eventually forget all about bucking me off.

"Then I met this wonderful equine chiropractor. She came out and worked on Goodman, and I began to understand the injury this poor horse had been subjected to."

"I wonder what happened to him? You got him at three, so something had happened early on in his life," I commented.

"I think the previous owner got on him and he weighed two hundred and fifty pounds. Goodman was a two-year-old and had a long back, so it wasn't strong. And maybe the guy tried to rope on him or something.

"The body worker worked her magic on Goodman. He shook his head, blinked his eyes, and blew out his breath several times, and from that time on he was a different horse."

I believe that. I had seen it numerous times on my own horses both in Indiana and with Christy here in Arizona. I think animals respond much faster to alternative type healing than people do because they are not burdened with baggage we humans have. I saw Christy work wonders on one of my mules and it was more emotional than physical. He had been standoffish and a little spooky. After his treatments he became a grand friend and was much quieter. So, I was a believer.

Bonnie continued, "After that I could take Goodman out in the hills and he was rock solid. I could point him where I wanted to go and he did—through brush or whatever. After I had some surgery and wouldn't be able to ride for a while, I had to make the hard decision to find a new forever home for Goodman who was now twelve. I sold him to a woman in the Long Meadow Subdivision."

Nadine piped up, "Oh, *Goodman*? I know the lady you sold him to! They live just down the road from us. I see him in the pasture every time I go to the mail box."

"Oh my gosh! Well, I told the lady to try him out for thirty days, and then pay me, but she called in fifteen days and said, 'Come get your money; I love, *love* him! I go to get my money and want to say hi to Goodman. He is eating out of a feeder and I walk toward him saying, 'Goodman, Goodman, good boy, come here!'

"He turned his head and looked at me as though saying, 'And *you* are…?' He wouldn't come over to me. Fifteen days in paradise and he was like, 'See ya, I'm good.' That is the way to find a forever home!"

As we chatted more about Goodman and how wonderful it was he found that forever home, Bonnie realized he must be about thirty now. With tears in her eyes she said she must drive up and see him again. I told Bonnie that knowing how well cared for Goodman had been was her gift for the day. We horse folk all love stories with good endings.

Bonnie said, "Here is another interesting horse story. I had gotten Nimbus when he was nineteen. He was an Anglo-Arab, and he had been a children's three-day-event mount. The day I got home from the hospital after my surgery, my husband came up to the house and told me that Nimbus was down in the pasture (meaning lying down) and wouldn't or couldn't get up. He was twenty-one at this time.

"I went down to the pasture in my bathrobe with a halter, put it on him and tried to entice him to get up, which he did, but immediately went down again. Colic was the probable cause of his discomfort. I had just recently lost two other horses I cared a lot about to severe colic. That was actually around the time I was learning about blister beetles. They come in like a swarm and can easily get into your horse's water source. They also can be harvested in alfalfa hay where they eat the flowers. When horses eat the hay, it can be devastating.

"I just didn't feel I could go through that again, especially right then, recovering from major surgery. I said to my husband, 'Go get your .45.'"

I interrupted her, "Is it hard to get a vet out here?" They were far from the vets that I knew about. In fact, that was the main reason we got a gun when we moved to Arizona. My thoughts were of my horses. What if one broke a leg, or like this situation, had painful colic. How long would I have to wait for vet care?

"Yes, it is." Bonnie said. "But a lot of it was emotional. I was 'wounded, weakened' and I just didn't feel like I could go through the ordeal of the vet visit. So, he went and got his .45. Now my husband Bruce is a very gentle person. Yes, we have weapons, but putting my horse down—well, he wasn't real keen about it. I told him 'ear to eye' (meaning drawing an x on the horse's forehead between opposite ear and eye and that is where you put the bullet. This is important because anywhere else can cause much pain and not kill the animal).

"My husband still isn't sure and asks, 'What if it ricochets?' I say, 'Press harder (into his forehead)!'"

About this time Bonnie notices both Nadine and I are looking rather pale. She smiles and says, "This has a good ending. He takes the gun and points it at Nimbus' head. In an instant, the horse leapt to his feet, pooped and went over to some hay and began eating! I am *not* kidding you! It's like he said, 'I'm good, *totally* good!'"

We all had a good laugh at the happy ending.

I said, "Since you read my other stories about ranch gals, do you remember Kimberley Knight's story about the gelding that she re-homed? He was slightly lame—too much to be a ranch horse, but OK for light riding. She found him a nice home, delivered him and left. Several days later the new owner called and told her she needed to come get him as he was desperately unhappy. Every time he saw a horse trailer go down their road, he ran after it.

"She went and got him, and told him that is what happens to lame horses. 'If you want to stay here you cannot be lame anymore!' And he wasn't! Maybe not one hundred percent, but not lame like he had been. I believe you, although I admit it does defy imagination."

"I had another strange, interesting experience with a different horse I wanted to re-home," Bonnie said. "I had a nice horse, but he didn't do these mountain trails well, he was a 'flatlander.' I found a potential home for him in California. I hauled him part way, where they met me and took him home. We signed a 30-day lease agreement to see if it was a good fit. Two weeks in, they called and said he was fighting with his neighbors and even going over the fence at them. I couldn't believe it. He had always been just a puppy dog here.

"I went and got him. When I saw him I was dismayed and shocked. He looked awful—skin and bones almost. I wondered if they fed him at all, he looked so bad. My sister boarded horses at her ranch near there and she thought she would be able to find him a home, so I left him with her.

"About three months later *she* called and said, "We have tried everything to get weight on this horse. We wormed him, had his teeth checked and nothing helps." I drove my rig over to California and brought him home. I felt badly. I had bought this horse out of the pasture when he was a weanling and now he was eight; he had spent his whole life with me. I felt like I had abandoned him. Back at my ranch with his herd mates, he was roly-poly fat and happy again within a month. Eventually he found his own forever home—with a female sheriff deputy he bonded with. He does flat-land crowd control and it is working out wonderfully."

I asked her if any other stories came to mind about the human interaction with horses. I was especially interested in troubled children. She had said they worked with emotional and some psychological problems in the equine therapy program.

I was familiar with horse riding therapy where sitting on a moving horse being led by another helped with physical issues; in fact, we had a program such as that in my home area of Middlebury, Indiana. It was called "Loveway." I wasn't sure how working with horses on the ground helped.

Bonnie's eyes lit up. "I have *the* story to tell you. I was contacted by a family that wanted me to teach their ten-year-old autistic daughter horsemanship. She had done therapeutic riding and it hadn't worked for her. In fact, it had the opposite effect. In that kind of riding, a helper has to keep a hand on the person to be sure they are steady in the saddle. With her moderate autism, she couldn't stand to have anyone touch her.

"I told them to bring her down and we would give it a try. They ended up bringing her down for weekly visits for about a year and a half. She didn't really like touching the horses; there was something disagreeable about the warmth and the hair of the horses. But what she loved was interacting with them as though they were people.

"So, we would do these dramas. She had an amazingly creative mind. I gave her one of the mini horses who she led around and we made structures out of the barrels and stuff I had in the arena. Then she had to give a performance from any structure she created. But the really amazing thing was what her mother shared after her visits.

"Her mom said that she did her math homework which previously she had categorically refused to do, she ate things she had not eaten before. She had a significant food aversion so this was huge. Her neurological system calmed down enough after her horse interaction that she would be better."

"How long did that last?" I wondered.

"About half a week. But the results lasted longer as time went on.

How it helps goes back to Rupert Issacson's work. There is something about the electrical nervous system of a horse because it is a larger system than ours. Some researchers thought a horse regulates their system, even their heart rate, to a human's, but not true. The person actually slows their heart rate and attunes to the horse."

I said, "That is why I like to ride now days. I used to compete; now I just want to relax on Susie, my mule. My son who has a stressful job managing money—who would really want to do that in this day and age—rides with me. As we go along, I hear him start to sigh. I love that because it shows he is unwinding. Actually, so do I!"

"Yes, it is the rhythm of the horse walking, or just swishing its tail. There are a lot of rhythmic patterns in being around a horse. Even brushing a horse has its own soothing rhythm. There is a neurological and electromagnetic recharge that happens."

Not that I really needed justification for riding my mule or horse, but those words gave it to me anyway. Even people who think of themselves as 'normal' can benefit from being around equines. As Winston Churchill said, "There is something about the outside of a horse that is good for the inside of a man."

Yes indeed!

BEV PETITT
Fine Art Equine Photography

Bev is an internationally renowned western photographer. She specializes in photographing wild horses, cowboys and horses, and Native Americans. Like most of the women in this book, Bev has loved horses and animals since she was a young child. She got her first horse when she was twelve, just a common horse, she said, "But I spent every waking minute with Mein Schatzie (My Sweetheart) that I could. Life was good! I rode him bareback, packed a lunch and left for the day to wander the bluffs around our home in southeast Minnesota."

I laughed. "Oh, too funny. I did the same thing. I got my first horse when I was fifteen. He also was just a common old retired workhorse. His name was Smokey and he was also the love of my life. My sister got a pony and we were a 'Mutt and Jeff' pair—a big old plow horse and a large pony wandering the hills and the forests of Tioga County in Pennsylvania that was right beside our farm. You know we had good guardian angels, because we really shouldn't have done that. We could have disappeared and no one would have known where we were! You probably did the same thing."

"Absolutely, and we'd be gone all day. No cell phones. Of course things were different in those days, but still things could have happened. I rode bareback too. I had a saddle, but the horse was in a five-hundred-acre pasture, so I would just jump on in the pasture and ride him home. I moved to Arizona when I was in my twenties, got a horse and rode in the desert when I could. One year my horse got a bad case of colic and died; my older dog who went everywhere with me and I loved dearly, also had to be put to sleep, all in a relatively short period of time. I was married at that time and my husband got a job offer to work in Asia. I had lost my dog and my horse, so I went to Asia with him, Hong Kong actually.

"I was just going to stay for a short while; I couldn't see myself living a long time in a large foreign city. We wound up staying for six years. I worked for a bank that eventually became Citi Bank. I missed horses terribly, all animals really. I went for walks in the huge city park and I'd find stray cats which I brought home. I found homes for them with Chinese ladies as I couldn't keep any for myself. They followed me; somehow, they knew I had a soft spot for animals. I was just born with a love of animals; I am hopeless, I guess."

"Me too," I said, "and it seems everyone I have talked to is pretty hopeless too!"

"Good, good. Thank goodness for a few of us," Bev said. "I am still that way. I can't kill anything; now I have this indoor-outdoor cat that is a rescue kitty, actually a whole bunch of them. I put in a little door so she can get in at night. Now she brings in mice and lets them lose in the house."

"She doesn't kill them first?" I asked.

"No, she doesn't, she brings them in and lays them at my feet and of course, then they run off in the house. One day she brought in a ground squirrel."

"Oh my! She probably thinks: I brought it for you, did you expect me to kill it too?"

"Thank goodness I have a husband who just laughs."

"Me too, my husband just shrugs and smiles at the situations I get into with animals."

Bev said, "My husband knew when he married me how I was and knows he isn't going to change me, but fortunately, he loves animals too.

"OK," I said, "back to Hong Kong."

"We lived there for six years and were able to travel a lot, but I really missed animals. I found this place that was an hour train ride away, where there were a bunch of rescued Thoroughbred horses that they used to teach kids to ride. When I could get off work soon enough, I took the train and rode horses!

"Next we spent another four years in London and I had no access to horses there, but we did get two Abyssinian cats. I was in heaven again—I had my pets. These cats lived for a very long time and moved all over with us, including coming back home to the states in 1996. We wanted a place in the country, rediscovered the Prescott area, and bought forty acres in Rancho Diamante. We had to live in California for several years, but came back here to camp on our property for our vacations. I bought three horses from Laurel Denton, who I know you also wrote about, and kept them with her and went to ride them when we came up here. Finally, my husband and I decided to build a little guest home on our property. We were tired of big cities and tired of moving around, so we just quit it all and moved to Arizona, probably in 2003."

"How did you get started with the photography?"

"When we lived in Asia, I was so captivated by it all, that I started taking photographs. It was so beautiful—sights of people, the land—it was all film back then, and started selling some of my photographs."

"Around here do you go out to the different ranches to take your famous horse photographs?"

"I have gone to the 7 Up ranch, owned by Kathy and Swayze McCrain, which is many miles up Campwood road, and is quite rough and remote. A lot of the pictures I have are because of Kathy's inviting me up to watch while they do ranch work. It is rough riding on the 7 Up ranch. They raise their own horses that grow up in the hills and *rocks* and that makes a huge difference in how they can travel when ridden in cow work. I used to take my own horse up to ride, but don't anymore.

"On a day's work, we would be up at 4 and out by 5, ride for two hours to get out to the cows, then they gather and brand, and it is 4 or 5 by the time you head back home. One evening Swayze came back in where Kathy and I were sitting and said that the guys were back and were going to break some colts. We went out to the round pen and I took some of the best pictures I ever got that afternoon. Quite a few of my pictures of their horses, ranch and cowboys have been published in *Cowboys and Indians*, and *Western Horseman*."

With all my interviewees the love of animals pervades their whole beings. Now I see why western photography is her love, and she is darn good at it. Many of her pictures have been sold to various hotels in several cities where prints are made and hung on the walls. It is probable that you might see one in a place you may stay. She told me many of her photography friends travel the world, spending eight to ten thousand dollars taking pictures and going to workshops. But lady luck can play a part in getting fabulous pictures.

Bev said, "Here is a fun story. I have a friend in Skull Valley that has a beautiful white Andalusian stallion. I just went over there one day and snapped some pictures of her horse running around, and I won more awards with that picture taken that day than I could ever imagine. He is absolutely beautiful and I caught him just right. Patience plays a big role in photographing animals.

"In a couple of weeks, I am going to visit a friend in Colorado and we are going to Western Colorado to take pictures of the Sand Wash wild horses that live there. We will go 'car camping.' I have a mattress for my car and we will be out there for ten days, then we are driving to Utah to the Onaqui area to photograph the wild horses there. I love the wild horses so much. In October I am going up to Monument Valley where I have some Navajo contacts.

"One year I went up there with a photographer friend and he knows the Navajos very well. I took a picture of Susie Yazzie, known as the matriarch of Monument Valley, which won all kinds of awards. She was a legendary rug weaver and very photogenic; I had a double page spread in *Cowboys and Indians* magazine with her pictures. She recently died in February, 2013; they think she was around one hundred years old. She was in a lot of John Ford's western movies in the 1920s to '40s. I got to know the family pretty well because of my pictures, so I go back up and camp on her property."

I asked, "What is your experience of how the Indians care for their animals? I hear many negative things on Facebook especially, which as you know, cannot always be believed."

"Well, it depends on where they are, and I can only speak to what I have seen. They do the best they can. They don't have much money, and hay costs $20.00 a bale. How can they afford that? They cannot grow any crops, there is no water; it has to be hauled in. In defense of them, I think that is being a little harsh. They have to let the horses run and get their own food. I rode a horse up there one day for twelve hours; she was a thirty-two-year old paint mare. She was strong—my Quarter Horses wouldn't have the stamina that this horse had.

"So how do they live on the reservation? What do they do? I don't understand this whole Indian thing very well. Do they get government support?"

"Yes, but I don't think it is much. They love their families, pets, and horses. They talk about their horses a lot and they like to ride them. You asked what they do. This particular group of Yazzis that I know, have taken a part of their land and fenced it off, made some proper corrals, and they run tours. When someone like you or me wants to go up and take our own horses, they have a place for them to stay. You have to bring your own feed and water, but they will take you on a guided tour. It is in a beautiful canyon area surrounded by big walls of rock and you can also bring your own camper.

"Some of the kids leave home and go to school other places, but there is a nice high school in Monument Valley with good teachers. Some have gone on to become doctors, lawyers, teachers, veterinarians. Some work in the tourist motels. They may live and work off the reservations, but eventually they may come back because of their close family ties. They dress modern. I send huge boxes of books and clothes to Susie's grandson. I think they got a raw deal. I am not much into politics, but I think we need to take some of the blame ourselves and not blame them so much.

"I am going up to northern Montana to photograph horses running in the snow. I am always looking for different horses and places to go without going to another country. Actually, when I lived in London, I did spend a week riding in Argentina with the gauchos. They couldn't speak a word of English. The land is very marshy and we rode through some with the water coming up almost to our waist. The horses were Spanish Barbs, really beautiful and they all looked the same."

"How did you find their cowboys different from ours?"

"Oh my goodness. For one thing they rode barefoot! Some even wore spurs on their bare feet. We had to ride through so much water, I think that is why they rode barefoot. They carried these big bats that they made carved out of wood. I didn't know what those were for until we got into the marshes and saw the alligators. They hit the water with those big bats, just to frighten the alligators, they didn't hit them. One day they butchered a cow and made a pit to roast it. What meat we didn't cook and eat, they put into big leather bags and took back to the ranch."

"OK, back to the West and our wild horses. Would you like to share in writing your love of the wild horse and your fascination with photographing them?"

Living with Wild Horses by Bev Pettit

He was big and fast! And he could turn on a dime in a split second. The black Onaqui wild stallion shows his sense of survival through the display of his many battle scars over his entire body. And those fiery eyes could speak – no, SHOUT – at you without hesitation.

53

This big guy made darn sure that I would keep a good distance from his "stolen" band of mares and their foals. And any other stallion that may encroach upon his territory to threaten his place in the herd would witness his wrath even more severely.

I've enjoyed photographing horses, both wild and domestic, for many years. But I had never "lived" with them, out on the range, day and night, observing them and watching their behavior so closely as I did on a recent trip to Sand Wash Basin in Colorado and to Utah on the Onaqui Range.

In September of 2016, I left the comforts of my Arizona home for a 2,000-mile journey in my trusty 4-Runner, traveling north to where the wild horses live. After two days of travel I arrived on the range at night, under a pitch-black sky, which added to the adventure. Slowly trying to find any sign of "civilization" I came upon a trail off to the side of the road. I slowly pulled off onto the trail, turned off the car engine and climbed in the back for a "good" night's sleep. Waking at daylight and looking out to where I had just spent the last six hours in total darkness was an eye-opener! Here I had parked, perched high on a grassy bluff, along the edge of a 500-foot drop off, down into a vast valley. My jaw dropped as I witnessed more than 100 wild horses spread out peacefully below.

This is where my journey began. A journey into the lives of wild horses that few others have the privilege of experiencing. I securely fastened on my back pack with camera and lenses while cautiously scaling the hill down to the herd below. I followed their every movement for the next five days as they grazed, fought, protected each other, watered, and slept.

I watched in awe as they moved in such precision and calm order along the edge of the watering ponds, taking turns to drink, mares and foals first, stallions casually keeping a watchful eye close-by. I relished every moment of this journey, while absorbing their majesty, freedom, independence, camaraderie, survival and grace. One thing to keep in mind—these are OUR wild horses. They graze on our public lands. We pay taxes on these lands. So I feel that it is up to us to make sure that the herds are "managed" well. I would encourage anyone who has an interest in seeing these majestic wild horses to add to a trip out west to their bucket list, real soon.

Bev and I said our goodbye, but several weeks later my thoughts turned to what I would use for the cover of this book, and I contacted her. The western beauty you see on the cover is "Jane" a local cowgirl, photographed by Bev Pettit. You may contact Bev through her website: www.bevpettit.com

Bev and Skeeter

MARY MATLI
Cowboy Poet, Writer
And
Cowboy

Mary is the first of the ranch gals I met who was not imported from another state, but born in the Prescott area and grew up on the Matli family ranch in Yavapai County, Arizona.

"How long did you live on the ranch?" I asked, thinking it would be well into her adult years, maybe she had even run it; she sure looked the part. Tall, sun-tanned, slim and muscled; I could imagine her being a ranch boss.

"Until I was fifteen. I had expected to live there and help run the ranch. I planned to go to Arizona University and study accounting, basic veterinarian classes, and auto shop. I knew we paid for these services and figured I could do them better and save money." She had a sad look on her face.

"What happened?" I asked her.

"Dad sold it. I left home when I was sixteen and lived in Prescott for my senior year of high school. Then I moved to Colorado when I was eighteen."

"You and I are now friends on Facebook," I said, "and I just saw a stunning picture of you and some beautiful young ladies, I am guessing they are daughters?"

"Yes, I met and married my husband in Colorado and three years later had daughter Briana. We traveled around some, living in New Mexico and Nevada. Daughter Stevie was born in Nevada. Eventually we moved back to Arizona and Jamie and Tammy, the twins, were born. A few years later my husband and I split up."

"Are your daughters and grandchildren interested in ranching?"

"No, they are interested in the heritage, but not ranching. Since none of them grew up on the ranch, that made a difference; however, lucky for me all of them live here locally except for Tammy who lives in Washington. She has twin sons. Between my four daughters I now have seven grandchildren."

"Tell me a little about your life before now. What did you do given that you didn't become the ranch lady you had expected?"

"I guess I have never been one for 'traditional jobs.' I worked with my past father-in-law for several years. We did remodels and built new homes. I worked for a heavy-highway construction company where I managed the construction yard, ran equipment, managed local traffic control and ran for parts that were needed. I also had several jobs after that which included inventory control, HR duties, and technician for customer trouble or information calls. I worked as a cook at a sports bar, delivery driver at Auto Zone and presently am an accounting tech at Arizona Archery."

As Mary rattled off her many job skills over the years, I had a new admiration for her. She hadn't become a rancher, but she certainly had filled her life with experiences. It would soon come to light that she would be using many of these skills in her future.

Mary met me at my home about twenty miles north of Prescott for our chat. She had offered to stop by on her way home from meeting with others to plan and organize the 28th Annual Arizona Cowboy Poet's Gathering. This is a big annual event which lasts for three days. Many famous local and not so local singers, poets and storytellers come to entertain. Mary herself is a poet, and this year was receiving the *Gail I. Gardner* award for poetry. It continues to amaze me how many folks here are writers, poets, artists or singers in the cowboy/girl fashion. There is definitely a concentration of talent in these parts!

"Tell me about your present home these days and what you are doing now."

"I moved to the community of Yava, twelve miles west of Kirkland near Hillside, in March of 2014. I have been so blessed to live here in the desert with rocks and boulders in my back yard. One day recently I was offered two good cow horses by a very special friend who could no longer keep them due to family circumstances. Now I have horses to feed and exercise. I said to another friend, Dani, who is the cook for the Necktie Ranch, 'I wish I could find a day-work job with these horses.' She knew that ranch was actually looking for someone and our schedules happened to mesh. I ride for the ranch every Friday."

"Tell me a little about the Necktie Ranch. It has a unique name."

"The Necktie Ranch is one of Arizona's oldest ranches and has been in the Carter family since the mid-1880s. Arden "Tripp" Carter III is the family manager and who hired me. Recently that family suffered an awful tragedy. Were you here during the Yarnell Fire?"

"Yes, we were. We had only been here for one year, and were still getting settled, knowing folks, finding out where important things are, and getting used to the 'lay of the land.' I remember that fire vividly because the storm that caused such misery was seen and felt at our home. I was outside and the wind suddenly picked up and blew with a vengeance from the north. We got a little rain out of it and I was grateful, not knowing what was happening a few miles away to the south."

"Yes," Mary said, "that was the fire that killed the 19 Prescott Hotshots when they were caught in a sudden change of wind direction. Tripp Carter's son, Travis, was one of the hotshots that was killed. He was only 31 and he grew up in those hills."

I feel so sorry for the families of all those who lost their lives. They were such upstanding and brave young men.

****

"Mary, what is a 'day-work' job?'" I asked her.

"It is just a day's work. I haul my horses to the ranch and do whatever needs doing for that day. Sometimes it is checking the cows, maybe hauling out salt blocks—then I can use both my horses, one to pack and one to ride—sometimes we gather the cows and calves to brand, which by the way, is still done in open country like it has been since the beginning of the ranch."

"Does the ranch use dogs to help gather and drive cows?"

"No, this one doesn't. There are instances where a dog sure could come in handy though. One day another cowboy and I were driving sixteen cows with calves toward headquarters. In that area the brush can be forbidding. It is high and thick. There is a place where two waterways converge, and in-between them was a tall dense thicket of brush. The cows all decided to hide in there. You could smell them, but you couldn't see them, and they didn't move an inch. How that many cows with calves could be so still is amazing. We decided the cows had won that round and left them there for another day."

I could relate. I remembered our childhood Jersey milk cows doing much the same thing. Mom planted a huge garden each year, and a lot of it was sweet corn. One day our small herd of five cows and a bull got out. We couldn't find them, but eventually they were spotted in the garden and in the corn. The funny part of it was we saw them accidently; they didn't move either as we looked for them. They even stopped chewing the cornstalks as we walked by.

When I asked Mary when a good time to visit for this interview would be, she said sooner was better than later as she was moving and taking a new job on a big ranch in northern Arizona. That sure sounded interesting. I have been trying to figure out where some of the ranches are around here and so far, have not done a good job, but I have "googled "many of them just for interest.

"Where is the ranch and what will you be doing?" I asked.

"It is the Diamond A Ranch in the Seligman area north of here. It also goes by the name of the Boquillas, or Bo."

That ranch was one I *had* read about.

The Boquillas Ranch is the largest working cattle ranch in Arizona and one of the top 25 largest in the United States. It is comprised of about 750,000 acres of which about 500,000 acres are private land owned by the Navajo Nation and 250,000 acres are Arizona State Trust land. The Navajo Nation leases it to the Cholla Cattle Company under the name and brand: Diamond A.

"I am really excited about this opportunity to go back to my roots and work on a big ranch," Mary said.

"What will you be doing?"

"I will be the cook for the wagon crew…"

Now my ears really perked up. Cook? Oh my goodness, that would be the farthest thing from my desire to do. I have cooked all my adult life and some in my childhood for family, and now would love to *hire* a cook. Several of the gals I have met recently say their retired *husbands* are the cook. How perfectly marvelous.

When I was around twelve, our family lived on a hilltop farm in Pennsylvania. Dad was a school teacher in a near-by town, and Mom who was raised in a city before we moved to the country, decided to be a real country lady. She never milked our cows, but planted a huge garden large enough to feed us and the many deer who visited. I hated working in that garden and volunteered to be the cook. That suited Mom just fine too. She had cooked enough to rather be a gardener.

One day I was making biscuits to go with a chicken dish. I remember I forgot the baking powder soon after putting them into the big old-fashioned wood burning cook stove oven. Horrified, I pulled them back out, put them back into the bowl and added the baking powder. No one knew except me and the oven.

Mary said that she had been told about the job by one of her ranch gal friends. When she was offered the job as cook, she said she couldn't do it unless it was a full-time job, not seasonal as in the "spring works" (branding) or "fall works" (weaning). Mike Ensley, the Cow Boss, decided to give her a full-time job.

"Mike asked me if I could do repairs, probably thinking that I couldn't, but I told him sure. He said, 'Well now, I think this is going to work out just fine!' It is hard to get anyone to go way out there to do things like that. I will also be a 'go fer.'"

There is no gender gap here, no need to be politically correct. Gals can "cowboy" too!

That would be where her carpentry skills would come in! In other words, many of the skills that Mary has garnered during her "previous life" would now come in handy in her new life—her dream job of working on a cattle ranch full time. I became friends on Facebook with Mary and saw an entry and asked for permission to include here because it speaks to Mary's faith and also to what I have been calling our "God experiences."

MUSINGS BY MARY

Do you have a dream or a goal or feel a call on your life? I know I do. I've been thinking about what holds us back a lot here lately. Is it fear? Is it that we think it's just too big & impossible? Do we think that our dreams won't fit in to what other people's expectations are for our lives?

Probably it's a little of all of those things & more. All I can say is that not answering that call, not chasing those dreams, not working for those goals will get you to a place where you are bitter & resentful.

I'm not saying "sell the farm & run off to join the circus" but if that calling is strong & persistent at least check it out. Research it, explore it, most of all give it to God.

If what you aspire to & long for is truly where you should be, doors will open & things will begin to fall in to place.

Did I ever think I would go back to ranching? No way, not until earlier this year. It seemed impossible. I didn't see, as a 52-year-old woman, many opportunities. But I prayed & prayed about it. This new job came to me, I had not been out searching. The door opened. I asked God to slam it shut if the move was not His will. It stayed wide open.

Explore the possibilities! I started day-riding to reconnect with my heritage & roots (& to help cover expenses of owning horses). I didn't even consider where that would bring me just 1 short year later.

In your exploration find something you can do that is part of or related to your dreams so you can at least get a taste of what it would be like. Still have that dream? Then pursue it! If it's truly your calling it will come together, just be patient & do what you need to in the meantime.

I can think of a thousand reasons not to follow this call on my life but not one of them, nor all of them combined, is stirring the thought of changing my mind.

Life is an adventure. It is finite & each day gone is marked as past. Honor His call & He will honor you with peace, joy, contentment & success.

Now, get out there & live!

****

When I wrote the first part of Mary's story, she was getting ready to take the job as cook on the Diamond A Ranch in Northern Arizona. Now, a little over eight months later she was back and I wanted to find out what it was like living and working on this huge ranch—the largest in Arizona and one of the twenty-fifth largest in our nation.

As well as information, Mary knew I was a sucker for good stories and so she began with one.

"When I was cooking for the fall wagon (fall roundup verses spring branding), the guys would take days off after paydays which were the first and fifteenth of the months. By the time these guys had worked together for twelve days, sleeping in bunks or tents with each other and eaten together—with the absence of other company, they began to get a little tired of each other.

"I told them they could ask for certain food and if possible, I would cook it for them. At first they wouldn't say anything. Later I found out how horribly some of the other wagon cooks had treated the

61

cowboys."

"Oh really? Like what?" I asked.

"They had to not be a minute late for meals 'or it would get dumped,' they couldn't wear their boots in the eating area, and other things too awful to write about here. I think it was all a control issue and it made me very sad to hear.

"Anyway, when they believed that I was not like the others, someone asked if we could we have breakfast for dinner. I fixed French Toast; I had seven guys and they ate two huge loaves of bread. And they got all sugared up. Two of them have this talent that you could give them a line out of just about any movie or song and they could pick up and go on with it. They got started and everybody was laughing so hard that we were all cryin'. I finally had to get up and go out.

"One of the other guys said, 'Miss Mary, your boys are getting outta control! I bet when you came here you didn't think you would be adopting grown men for sons!' I said, 'No, but I sure prayed for it.'"

"I can see that," I said. "I could see that having someone like you as a 'mother figure' could be beneficial. How old were they?"

"They ranged from eighteen to twenty-seven."

"Are these young men ones who come just for the season?"

"Some were, but some were 'camp men' who lived there year-round. They had cow camps they were responsible for, but some also helped with the wagons."

I said, "OK, working on a huge ranch such as this is definitely different from Kim and Dave's smaller 'Mom and Pop ranch' for instance. We need to explain some terms. I have done some reading about Western ranches, but to refresh my memory, a ranch like this one is broken up into what you call 'cow camps?' And they are sections of pastures which are hundreds of acres?"

"Umm, up there the average size is about 70,000 acres per pasture and typically there are maybe seven pastures."

Well, I missed that by a mile!

"How many cowboys are in one of the camps?"

"Just one."

"*Just one?* Holy cow. What are they supposed to do? How many cows in one of those typical pastures?

"Depending on the time of year, certain ones will have none."

"Well, then that would be easy!"

"But that is the time they have to get everything done. Fences fixed and things like that.

"Cody, one of the men, was responsible for over half of the bred heifers (first time mommas) this winter. He had to watch for calving, and when they needed more feed, haul hay to them. They were pastured forty miles from camp, so in the morning he waited until it started to get light out and had warmed up enough that he could break the ice in the stock tanks as he went.

"It gets cold at the Big Bo, they are a higher elevation than we are in Prescott, and even here winter mornings could be cold. All the water tanks could have ice on which the cows would find hard to break, thus, a cowboy would have that duty."

I asked if he rode a horse, ATV or used a truck.

"*No* ATVs are allowed on this ranch, which is kinda nice. They tear up the land too bad. It is bad enough with the pick-ups."

"Getting back to the cow camps, normally how many cows would be in one?"

"The northern camps during the winter have probably three to four thousand head and the way it divides up there are 200,000 acres per camp."

I said, "Let's start with spring at a cow camp. Is there still just one person there and later more move in to help? I don't understand this like I do Kim and Dave's operation. That I understand perfectly. They do all the work and are lucky if they can get a few cowboy friends or find competent seasonal help to aid them!"

"The wagon is based out of Rose Well Camp which is basically the center of the ranch. The first thing in the spring the wagon crew will bring in four to eight guys depending on how many they can actually get."

"What is a 'wagon crew' exactly?"

"They are the seasonal guys. And there are some places that are still using a team of horses and a wagon. The wagons are portable so they can be moved place to place. At this ranch the cook wagon is actually an old milk truck and it is all set up with a kitchen and tent with a wood stove that is towed behind a pick-up so we can move from place to place. Where we move to depends on the 'Cow Boss' who is in charge of the cattle."

I asked the procedure of getting started in the spring after the wagon crew is hired and if the new guys usually have cowboying experience and skills and if they are young.

"Most of them do have experience but sometimes you will get a guy who doesn't, but they *have* to know how to ride! You will be on a horse for twelve to fourteen hours a day. The camp men (year-round cowboys) really know what they are doing. The new ones can learn on the job, but they have to be willing."

"I heard from a couple other ranch owners that getting good help is getting harder and harder because nobody wants to do that crazy hard work," I said.

Mary replied, "I don't know that it is that necessarily, but they don't get paid all that much and it is hard work plus you are gone for months—long enough for a stretch that if you do have a family and horses, dogs, maybe cattle, you have to make arrangements for all that. It isn't so bad for the younger ones who still live at home.

"They start by the end of March and finish the end of June or early July. There are a lot of good, steady, better paying jobs in towns which they take first. Sometimes a guy can work in a wagon crew between his other jobs. Right now, they are not finished with the branding and some of the guys have to leave for their other job commitments. Typically, you don't have the same guys for two seasons, they don't come back."

"OK, this is spring, we have the crew hired, the cows have already calved and the regular cowboys have taken care of that, so now what?"

"One of the first things they will do after they get their horses shod that they were assigned, is go round up the bulls that wintered away from the cows, and haul them via semi-trucks back to their cow herds."

"How many bulls, what kind are they and how many cows to a bull?"

"The pasture I knew about had two hundred and eighty bulls. They are Black and Red Angus and now they are bringing in some Charolais bulls to cross with the Angus. Typically, there is one bull to ten or twelve cows. They lost almost two hundred head of cattle to Trichomoniasis, a venereal disease the bulls get and transmit to the cows."

Trich, as it is commonly called, causes infertility and occasional abortions. It is caused by a small motile protozoan found only in the reproductive tract of the bull and cow. No vaccines are available and once a bull is infected it remains so for life, but shows no sign of the disease. It is detected via microscopic examination. The cows will recover by themselves, but loss of calves by abortion or failure to re-breed is a costly issue.

"Since the bulls carry it, they have to test every bull every year. You test the bull, hold them in pens until the results come back which takes up to two weeks. Any bull that tests positive goes to the killers. The meat is OK for people to eat."

"Wow that can be a costly problem!"

"Yeah, you take bulls that cost twenty-five hundred dollars apiece and there are two hundred of them, plus the cows that didn't get pregnant; that adds up."

"If you buy a new bull that tests OK and turn him out with a herd, can he get the disease?"

"Yes, if a cow is contaminated and a clean bull breeds her, then he most likely will get it. It is a vicious, vicious cycle. And you have to keep really good records of where a particular infected bull was—in what pasture—so you know about the cows. Blame is put on the Indian cattle that come over the fence and maybe that happens too, but certainly not all of it."

"What Indians would that be?"

"The Hualapai border almost all of the western edge of the ranch; the Diamond A leases many thousands of acres from the Navajo.

I remembered hearing about the Hualapai because my husband, Hal, had taken a local trip to Peach Springs on the western edge of the Grand Canyon. This part is owned by them and they do a touristy business there. In fact you cannot enter if you do not have a permit. Hal actually got to touch the Colorado River on that tour.

The Hualapai reservation encompasses about a million acres along 108 miles of the Grand Canyon and Colorado River. Cattle ranching, permitting hunters, and crafts make up their livelihood. They have no casinos. Knowing the disrespect cattle have for fences, I could see that their bulls could intermingle with the Diamond A's.

Mary said that the elk are terrible about tearing up a lot of fences too, and there are a lot of elk in that area.

I wondered about elk conservation versus hunting. What were her thoughts? The elk were desired there, weren't they?

"Well, it would be nice to thin out that herd. There are thousands of them up there. That is one of the best hunting places in Arizona. There are a lot of big trophy elk in there. Right before I left, I was watching two bulls that lived in the canyon where I was. The other elk had antlers about a foot long, but these guys were three-foot-long and still in velvet. By fall they would be huge. The hunts are strictly controlled by the Navajo and they also charge an impact fee. I think it is five hundred dollars, whether you get an elk or not."

"When I knew you were going there, I investigated the Diamond A," I interjected. "It sounded like years earlier just about anyone could hunt there. But then some limits were put on it."

"That is because they abused it so much. The guys that get to hunt up there now have a ton of money invested in it. The Navajo have limits and Game and Fish does also. Only a certain number of elk tags are available and they are expensive. Our elk population got really knocked down and that is why they have such stringent regulations.

"For every elk that is one less cow you can put in there, and twelve jackrabbits eat as much as a cow."

"Now, since we are talking about wildlife, let's throw in the coyotes. I would imagine you want some predators to eat the rabbits."

"Yes, you want predators to a certain extent, but when you are one of the camp cowboys trying to help a cow birth her calf and you are alone out there only with your horse, and you have to beat off seven or so coyotes with a stick—that puts a different perspective on the whole thing."

"They are that brazen?" I asked.

"Oh yeah. They don't see humans very much so they are not afraid. We have taken out many because when they get numerous enough to run in packs, your calf population will be decimated in no time. Also when they run in large packs, they will 'sport kill.' Some people say coyotes don't do that, but they do. The rule was that you *never* shoot at them unless you know it is a kill shot because if you do that two or three times, they get real smart and they disappear—don't go away, we just won't see them.

"Why don't you take me through the 'spring works.' What happens first?"

"About six to eight new guys are hired to work with the regular camp bosses. They are given a string of seven or eight horses."

"Are they Quarter Horses?"

"Some are, some are a mix. They are working on improving their horse program. This life is hard on horses. They are turned out all winter, but they are fed hay if pasture is lean. When spring comes, they are put in holding traps which are as large as the ranch I grew up on—ten

66

thousand acres. From that area the 'Jigger Boss' takes the horses to be used for the next two days.

"Next they 'put them on the ropes.' A rope corral is made by using metal posts with a rope around them. The horses all line up around the enclosure facing out, with their butts toward the corral."

"How in the world do they get them to do that? What is their reward? I can just see my mule saying, 'You want me to do what?'"

"Luckily the old ones teach the young ones, there are some horses that have been there quite a while. It just becomes part of the routine. Only the jigger boss ropes the horses out. The jigger boss is over the guys, the cow boss is over the cows and how the works go."

"So those two people better get along!"

"Yeah, that really helps, for sure." Mary chuckled.

"The jigger boss asks each guy which horse he wants for today and tomorrow. The way they throw their loops to catch a horse is different from roping a calf where you swing from your shoulder and throw out. To rope one of the horses, he swings backwards and throws over and it comes down over the horse's head. And you watch these horses that have had it done a lot, they will duck into it. It is a light small rope, and very seldom is one hit in the face. But it is a real talent to throw like that because you are standing back fifteen to twenty feet from the horses, which are also shuffling around a bit. Then he leads the horse out and the cowboy puts his rope on and takes it away."

I wondered how each cowboy would know what horse he wanted to ride as they didn't know the horses. Mary said that when they are hired, which is mostly over the phone, the bosses try to get a feel for what their skill level is, and then someone who is on the permanent crew and knows the horses helps get the cowboy with the proper horse. Usually, the horses are even assigned before the help gets to the ranch.

I asked what the horses were fed. Mary said for that last winter there was enough grass for the first half, then they fed grass hay. Feeding alfalfa would be too big a dietary change from the native grass pasture which they got when turned out, and they do not get grain, just all the good hay they can eat.

"OK, each cowboy has been given his seven horses, now what?"

"They have to put shoes on all of them."

"They don't have to *shoe* their own horses, do they?"

"Oh yeah."

"So that is one of the criteria for being hired? Ouch."

"You either have to be experienced or willing to learn—quick. After they are shod, the cowboys ride them a little to get acquainted and some haven't been ridden in several months. This year what they did was to trailer out from Rose Well camp to wherever they are going to be branding, and that is usually determined by where the best set up with holding pens are.

"After those calves are branded, they put that bunch of cattle in a different pasture and go on to another good holding location and do it again. Once the whole area is done, they are all moved to their summer pasture, which can be a thirty-mile drive and can take two or three days."

"Are there roads the cows follow? Do all the cowboys move the cattle?"

"There are some roads, but where not, the older cows know where to go; they know where the next waterhole is. And if you have a herd that is fifteen hundred head, you might be strung out for seven or eight miles."

I commented that was just like the old-time cattle drives and asked if it was hard for just seven cowboys to do it.

"The hardest part is to get them started off. They drink in the morning, eat, wander around a bit, and then want to bed down. But there are enough old momma cows that know the drill and that helps a bunch. It is really neat when the cattle are moving and you come over a ridge and see five miles of cows single file in front of you. I have pictures of that. Single file is the best way to move cows. If you try and bunch them up, it just gets confusing and dusty. The best way is to do what they do naturally, which is single file. If you get a good lead cow they will travel as fast as a person walks."

Well, that *must* be the truth because I think every cow lady has told me that. Don't hurry them!

"What happens at night?" I asked

"They stop at water and graze and sleep, then in the morning it all starts again. They can spread out quite a bit at night, so you have to round them up again. Sometimes you miss some. It is flat out there, but with a gully here and there, you can miss fifty head if they are in one of those."

"I understand every cow has to have a brand or you have big trouble selling it. Why is that? Too many rustlers?" I asked that with a grin on my face, but Mary said, "Basically, yeah. There is a saying that if you want to eat your own beef, go to a neighbor's barbeque! To explain more, the cattle are going to cross the fences (or go through them) and it just depends on how honest everyone is. When you do spring branding, you try very hard to get all of them, but there is always a certain amount that you miss. That is why branding can go on all season long."

"What happens in the fall?"

"Another crew is hired for fall works around the first of August. In between the spring and fall there are a couple of months where everything is pretty settled, no water tank ice has to be broken, cows are in summer pasture, horses are turned out, and that is the time when the permanent camp cowboys will go on vacation, go see their families.

"There is no down time in winter between fall and spring works. The ranch elevation is 6,800 feet and it does get cold and snows. There are lots of water tanks to de-ice and the cows begin to have their calves in February, sometimes in a snowstorm. Calving takes a lot of work. Usually it is the young cows that have problems, but it can be an older one too."

"If a cow needs assistance, does she cooperate?" My own special cows were gentle and easy to help, all bets were off on range cows in my mind, but did they know they needed help?

"No, they gotta rope and 'tip her.' They rope them and flip the rope again so that it goes around their front feet, then they get them down, tie their legs together in some fashion and then they can assist with the calf."

"Does their horse hold the cow like seen in photos and paintings?"

"Well, you hope. The regular camp cowboys do get the best horses and many times they will have several of their own horses that they really know. A lot depends on a well-trained and good-minded horse partner."

"Is calving on the ranch a big problem?"

"A lot can happen to cause problems, but one of them is too big a calf. The bulls they were using were supposed to be 'easy calving', but they had some calves that weighed a hundred and forty pounds on the heifers. That is way too big for first time mommas. A couple of times they had to do a cesarean. The cow doesn't always survive that."

Cows are tough beasts. Nothing like a horse who could faint at the thought of having a cesarean delivery, which doesn't work out as well as with a cow. I had a couple of beef heifers in my early days on our farm in Indiana. I watched one of them labor for several hours (my bad).

Finally called the vet, an old timer who had been there and done that many times.

Dr. Weldy did a C section as the calf was too large and he had determined that it had already died. With the young cow still standing, he gave her a local anesthetic, cut the area on her side, delivered the calf, and poured a bottle of antibiotic in the cavity. The heifer was pretty nonchalant about the whole affair and was soon eating hay. I learned a hard lesson that day: Watch your heifers and always call the vet first.

Many years later we had again had some other young beef cows and I poured over the bulls used in the artificial insemination program, looking for an 'easy calving' bull. Found one highly recommended, and bred both heifers. This time I watched them like a hawk, had them stalled deep in clean straw in the barn and had the vet on speed-dial. Sure enough, the first one went into labor and struggled. As she turned those big brown eyes on me, pleading for help, I called the vet and fortunately he was close-by. With his assistance we soon had a big baby boy. Where was that 'small calf size?'

A few days later the next heifer went into labor and the same thing occurred. A too-big calf. Again, all turned out OK, but that one was even larger and harder to pull. Enough of this, I thought, and next time bred my heifers to a Jersey bull (A small dairy breed) and the calves literally fell out. Another lesson learned. That was why some of the other ranch gals had done the same thing by breeding their cows to Longhorn bulls with smaller calf weights.

"Mary, you were actually hired on as the wagon cook. As I said earlier, I shuddered to think about doing that. Please tell me how that worked. It isn't like you had a nice house where you could cook and feed the men, right?"

"Actually, most of the time I did. Most of the fall works happened at Rose Well. At Pica, another camp, I used an old milk delivery truck which was outfitted with what I needed. And those two camps did have electricity so I could use a crock pot and then go riding with them!

"You were feeding eight to ten cowboys?"

"Yes, and but most of them were not big breakfast eaters, especially around three a.m. when they had to get up, but I made breakfast sandwiches and wrapped them in foil. They could put them under their truck's heater and warm them up and eat when they wanted to. Like my dad said, 'You need to be where you need to be before it gets light,' then you ride out at daybreak so you can see the badger holes and other dangers.

"Every wagon cook has their own ideas. The one before me like to bake, I didn't, but I did try to make deserts and used the crock pot a lot. The guys joked that they were all getting fat, and that wasn't supposed to happen! Since a lot of cow work was done close to Rose Well, I could go out and be a part of that and then leave and make the meal.

"The thing that was the most eye-opening was what the cowboys thought was expected of them by me, the cook. I was asked what time they should come for the meal. I told them, 'Don't worry, it will hold. Whenever you are ready.' When they came to the door, they asked if that was the right door, and if they could wear their boots. When I started hearing the stories of past cooks, it was heartbreaking. There were so many rules: You have to be here at twelve because at twelve-o-five, the food gets dumped."

"Really? On a ranch? Good gracious!"

"The only thing I was strict about was breakfast because they did have to get up and get going. Otherwise, time would get pushed back farther and farther. I said lunch was at eleven, but whatever I make will hold. They were like, 'Really?' Another cook got mad and would only fix salads. Finally the jigger boss said, 'These guys need some meat.' So the cook took hamburger, fried it up, didn't drain or season it at all, put it in a bowl and plopped it on the table. And then would send six guys out with one sandwich and one apple between them!

"Another cook started a pot of green chili stew the day before the wagon started and then kept adding to it. That was the menu three times a day for months."

Mary chuckled. "Here I am fixing roasts which are actually easy, chocolate crème pie and cheesecake and stuff like that. The guys are like, 'Wow!' I tried to cook a whole beef shoulder at a time…"

"How did you do that, have a pit? —just kidding."

"I wish! No, I had a big oven, but usually I cut it up and used the six-burner commercial cook top, and I would try to cook all of it. We would eat it as roasts for a few meals and then I could do shredded burritos and stuff. After all the bad things that had happened with past cooks—in fact one even had such a horrible reputation that it got all the way to the Canadian border—I tried to be creative with my meals. It was criminal what these young guys had had to put up with."

71

This summer after the spring wagon, Mary decided that she would move on. Mike, who had hired her, had also moved on and things were not the same. It is hard on a huge ranch where the owner isn't involved with day-to-day issues, to always have things work to everyone's satisfaction. In my opinion the Diamond A Ranch lost a fabulous cook and a super, wonderful pseudo-mother to young cow hands when Mary left.

Always resilient, Mary is now again in Prescott. Who knows where she will next plant her cowboy feet?

Written by Mary

Have you ever watched coffee perk in a glass coffee pot?

Sunday, I got to stay home, a day off. As the sun came up and greeted me through the kitchen window, I put my coffee on the stove and got lost watching it. The sun provided me with an opportunity to see a process of change that I'd not taken the time to see before. The water starting to move as the flame changed it from cold to hot. The molecules excited by the heat. The first brown drops of coffee from the basket holding the grounds. Changed. No longer cold, clear water, now hot, dark and rich. Ready to warm my hands when I wrap them around the cup. Never to return to its former state.

I thought about what excites my molecules, what changes me into something different, never to return to my former state.

This land changes me. These cows and horses change me.

This ranch is not a paradise. There is no natural water, no rivers, no streams, not even one spring on its almost 60,000 acres to bring vital water to the surface. Any water here is caught when we are blessed by enough rain to run in to the dams or it is hauled. There are few spots that most would call beautiful. It's harsh, rocky, hard on horses. It's subdivided, houses here and there. Fences in various states of decomposition. The skeletons of shattered dreams abandoned to decay and packrats by folks not prepared to live life without all the conveniences. Home Owners Associations, 2 of them, formed by the more monied residents who want to live out here but have no concept of ranching, cattle, grazing rights or open range laws. People and traffic colliding with ranching and cow work and texting the boss at 1:15 AM to inform him that there is a lonely cow near her house that we should come and get right away because the others must have left her behind (we had just weaned 300 head of calves, yes there was bawling).

Yet despite the terrain, the lack of grass (or anything resembling edible green), the weather, the water challenges and the people, the cows thrive. They are fat and spend their afternoons sunning themselves and chewing their cuds. They go about their daily business peacefully in preparation for the arrival of the calves they are carrying. The 2 or 3 months that they have only themselves to take care of are spent grazing and resting. The calves we weaned last month are gaining at a startling pace. They are a tough, hardy lot making much out of little.

The work changes me. My days no longer spent behind a desk, with the constant people noise, keyboard clacking and phones demanding attention. No commute, no traffic lights, no watching the commuter next to me pick his nose. No TV, no electronic noise, no commercials informing me that what I have is not the latest, greatest model. No street lights, no sirens, no drive throughs, no $7 cups of coffee.

My days start early. Long before the sun silhouettes the San Francisco Peaks. Before there is any noise. I am welcomed to each day by the breeze sifting through the juniper, the clatter of elk hooves leaving the dam when I startle them. Utter quiet. Unbroken by human sound. The hint of sunrise on the horizon. And I am changed. I am peaceful.

When I chose to live this life and do this kind of work 15 months ago, I didn't know just how much it would change me. How peaceful I could get, how I could be inspired by cows just being cows. How much I had missed 16-hour days and the physical weariness that comes from using my muscles all day. How calm the early morning is when there is no interference.

This life excites my molecules. Despite the challenges, the changes and the aches and pains, I don't dread the day or have that miserable knot in my gut when I slide my card through the time clock.

The sunrise, watching the wind change the clouds, the calves that encircle my truck wanting breakfast, the little white-faced heifer that will eat cake from my hand, the feel of a good horse between my boot heels, and cows just being cows and growing food excites my molecules.

Life matters and our health, both physical and emotional, are directly linked to our sense of well-being. And it's short. Passing us by at break-neck speed. Each day is what we make of it. Not all days will be good but we have to look at the averages and determine whether or not we are on the plus side.

I've sacrificed for this life. No 401k, no insurance, no big paychecks, no warm office to spend my days in, no retirement plan. I'll work until I go face down in the dust, hopefully from the back of a good horse. All that I will leave to my descendants is my love, my work ethic, my reputation and a few trinkets picked up along the way.

I'm not saying that anyone should choose as I have, to relinquish what brings you security, to say to hell with it all, but, in your life, just don't forget to keep the molecules excited.

****

Several months later I again met with Mary and continued her ongoing saga of being a cowboy in a man's world.

"The fall after I left the Diamond A, I got a call from a guy I had known through the Cowboy Poetry group and he wanted to know if I knew anyone who would be interested in a job that was part ranching and part working on a pipeline on a ranch north of Williams, Arizona. I said, 'Yeah, me.' I stayed there for five months—as soon as I got there, the ranch was put up for sale. Both my boss and I agreed that if another opportunity came along for me, I should take it."

I said, "I remember seeing on your Facebook page that you were driving a big water truck."

"Yeah, and it was an experience because Highway 64 between Williams and the Grand Canyon is really busy. In 2016, the Grand Canyon had 3.6 million visitors and about ninety percent of them got there on that road. So many of them are foreign, and if they get a traffic ticket here, they don't care because they will be gone. The cops up there say the average speed if they stop somebody is 120 mph. And you put a four-thousand-gallon big water truck out on the road that caps out at 53 mph, it kinda causes chaos because the drivers are going to pass—they don't care if there are cars coming or not, and the tour buses are just as bad, they are terrifying. Every day was a whole new adventure; it was scary, I had never driven anything that big before, and there was no place out there to learn to run through all the gears, except out on the highway."

"How many gears were there?"

"It was a ten-speed semi-truck, seventy-two thousand pounds, loaded. There would be times that it took me fifteen to twenty minutes just to get out on the highway because it was so busy."

"Oh, mercy. How long were you on that road?"

"It was eleven miles each way to go up to Valle to the well and then back to the ranch to water the cattle. That well at Valle is supposed to be 12,000 feet deep. There was no natural water on that ranch; I did finally find one little seep that in a really, really good year might almost make a spring. All the places around there have to have their water brought in."

I told her we go to the Grand Canyon when visitors come, but now I will be looking at that road through different eyes after talking to her. She said that area is one of the most dangerous stretches of road in Arizona. Her current ranch is off of Highway 93 and that also is dangerous because of people going to Vegas from Phoenix driving at high speed with Friday and Sunday nights being the most "horrible."

Mary said, "Next I went to the Pipeline camp which is part of the C Bar S Land and Cattle LLC, it is the most southwest camp and is in Yavapai County."

"What is a typical day on your new ranch?"

"I am on the place all by myself. I have around eighteen miles of pipeline that waters the whole place that is spring fed, and I have to be sure it is working properly so the cattle get water."

"It is a mechanical job then; do you have to get out there with your wrenches and blowtorch?" I asked.

"This one is pretty easy. Where I was before, at Howard Mesa, near Williams the water line was five or so feet deep, so if it leaked, you had to have a back hoe to dig it up, and it might leak for a week or two before you saw it make the ground wet. Now at the Pipeline, which is low in the desert, it rarely freezes, so if it is buried, it is only a foot underground, and you can see the leaks quickly—or the rabbits will show you where they are. They dig the wet spots to get water."

"Have you had to make repairs?"

"Yes, frequently. Some portions of the pipeline are roughly thirty or more years old, so it is a high maintenance deal. Most of the time the repairs are simple, the line is PVC, but the biggest problem is shutting off the water back up the line and waiting for it to drain out so you can repair it. Also you have to make sure your water storages don't drain out because of a leak, because it takes *days* to refill them, that is why I check it almost every day, or check the storages to be sure they are where they should be in case I have to go to town or be away for a while."

"About how many cows are you responsible for?"

"Maybe around sixty-five pair, plus some replacement heifers, and some bulls."

I said, "I hate to say this, but what is it like being a *woman* and out there all by yourself with all these cows and the pipeline?"

"I don't know, it is a responsibility just like any other job. The nice thing about my boss is that he is really helpful when I have a problem, and if I cannot fix it, he is very responsive. I had a problem with my house water which is off a well with a solar pump. You try to be sure there is no problem anywhere else, like a leak, before you pull the pump out of the well. Finally, we did have to pull it. But he is good about telling me what to do. With the house water, finally I just had to say, 'I give— you are going to have to come and see what is wrong.'

"With your cows, what do you have to do with them?"

"Keep them healthy; keep the mineral and salt available, and water of course."

"Do you ride around them on a horse?"

"Usually I use the quad because it is faster. Most of the country isn't difficult, but I do have a couple of mountainsides that are not great for the quad or a horse either! Now that the weather is a bit cooler, the cattle are hanging out near Date Creek for the winter, and most of them I can see on the quad."

"That is the same Date Creek that runs through Kimberley Knight's Date Creek Ranch?"

"Yes, they border the Pipeline on the east."

"Do you have to worry about snakes, has a cow ever been bit?"

"So far I haven't. Every now and then you will see a cow that has been snakebit, but they grow up in that desert and usually leave the snakes alone."

"I suppose if a cow was bit, she would die?"

"Not necessarily. If it was a green Mohave, then likely yes, as their venom is entirely different and very deadly (neurotoxic-hemotoxic). The animals are smart. I was riding a mare one day on one of the other camps on the ranch and started to go up a mountain path, when the mare spun around, and then I heard the rattlesnake. She had smelled it before we got to it and that is the advantage of having horses that are raised in the area.

"Stephan, the owner, has been buying quite a few of the

mustangs from the Wild Horse Inmate program in Florence, Arizona. Inmates work with professional horse trainers to train the BLM mustangs so they can be adopted. They are great little horses—tough, sure footed, and well broke, but not trained to do cow work. I rode one and at first was skeptical because he was small and 'light.' I wouldn't have wanted to rope off of him, and he really didn't know anything except how to be ridden, but we got out there on the side of the mountain waiting for the others to make a bigger circle, and he never missed a step. The thing that is really neat about the mustangs is that they are always watching, always looking. He never danced around or got silly, but he never stopped looking around, being aware of his surroundings."

"Do you have very many mustangs?"

"I think there are maybe ten or twelve of them and they are all geldings. Stephan also has a huge white mule that has some age on him now, but there are pictures of him packing big rolls of pipeline."

I said, "Now you don't have to do too much 'horse stuff,' most of your work is on the quad?"

"I've got three horses down there now. One mare came out of town and I am trying to accustom her to ranch life. I think she is bred because he has a stud and they had been together in the pasture and now she is a round barrel. I have horses there but don't use them a lot in the summer because it is too hot. The rest of the year I ride a lot more."

I said, "I remember earlier when I talked with you, you weren't too keen on using dogs with the cattle, mostly because of the training, or lack of training. I understand you have changed your mind here because Stephan uses dogs. What kind of dog?"

"He has Catahoula. They have a short coat, are longer legged and stocky with a good nose. He has tried longer haired dogs in the past but the desert is too hot for them. The Catahoulas are tough and work well for him."

According to the internet, the Catahoula was originally bred as a hunting dog used for the wild boar that were local to its origin in Louisiana. But as working dogs they have been used to track and hunt many animals including mountain lions, which is where I had first heard about them here in my part of Arizona, and bears. Their herding instincts are also very strong, but they use *intimidation* to control their herds instead of the way Border Collies and other herding dogs do. The size also varies from thirty-five to eighty pounds.

I said, "Explain how the dogs work."

"Usually he will take three or four 'catch dogs' which take off away from us and go look for cows. When they find some, they bark but hold the cows close to where they find them—not much will get away from them—until we get there, then they take off again searching for more. We drive those cows to a hold up and then listen for the dogs to find more. Right now he has an awesome pup that Stephan says is just getting in the way, but he is learning from the other dogs what to do. He has one dog that is his head dog and if there is a cow that wants to really get away or fight, he sends this dog in to put a stop to that. He is crossed with something else, but I don't know what it is. He doesn't leave when the other dogs do, he stays with Stephan. He has a totally different job: once we are moving the cows, if one doesn't cooperate, he steps in. It's really neat to watch. Stephan never raises his voice; the dogs just obey him."

"Stephan is a 'hands on rancher' then?"

"Yes, he is probably out there more than the rest of us, but there are only four of us."

"It seems amazing to me that four of you can take care of that many cows."

Mary asked if I had seen *Ranch Album* a DVD made by a local rancher, Gail Steiger, in 1987, but still very applicable to the area today. It had been released as a PBS special and follows the seasons of cattle ranching in Northern Arizona. I had, and show it to visitors frequently. Mary said her area was like that, only even rougher in places.

"The Santa Maria, and the Walking A ranches, which are north of where I am, the Santa Maria River runs through there and off to the West there are cliffs and at the bottom of the river, the boulders are the size of this large table."

"And you need to get in there to get the cows?"

"Yes. Where those cows are is so remote and rough that a lot of them haven't been handled much, and they don't see a lot of people. You make a noise and over the hill they go. That is when you hope the dogs are around! You cannot take a horse and go chase them, those rocks, even for a rock savvy horse, can be deadly. It is *beautiful* country, but it is rugged. There are old copper, turquoise, silver and even uranium mines out there; it took real tenacity to get back in there, especially back in the old days. In one spot the road is really narrow, and if you look down right off your knee as you sit on your horse, you will see a little tiny aluminum travel trailer down there in the canyon that didn't make the corner!"

I said, "I have to wonder how you can make a profit running cattle on that really rough country."

"You can. Those cows work hard and they make a lot out of nothin.' On land like that the leases must be pretty cheap. Folks buy some ranch land, but then see how hard it is to work, and then sell or lease it. Stephan's family came from the Dakotas, but he has been here in this country since he was two, and he has learned how to make it work. How you can take a little seep of water on the side of a hill, dig it out, put a pipe in there and water an entire ranch.

"When I first got to the Pipeline in March, we had to go to repair a water gap—a place where the fence goes over running water and sometimes it gets debris all tangled in, or torn down. That area was so incredibly rugged. We were riding on the quads, and I had only ridden a quad once before and just been riding one for a few days there. I was trying to follow the others down what was almost a cliff, straight down, hearing a friend 'in my head' saying, 'Quad 101, here's what you do,' but I 'safetied' up too much, locked up the brakes and it was so steep, it just came over. It landed upside down; I was flicked away from it and went down on both hands around a Cholla cactus! Luckily, I had on cotton gloves; I peeled them off and one of the other guys spent about twenty minutes with a pocket knife picking the Cholla out of my hand. They picked the quad back up and I was good to go. If I had been alone, I would have been in trouble because I could never have gotten it up by myself."

"So, did you learn how to go down hills, or rather cliffs?"

"I did."

"What is the secret?"

"Don't stop. I put the brakes on too hard when I should have just let it go. We had been going down, down, down and down some more, and I just chickened out and tried to stop so I could look at it, because it was just almost daylight at that point, but with all my tools in the back, it just came over."

"Oh, Mary! You were doing this in the near dark? How scary."

"There are spots out there that I still look at and go around until I get sick of doing that and figure out *how* to get down—or up them, because that's almost as scary. And you are out there all by yourself, so if you get hurt…"

"Does the cell phone work out there?"

"In most places it does. If I go out horseback or not, just making my normal route around the water where they can track me pretty easy, I leave a note on the kitchen counter about what I plan to do and when I should be back. If anyone tries to get a hold of me, at least they know where to go look for the horse! If you get hurt out there you are 'SOL' (shit out of luck). If I see something that I am not comfortable doing, I just back away until I can feel comfortable with what I am going to do. Barring any accidents, I figure at my age I probably have five to seven years that my body is going to let me do this."

"Is where you are now, the most challenging or dangerous place that you have been?"

"Probably. It has terrain and resident challenges with the snakes and things like that, so it likely is. The snakes never hibernate down here in the desert. When I first got here in March, I saw one rattlesnake, and then nothing. I was told that was because it was too hot for them—well, not them, but what they *eat*. Their prey is all holed up to keep cool. That is the thing I have to remember. The growing season here is backwards from what I am used to. I have this little back porch I like to sit on in the evening, have a cup of coffee, check my phone messages because that is where it works the best, let the dogs chill for a while. One evening I let them out and then I heard it, right up against the side of the house. I killed that one and the next night I came out of a room into the kitchen and heard another one. It sounded like it was in the house, but it was on the walk; I heard it through the sliding glass door screen. But now that winter with the cooler temps is coming, I will likely see more of them. Spring and fall are really bad because Stephan usually kills seventy-five or eighty a year.

"Stephan was supposed to come over and check something at my house, but he called and said he was sorry, but he had something going on over at his house. His house is an older one also. One night he saw a little rattlesnake in the house, killed that one and then later killed another one. What happened was a female snake had gotten in and laid her eggs in the house. I said I would be living in my truck!

"He said, 'Well, I felt like a real wimp, but last night after I killed three of them in fifteen minutes, I went out and slept in the trailer.' He had to pull all the cabinets out of the kitchen because that was where they were coming from, and plug up all the holes, cover with plywood and put everything back. He said if he saw another one, he was just going to take a match to it, or switch camps with someone! I said, 'Don't

80

look at me!' He said he always keeps a lot of outdoor cats around to keep the mouse population down so the rattlesnakes don't get in his walls and attic as much! Where he is, it is really bad with snakes. I guess I will find out how bad mine is when the weather gets cooler. I will be investing in a bunch of snake killing shovels and place them strategically around the place."

I said, "I usually ask for snake stories when I talk to you gals, but that one takes the cake! Are you happy there? Do you think you might like to stay?"

"Yeah, it is funny. I had heard about that camp four years ago when I met Stephan after not seeing him for years. We had actually gone to school together. He talked about that camp, and then a girl I knew went to work for him. I had never seen it, but it sounded like something that would be idyllic, never thinking I would be qualified to handle a camp."

Mary said she was planning on going to the Legacy Horse Sale in Prescott later that evening, but wasn't buying anything as they were way too expensive. Also, she said, "I had five horses when I left the Diamond A and I had to sell all of them, and I do *not* want to do that again. I had a special little mare that I loved and was worth a good deal of money, and I gave her to someone I trusted to take good care of her. I don't want to be in that position ever again."

I said that I understood and agreed. I now have one horse and four mules and figure, God willing, they will all be buried here on the ranch. I had raised, bought and sold my fair share and now all I wanted was to be sure the ones I had would always be cared for until they died.

By Mary Matli

You don't see me

You don't see me
I am of the drive-by people
65' from the yellow stripe
On an old gray
Not for trade
We follow 30 head of good 1st calf heifers

You don't see me
You see
Unmanicured sunburnt grass
Vast open miles of…nothing
No shopping malls
No super-size it
No double-shot make it skinny
No neon flashing to hypnotize
In a gotta have it right now store
Emptiness
You don't see me

I am in your way
72,000 pounds
Cat diesel screaming
4,000 gallons at a time
Keeping you 10 below when you want 10 over
A black smoke rolling lumbering
Roadblock that you'll
Risk your life to get around
Get on down the road to the
Next attraction
No, I won't take the ditch for you

You don't see me
My rain drenched face
Upturned

Hands full of precious mud
After 100 days without
Or my tears
They fall on the still wet hide
Of the calf I couldn't save

Boots walking the floor at
Midnight trying to
Balance too many and
Too few
Where is the grass?
Where is it not?
Can baby calves walk that far?
And how many days 'til we
Ask them to walk again?
And where do we go…then?
You don't see me

You can keep your multi-line madness
Fax clacking
Copier-reeking formaldehyde-scent carpeted
Star rated suffocation boxes
Out here
I can take a deep breath
Without feeling like I'm stealing
Your oxygen
I feel the sun, the wind
I bury my face under a horse's mane
My world is right and I am home
I am grateful
You don't see me

I ask now
When you fill your cart
With bounty of sustenance
Suited to your tastes
Your cravings
Say a little prayer
Say thank you

Remember us out here

We give up shopping malls around
The corner
And soccer practice
And paved roads
Electricity
Big screens
Paid vacations
We give our youth to sun
And wind
And worry
We live and die by conservation
Legislation and an annual
Paycheck
We fill your shelves
Your backyard BBQ is a
Smashing success
The ranchers
The farmers
The drive-by people
Can you see me now?

CHRISTI SILVERBERG-ROSE
Bethany's Gait Ranch

I heard about Cristi Silverberg-Rose and Bethany's Gait Ranch through Bonnie Ebsen Jackson when I interviewed Bonnie about her horse program. Cristi's program works with restoring the lives of those who have served in the military, first responders, and their families. The program specializes in PTSD, traumatic brain injuries, adjusting to civilian life, and the secondary trauma experienced by spouses and children. A unique thing about Bethany's Gait is that it is also a horse rescue.

As Cristi says, "We have found that bringing the rescue horses together with the people offers a unique situation where horse and human heal through a bond that is developed based on unconditional love, unwavering trust and a keen understanding of what the other has been through.

"The majority of the horses have lived hard lives that may have included abuse, neglect and/or severe health issues. In most cases clients are given the chance to choose the horse they want to work with, which helps develop a closer bond."

Two of my first questions were about the name: Bethany's Gait. How did that come about? And what created the interest in the first place?

"This is actually our ten-year anniversary using horses to help others. Initially we felt called to start Bethany's Gait for foster children. We were living in southern California at that time. Many years ago, I had met a little girl named Bethany. I was a single mom and I had to sell my own horse because I couldn't afford diapers and hay. I saw an ad for volunteers to help with a horse program and foster children. If you helped, you could also ride. They were a summer camp during the week, and on the weekends, they had the children come out from the county home where children were taken until foster homes were found for them.

"While I was there, I met this little girl, Bethany. She was a beautiful, sweet little girl, but whatever had happened to her had caused her to completely shut down. After a couple times on the horses she started opening up, talking, laughing and being a little girl again. We really bonded on those Saturdays, and I realized that these kids need more than one day. I wanted to help and do something right then, but God's timing isn't our timing. My pastor said to me that God wouldn't want me to abandon my own young child to help abandoned children.

"Fifteen years later I met my current husband and the time was finally right. I was able to quit working and he could support the family. We started our program and named it after Bethany. By that time, I had lost touch with her and there was no way I could find her. Our program went through several transitions. For a while we worked with people with addictions, but I discovered I just did not have the heart for that. Finally the military: my husband had been a Marine for twenty-four years and my son is currently serving.

"Growing up in California there were three Marine bases, a large Navy base, and a Coast Guard base, so military was a huge part of my life. My husband had one of his guys commit suicide when he came home from a deployment, and he realized that what is being offered as help isn't enough. Sitting across a table from a therapist doesn't always work. He said, 'First of all we are guys and second we are Marines. We are suck it up, grab your gun, and keep moving.'

"He saw what was happening with the horses and the children and thought maybe we should try something with the military guys. He actually helped me put together the initial program. He is *not* a horse person! He is a dog person. He rides twice a year—on my birthday and Mother's Day. But he saw the benefit of the program."

"This is all in California?" I asked.

"Yes. That program really grew; we were working primarily with active duty military. Then my son went to Embry Riddle here in Prescott. So we came out to visit him for four years and got to know the area. My husband, Hoke, is from Kentucky and I knew he would never be happy staying in California forever. Prescott seemed a nice compromise because I did not want to move to Kentucky! And we both began to feel the pull to come to Prescott. We felt we were needed here.

"When we first got here, I said to God, 'You have really opened my heart to the young Marines, soldiers and sailors. Why are You putting me here? The closest base is Luke Air force Base two hours south of Prescott. But then I met Colonel Fred Cone who runs the veteran's program at Embry Riddle, and he said, 'You know, I got a lot of young guys that come here to go to the college, and they are really, really broken."

"You mean, they have been in service and now are home?"

"Yes, they are using the G.I Bill to go to college there and also Yavapai College. Thirty percent of Embry Riddle students are veterans. Most of them served during Operation Enduring Freedom which is Afghanistan, and Operation Iraqi Freedom, so they are the younger guys, which is where my heart is. But now it is the older ones too. I just care for them all. The work we are doing here is so much more needed than what we were doing in California.

"We soon realized that both male and female veterans are in need of help and are just not getting what they need from the VA. You wonder if what you read is really correct, but from what we see and hear personally, it is bad. Especially when they call the crisis line and are told to call back later. What we decided was that we would just wrap around the whole family. We work with the veteran and their spouse and kids if they have them. Right now, I think we have ten families."

"Do you have a therapist in your program?"

"We do. She is a Navy veteran; she is younger and a mom. She gets the struggles the families have. She is awesome. I love her. We found that having our therapist and volunteers come from a military background is extremely important. The military has its own culture, and if you don't understand it, you are not going to get the respect or trust that is needed.

"We have one single guy who helps as well as gets therapy. He is estranged from his family because he had a rather tumultuous childhood. He had been blown up twice and experienced some pretty awful stuff. He was deeply scarred by that. But this has become his family."

"Tell me how these folks find your program."

"Mostly by word of mouth, some from the VA. There is an Ethos Ministry that is a Christian support group for combat warriors. A lot come out of that group."

I said, "Boy, it seems like you would have so many people that need to come, that you could not accommodate them all."

"Well, we haven't gotten to that point. Sometimes it takes the new veteran time to actually get out here because horses can be large and scary if you aren't familiar with them; and frankly, many don't like the idea of getting any type of *therapy*. That is why the mentorship program works well."

"So how does the therapist actually work with a veteran in this program?"

"We have three separate programs. One is the Equine Facilitated Psychotherapy (EFP) Program. The therapist will be paired with an equine specialist, a person who is also certified in EFP and is an experienced horse person. Their primary role is to be sure the client and horse stay safe, but they also participate in creating exercises and the therapy process. EFP does not necessarily involve riding the horse. Many times, things will come up while they are brushing the horse, or trying to clean out the horses' hooves. They might get frustrated because the horse keeps pulling his foot out of their hand. If this is an equine therapy session, the therapist can explore further. They can talk about why that situation is frustrating to them and how it might relate to other things in their life that is frustrating. This is different from sitting in an office and asking about their frustration—'what is that like for you?' They don't even realize they are 'in therapy.'

"Right now, I am working with a spouse who was pretty severely abused as a child and when she is in a situation where she doesn't feel in control, she struggles tremendously. She got on a horse and had a panic attack. She couldn't move to get off the horse.

"This is a young couple where he was the sole bread winner, a very traditional marriage like something you haven't seen since the fifties. They were high school sweethearts, married right out of high school, and he took complete care of her. Then he got blown up, and now what? She went to school, became a nurse and became the breadwinner, and he felt like he wasn't a man anymore.

"When she froze on that horse, she needed him. And I said to her husband, 'I need you to come over and help your wife.' He climbed up on the mounting block and talked to her, put his arms around her and was able to be that supportive husband who took care of her. That was *huge* for their marriage. I had absolutely no idea that was going to happen. I thought she was going to get on the horse and we were going on a trail ride! You can say that God is in control of many of these situations. He knows what they need.

"They have now bought a small ranch, along with horses and several other animals. I go over there and ride with her sometimes, and some days she comes here. Her fear level is fading. This all gave the husband a purpose and a chance to feel like he was the head of the family again. This is how our program revolves around each family as needed. We stay open to what we can do to help in any way it presents itself.

"Another program is our mentor program where the client is paired one on one with a mentor to learn horsemanship. We pair a veteran with a veteran, and if working with a spouse, another spouse or a veteran. For the kids we can use pretty much anybody. Most of the time they just want to braid the pony's tail—because most of them are girls. Sometimes the mentor program brings out the desire to join the psychotherapy group and do more in depth talking of their issues.

"For the first time, we just did a camping trip with three of the guys in the mentor program."

I wondered if this was still therapy or just fun.

"Oh, absolutely both. On one of the trail rides that weekend, one of the guys said he had to hold back tears because he couldn't believe that he was out in this incredibly beautiful place on this horse that he just loves. He is *extremely* bonded to one of my geldings. He said he just sat there and started thanking God for letting him survive and be able to enjoy this. He didn't believe he could be so blessed after the things he had done in the war. It was this huge epiphany for him."

"Yeah, a big healing, I would imagine. I can only imagine what he and others have gone through." I said.

"Right. A lot of them have told me that just being out in the wilderness where they can be alone with their thoughts is really huge for them. I am assuming that the packing trip that we are planning in Utah will be more of the same. I am not going, but we probably will send the therapist along.

"My husband, Hoke, who is not into the horses, is really into taking care of the ranch. He worked placing rocks for walkways and water control for a year and a half, and realized how therapeutic that had been for him. Some of the guys come out and say they don't have any interest in the horses but would love to help with the stuff out on the ranch. On Saturdays when he is here the guys can pull weeds, place rocks, or fix fences with him."

When I made the appointment to visit with Cristi, three of the guys were planning on being there also. That did not work out, so I asked Cristi to share their stories. The first is about a young Army Veteran.

"He grew up in a family that he probably would have been taken out of if CPS had known what was going on. They kinda lived like Gypsies, camped a lot, and he didn't go to school regularly. He joined the Army to get away from his abusive parents. While in the Army he was the one who had been among those who had fired upon a village, killing the women and children. Because of this he was terrified to be alone with children; he was afraid he would hurt them.

"Now to us this doesn't make sense because we know he didn't purposely do that. But a lot of what affects those soldiers doesn't make sense to those who do not understand. He also got blown up while he was driving and has a traumatic brain injury and PTSD. He is extremely intelligent so that is very difficult for him. When he got back, he did go home because he had nowhere else to go. He was so damaged he just lived in the closet. His mom would bring him food; he was terrified of everyone.

"Eventually he got hooked up with Ethos Ministry which is a Christian support group for combat veterans, and then found his way to us. His big thing was last year he rode in the Veteran's Day Parade. He said if anyone had told him five years ago that he would be doing that, he would have said, 'You are crazy because I am never going to put myself in a vulnerable position like that.' He is going to school to become a social worker, and he wants to be a part of an equine therapy program and has gone through that training.

"He found that worked best for him—being with his peers, who can say, "I know, I understand, I am here for you, I got your 'six.' He has come a long way in the two years he has been with us. He does still have periods of time where he 'goes into his cave.'

"Because of his close bond with Big Tucker, the horse he chose from the program, I can text him and say, 'Tucker needs you.' There even was a time when Tucker colicked and I called to let him know. I always let the guys know if their horse is ill, because they become so attached and need to be in the loop. So he came out and stayed the night, going out regularly to check on his horse, who thankfully recovered.

"An incident came up the other day that was a helpful lesson for him. He wasn't paying attention to the horse's language and Tucker kicked at another horse, causing him to fall off. The lesson for the veteran was to pay attention to what others are communicating; it might not be what he thinks it is at first. And he has issues with disciplining Tucker because of his childhood. There had been plenty of time for him to stop Tucker from kicking. The horse's ears went back, which is a sign of being upset, and next he kicked.

"Another veteran, who is a Marine, comes from a very traditional Mexican family and also had a rough childhood. His dad has just recently come back into his life which is awesome for him and his kids. The first time he got hurt his traumatic brain injury was misdiagnosed and he was sent back into combat. The second time he got hurt, he came back home angry and frustrated with his short-term memory loss and difficulty concentrating. Without a clear diagnosis, this caused issues in his marriage and he and his wife actually separated for a while.

"He was on the verge of suicide and ended up going into residential care for a couple of months. During that time a lot of healing occurred with them and they got back together. Samaritan's Purse is the organization that got them started with their healing. They do marriage retreats for married couples in Alaska. At the retreats they participate in a variety of outdoor activities, including river rafting, fly fishing, hiking, etc. That was where things really clicked for them because this Marine veteran got stuck in the mud and for hours, they couldn't get him out.

"Physically or in a vehicle?" I asked.

"Physically. He was fly fishing and I guess his boots somehow got stuck in the mud."

I thought that was a pretty strange thing to happen, so I googled "fishing and stuck in mud," and yes, I guess it happens.

"His wife said that was when she realized that she couldn't lose him; she couldn't go on without him. She thought he was going to die— stuck in the mud in Alaska. It was a turning point in their marriage. His rescue is a story in itself. Along on that trip was a female Navy amputee who had lost an arm. She was in a canoe and saw what was happening. She told them to get her out of the boat so she could help him, but they wouldn't do it. I guess they were afraid she would be hurt.

"She told his wife, 'If you don't get me out of this f..king boat, your husband is going to die. So she helped her get out, and she took a knife, went down into the water and cut his boots to relieve the suction. Apparently, the people running the camp didn't know that the only way to get him out was to cut him out of the boots. They had just been trying to pull him out. For the female sailor, that was huge. They have a reunion each year and she told the wife, that while the situation had been horrible for her and her husband, it had given her back her confidence and helped *her* immensely.

"The other veteran who would share his story was a Sergeant Major in the Army and lived in Georgia. His wife wanted him to come to this area because he has family here, and she hoped they could help him, as she couldn't. He came out to volunteer as a mentor and as he did that, he realized that he was getting help too. He and my husband, who was a Lieutenant Colonel, have become father figures to the younger guys because so many of them seem to have problems with their dads."

"That is probably why so many join the military in the first place," I said.

"Yes, they are looking for a family. And it really helps the older ones because they can help the young ones. After they get out of the military, their rank is no longer important and they don't get the respect they got before. This particular veteran has been around horses his whole life and wants to start a therapeutic ranch of his own."

"How do you help the spouses?"

"Well, everything is out there for the veterans. Many programs do not help the spouses, however. The money is *specifically* for the *vets*. They kinda get left behind. All the programs that we offer the veterans are also offered to the spouses, as well as their children and even grandchildren. We have just started a three-day retreat that is specifically for the spouses to help them understand how to best support their husbands while ensuring the well-being of themselves and their children. Some programs are for a certain length of time, but ours is open ended. They can stay as long as they need.

"It seems like it works out that you do not have too many at once. Again, perhaps God helps with that."

"Yes, some move on. Many were here at Embry Riddle or Yavapai College and go on to their new jobs, or back home."

"Tell me more about the horses."

"We rescue horses from abandonment, abuse or neglect, those who are truly in danger. Our two newest rescues were two little fillies that we saved fifteen minutes before they were headed to slaughter. Because we only have five acres, ten horses is our limit. If the horses we rescue work for our program we keep them; otherwise we adopt them out. Sometimes the horses are so abused that to work with a number of people is just too hard for them."

I said, "Oh, I know. It is hard enough to go out and *buy* a 'perfect' horse for a program like this, let alone use a rescue horse. It has to be challenging."

"Yes, it is, but we work with the horses, and we have some really great trainers who help us, and we can work through a lot of problems. The other thing is that the veterans have this understanding about trauma—'I know that look in your eyes. I get it.'"

"I can see that. And not each horse needs to be ridden. They can just brush, handle and love on them, right?"

"Right, four of our ten are not ridable because two are too young and two others have health problems, but they still can contribute. Sometimes I have to make decisions based on the animal's well-being. For instance, I might have a horse that is just 'burnt out.' It had been ridden earlier in the day and for the afternoon, it just was not in a good place, or it might be lame. They choose the horse they want to work with and if it happens that when they come for their session, the horse shouldn't be ridden, then they have to do something else with it."

"You mentioned 'Horses with Heart.' I have heard of them, how are they different from your program?"

"Bonnie's and our program work more with mental problems, and they work primarily with physical ones, and they both work with a broader population while we are specific to veterans and first responders."

I asked Cristi to share something about her horses and the program. This is from her website.

Stepping Out in Faith...
June 28, 2016
Cristi Rose, Bethany's Gait Ranch

It all started with a Facebook post two days before Thanksgiving in 2014. I was sitting at the MVD waiting to register my son's truck when my sister tagged me in a post about two fillies who were about to go to slaughter—literally. They were set to be killed at noon that day. I looked at the time and my heart dropped; it was 12:45 p.m., they were already gone. Forlorn, I looked at the post again and realized the fillies were in Nevada. I was in Arizona; Nevada is an hour behind us. They still had 15 minutes!

I knew we couldn't take them; Bethany's Gait was at capacity. I began praying frantically, asking God to have someone step forward to take the babies. One was a roan paint, the other a gruella, and they were just a year old. How could someone have turned these sweet little things over to die? I kept checking the post every few minutes but still no takers. I prayed again for God's will for them. Then very clearly God said, "Take the fillies." I knew my husband and my Board members wouldn't be happy so I argued with God. Well, as any good Christian girl knows, you never argue with the big guy! He said it again, "Take the fillies." Deciding the most important thing was to be faithful, I private messaged the feedlot.

No sooner had I hit "send" when my number was called at MVD. I thought, "Great. How am I going to pull this one off?!" As soon as I sat down, I got a message back from the feedlot saying the vet was there and could do the health check and coggins, but I had to get payment to them as soon as possible. Fabulous. I was about to start an MVD transaction that would no doubt take forever and likely with a clerk who could care less about two fillies!! Silly, unfaithful me—I should've known God would pave the way.

I shared what I was doing with the clerk, thinking she'd either be annoyed or think I was insane. Much to my surprise she was excited to be part of it and was happy to pause while I set things up. She'd start on a transaction and would patiently wait while I set things up on PayPal or responded to a message. She celebrated with me when I knew they were safe. She smiled as I walked out of MVD and into the adventures of two little fillies who I later named Daphne and Delilah—now I just needed to get them to Arizona!

It took me about a month to find the right hauler. It had to be someone with a real heart for rescue horses, and with patience to deal with these babies who had never trailered before. A friend recommended Gilfry Horse Transport and after one conversation I knew they were the right company. Again God had his hand in it! We were having more snow than usual that year and it was impossible for them to get to us. So they diverted to their ranch in Phoenix where they took care of the fillies for two days. We weren't charged for those days and I was sent pictures and given daily updates by Ofelia Gilfry.

Daphne and Delilah arrived on New Year's Day 2015. In the year and a half since that time they have brought joy to and helped heal many of our clients. They are growing into beautiful mares and serving God's purpose. It's scary to think what could have happened to these healthy, beautiful girls had I not decided to be faithful. They have already made such an impact and their work has just begun! In closing I'm reminded of Hebrews 11:1, "Now faith is confidence in what we hope for and assurance about what we do not see." And Proverbs 2:8, "...for He guards the course of the just and protects the way of his faithful ones."

Amen to that.

PAM PIERCE
Bar Triangle Ranch

I met Pam because her husband, Mike, raises some of the best local grass hay. Because we have mules and the more economical alfalfa hay (because so many irrigated cuttings can be made in the Phoenix area) is too rich for my more sedimentary lady mules, I needed grass. A neighbor told us about Mike's hay and we have been happy customers. One day when Bob and I went to pick it up out of the hay field, I brought along one of the books I wrote: *The Horse That Wouldn't Trot*. It is about our Tennessee Walking Horses, and I had been told Pam had a Walking Horse.

I gave the book to Mike for Pam. Several weeks later I got a call from Mike wishing to purchase my other two books. As far as I was concerned, having a rancher of Mike's status wishing to buy my books was noteworthy. I was thrilled. He said how much he enjoyed them and endeared himself to me forever. I had not yet met Pam, so I said I would bring them over so I could meet her. On the appointed day Hal, Bob, and I went to Middle Place, the name of their homestead and the part of the Las Vegas Ranch that Mike inherited from his father, Delbert Pierce, now called Bar Triangle Ranch.

Delbert Pierce had ranch land in Phoenix which he sold and in 1962, he moved his family to Las Vegas Ranch north of Prescott. The younger son, Steve, moved with his father, but Mike who was in college at that time remained in Phoenix area.

Armed with two books and lots of interest, we knocked on the door. Mike welcomed us to the back patio where we met Pam—and lots of chickens. I knew at that moment I was really going to like this lady.

"Sorry about the chickens," she said, "but they have free range and sometimes think the patio and even the house belong to them."

I enjoy chickens. My sister and I had a special pet rooster named Tut-Tut when we grew up, so having chickens strolling about as we chatted, ate cheese, and drank wine was cool. Dogs were also under foot, sometimes chasing the chickens, getting yelled at and demanding petting by everyone. A cat snoozed in one of the chairs. Just like home. I loved it.

Pam's story of being a ranch woman is different because she is a professional lady. She was raised in a farming community near Council Bluffs, Iowa, rode her friend's horses, and worked detassling corn during the summer months. That area had large seed companies such as Henry Field which grew seed corn. Detassling was needed so that the right pollination would occur. It was hard work and made going to school look like a lot more fun, she said.

Her dad was a country doctor doing all the required things a country doctor must do—which was about everything. To say he was busy was an understatement. When he was fifty, he moved to Phoenix, retrained to become a psychiatrist and began to practice there. It made sense that Pam would follow in her dad's footsteps, go to medical school and train to become a psychiatrist. Eventually she also moved to Phoenix where she met Mike, who was an attorney.

"How did you end up on Middle Place since you both had successful careers in Phoenix?" I asked.

"It just sort of evolved. We began coming up on weekends and loved the peacefulness of this beautiful land. We began to dislike having to go back to the valley. At some point I had the opportunity to take a leave, telling my department chairman that I would be back in six months. Six months became a year, then five, and now it has been a *long* time. We just decided the ranch was where we both wanted to be. I continue my work here in Prescott two days a week, and that is fulfilling, but I do love the ranch and I am fortunate to be able to balance both."

I knew the Bar Triangle raised hay and cattle, and Pam added that they also raised and sold horses. "We probably have forty now but have had as many as seventy."

"Tell me more about the chickens," I said, "how did that get started?"

"Well, they just sort of happened. Over the years people have 'given' us a variety of animals. A ranch hand, now our foreman, gave us some chickens. There already was an old coop with fenced yard; we spruced it up a little and moved the chickens in. They are 'free range' meaning they wander during the day and return to the coop when the sun goes down. I just enjoy watching them and appreciate the wonderful fresh eggs. The eggs are different colors: brown, white and even blue. Most of the hens are friendly. The other day I went in the house, sat down to enjoy a book and heard the gentle clucking of a hen. I spotted her sitting on the floor near my chair, happy as could be. Sadly for her, she had to leave."

Next I asked Pam about snakes. There is usually a story or two.

"Yes, we have rattlesnakes, and if they are close to the house, we kill them. The guys riding around the ranch kill what they see. One day I was out walking with a friend and one of the ranch hands rode by on his horse. I told him I had just seen a rattlesnake and he replied that they had killed twenty-seven already that summer. When they monitor the cattle herd on horseback, they kill them because the snakes can inadvertently bite them if the cattle 'step wrong.' On the other hand, bull snakes are helpful in that they eat rodents. At least once every summer we find a bull snake in the chicken coop swallowing eggs whole. We move *them* to a different pasture."

"What are your ranch duties?" I asked her. "Do you do anything with the animals?

"Well, the ranch hands do the hard work," she explained. "Sometimes I can help when cattle are being moved by planting myself in a strategic place and waving my hands to dissuade them from making a wrong turn. On days we do the branding, everybody helps. My job is often to swing open the chute door to let the next calf into the squeeze chute (it is then rotated horizontally for the branding). I also give vaccinations to protect from various diseases. Our animals do not get hormones or antibiotics. I also help with the hay-making mostly by going to town for any parts needed and getting food for the guys."

"Tell me about your cow operation."

"We have about 300 cows, and as many as 20 bulls, I think. They are Angus and Herefords and some are crosses of the two. All the bulls are pedigreed Angus. We wean the calves at about 8 months and sell most of them at auction, but also some to individuals who want healthy beef, and also that way they get the meat cut the way they want it. Some calves go to 4-H kids and many have been quite successful with them. The kids come to the ranch where several have been rounded up for them

98

to look at and choose. Most of the kids are local, but we have had some groups come from Tucson."

Pam paused and looked pensive. "When we sell our cattle at auction, they go from our welcoming pastures to…well, someplace beautiful. I know, because I just decided that. That is the best way for me to deal with raising cattle."

I said, "The other day I took a beautiful picture of one of your cows. It was speckled with *long* horns. I later spoke to Mike on the phone and he said that longhorn cattle were a hobby with you guys."

"I sort of look on them as 'art on the hoof,' they are just so pretty. Watching them and the horses walk back and forth in the back of the ranch home is such a pleasure. We have some longhorn/angus crosses also because longhorn calves are smaller and easier for first time calving heifers to deliver. We breed them to a longhorn bull. They grow as big as any other calf, but the birthing is much easier. The resulting calves are also very hardy and the meat is also leaner, which some people like."

Pam continued, "We bring the first-time mommas (heifers) to corrals near the barn where they can be checked every three hours for possible difficulties. We use the pens near the foreman's house and it is generally he who has that duty. One year (several years ago) he was recovering from surgery, so I offered to help. It was a cold January with the thermometer reading close to zero and even below. I put up a camping tent in the barn and put lots of blankets over the top. I had a lawn chair with a mattress on it and a heater inside. Every three hours I would do my duty and go out with my flashlight and check the backsides of the heifers to see who was in active labor. In that sense I guess I *am* a ranch woman, as I really embraced all this, found it fascinating and enjoyed it sort of like I was going back to my roots of being a 'country gal'."

"Pam, you mentioned the old cemetery that is on Steve Pierce's land. We drive by it all the time when we enter our subdivision. Who is buried there? Is it a Pierce Cemetery?"

"No, not Pierce, it is a settlers' cemetery. I once told Mike's father that I would like to be buried there. He said, 'You don't want to be buried with cattle rustlers and those who died by the gun!' Actually, the family names aren't desperados, but rather the settlers who homesteaded here, but it made for a good story."

Sometime after our conversation I came across an article about some of the old cemeteries in the area. This particular cemetery has several names: Williamson Valley, Las Vegas, Granite Mountain, or Pierce Cemetery with tombstones dating from 1880 to 1922. Shortly after we had finished out chat, Pam called asking me if I had lost a sheep, or knew of anyone who had—she had one on the ranch and it was a mystery. I asked her to write about it so I could include the story. It remains a mystery to this day…

Pam

Zeus and Ewe

There is always an element of surprise on the ranch. It may be your eye catching the cattle in the morning light on green pastures. It may be the movement of startled horses "stampeding"—where you *see* them running, and *hear* and *feel* the sound and vibration of hoofs. We welcome the migration of ducks and shore birds stopping off at our pond. Beyond the pond is a hill—Ponder Hill—where I have a zigzag trail to the top. I use it for exercise, traveling up and down several times. A couple months ago, from the top of Ponder Hill, I saw an animal in a nearby pasture. It didn't fit. Too small to be a calf. Not a pronghorn. I approached to find a Suffolk sheep, ragged and thin. Nephew Michael lassoed her and brought her to the barn. She was at least two miles from any road and she was a mystery. Unable to locate an owner and worried

100

about her mental health, we brought over Zeus, a Boer goat, owned by our foreman's son. Zeus and Ewe are now fat and happy, roaming at will—but never far. It is with amusement and pleasure that Mike and I watch them hang with the cattle or wander through our yard trimming the roses.

Our lives are rich with the beauty of nature and all our adventures, big and small."

That is one very lucky sheep. However in the world did she end up at that ranch and escape the coyotes and other predators? How did she get through the fence? Did someone "dump" her like some little roosters I found? Sad to think anyone would, but delightful to know others like Pam and Mike would open their home to a wayward sheep.

Pam summed up her life on the Bar Triangle by saying, "Now, after the better part of fifteen years, I cannot imagine living anywhere else. The smell of hay and sun, the grace of the cattle and horses in the pastures, (and now a goat and ewe) the seasons, the vistas, and maybe the biggest plus of all, our ranch is such a treasured meeting place for family and friends. *This is* my home."

CYNTHIA RIGDEN
Western Artist, Sculptress, and Rancher

I met Cynthia through Mike and Pam Pierce, and Pam escorted me to Cynthia's ranch near Kirkland, Arizona. The Rigden Ranch is about 3,900 feet elevation, which is about 1,000 feet lower in elevation than we are in Prescott, but still considered "high desert" and the vegetation is similar. Cynthia lives in a quaint, rustic ranch home with the first portion of the home being built in 1876. Her dad was born there in the house and although Cynthia was born in Prescott, she has lived most of her life on the ranch and in that home. She went to a one room country school in Peeples Valley for seven years and says she was a senior in high school before she wasn't just reviewing what she had learned there.

"Pam told me you have Longhorn cattle for pets and as models for your painting," I said.

"Yes, I keep some of the big steers for my painting, but others are crosses with the Longhorn that we market. We had a lot of trouble with calving with our straight Herefords, so we started crossing with the Longhorn which produces a smaller and easier birthing calf. Over time by keeping my cross bred heifers and breeding to a bull I liked, I have developed a special breed through these crosses for my ranch that I like very much. They have the dispositions and body type I like."

"What is it that you like about the Longhorn cattle?"

"They are basically very gentle and smart."

I said that I didn't ever think of Longhorns as being gentle, but Cynthia replied that it is the movies that make us think that about them. However she added that they can be wild-natured and she has selectively bred hers to be gentle. As most of these western cattle, they can be very protective of their calves, so that has to be considered.

"Several years ago, I had an interesting experience with one of my cows. I was on my horse checking the cattle and a cow ran up to me and she was bawling. I had the dogs with me and thought she was upset with the dogs. Her calf wasn't with her, but that wasn't unusual, most of the cows leave their calves with a 'babysitter' while they graze.

"I started out in the direction I was headed and crossed the creek, the cow went in another direction, but when she turned and saw that I was going away from her, she headed back in my direction and was still bawling. Finally, I realized that she wanted me to follow her! So, I followed her and found out that her calf had fallen in a ditch. That cow had stuck with me until she made me understand she needed help.

"I tied up my horse to a bush and crawled down into the ditch. All this time that cow is standing by my horse. When I got the calf out, the cow sort of nodded her head and took off with her baby."

"That *is* amazing." I agreed.

"Yes, many times when people think cows are stupid, they actually are not as smart as the cow!"

I remembered Kimberley Knight and Kim McElroy having much the same thoughts about cows. No, they are not stupid.

"Tell me a little about your ranching operation."

Cynthia answered, "We have about 8,000 acres here and maybe 200 cows. I have live-in help year around and we hire more help for spring and fall works. Back in the day we used to have big neighbor get-togethers and help each other, but now with the local auction, you can sell animals when you want to, it doesn't have to be a big roundup and sale.

"We really like our Longhorn cross cattle for market animals because they take care of themselves and are thrifty. They are deceivingly large. I had a man want one of my bulls to cross with his Corriente cows so they would have long horns, but when he found out that the bull weighed 1,300 pounds, he said that would be too large for his cattle."

I was interested in how Cynthia got started painting. She had a lot of art in her home, and I had seen some displayed at the Phippen Museum in Prescott. Much was of her horses and the Longhorn cattle.

Cynthia said, "Well my grandmother on my dad's side and my mother were both artists. That flower painting over there is one of my mother's, and some of my grandmother's are in the other room. My grandmother was pretty well known for her art. She was a member of the 'Monday Club.' Monday was the day everyone traditionally did their wash, so a group of local gals got together and painted instead of doing wash. They became pretty well known, and some became quite famous.

"I just grew up with all the 'tools' around me and did drawings when I was two. I got into sculpting when I was in college more or less by accident because the classes I wanted didn't fill with enough students, so I signed up for a sculpture class. My favorites to sculpt are cows and horses—don't do many cowboys or wildlife."

"Without asking your age, how long have you been doing art?"

She chuckled. "Well, close to seventy years if I started when I was two."

"When did you sell your first piece?"

Cynthia said, "I guess family and friends bought some pieces for a dollar or two, but I didn't sell in a gallery until I was in my twenties. This was something I always knew I wanted to do; basically, portray the animals I knew. I've done a couple with people in, but really never cared to, and I don't do wildlife. But it just grew into a life vocation."

"I know you said you didn't do much wildlife, but tell me some about your local wildlife. When we drove in, we saw a little sign that said: Elk Crossing. Do you have many elk at this elevation?"

"We had a real problem with them for a while. I don't know if they brought some in and turned them loose, or they just migrated in, but they tore up our fences. Do you have them in Prescott?"

"Yes, we do…"

"They are not native up there either. They migrated from the White Mountains some time ago. We had an irrigated strip out here that wasn't ours, but there would be about twenty elk out there. In the morning you would hear them bugling and sometimes fighting, but every time they left, they would mow down the fences and then they taught some of my cattle to jump…"

I gasped. "No kidding! Oh my goodness."

"Yes, and I have one bunch of cattle that I just cannot control. My plans to keep certain cows and bull together just evaporated and once a cow or bull starts jumping you cannot stop them. I even had to sell a very nice Longhorn bull that actually I got from Mike and Pam Pierce because he wouldn't stay on our ranch. The neighbors weren't too pleased, so I had to get rid of him. The Longhorn and Longhorn crosses are very athletic!"

"Tell me some about your horses. Do you still ride?"

"It's kinda funny that I have always loved Thoroughbred horses. There is a great prejudice against them as cow horses. The Quarter horse folks tried to make their breed look better for working cattle by running down the Thoroughbred horses. Everybody believed all this stuff, forgetting that the Quarter horse is really just a 'short running' Thoroughbred.

"Carlos, my ranch man, had this horse I called Slewpy because he is a grandson of Seattle Slew. He won a *lot* of money in big roping contests on him. A lot of horse people kept trying to buy him, and asked what his breeding was. When told he was a Thoroughbred, they said, 'Oh you cannot rope on a Thoroughbred!' and Carlos was thinking, 'But I just beat all of you…'

"My grandfather had a Thoroughbred stallion when I was young and I just fell in love with them. He crossed him on whatever mares they had and ended up with a good bunch of horses. I have gotten a lot of them just off the track and re-schooled them for my ranch horses."

"Really? I am surprised that that works. I know some make jumping horses, but roping and chasing cows—that is sure different."

Cynthia said, "Yes, they are glad to quit running when I get them. I turn them out on the ranch for a year, and I just pretend they have never been ridden. Then I start them just like I would any breed, and in about a year they are fine. It is actually harder to get a roping horse to quit being a rope horse than to get a race horse to be a cow horse."

"How do you mean?" I asked. That seemed strange to me.

"If you are riding a rope horse and a cow breaks out of the herd and you just want to get it back in, he is off after it whether you want that or not and when you try to hold him up, he just goes to lunging forward. Most of the race horses have been galloped slowly and fast, so they know how to rate down their speed. But a rope horse, well, he just wants to catch that cow! By the time you get him settled down so you don't fall off, that cow is way, way ahead of you."

"As well as doing all your art work, you actually did part of the ranch work?" I asked.

"Oh yeah, I ran it for years. My dad was blind for about the last thirty years of his life, but he kept on riding for another twenty years or so. He just rode with me; he knew the country so well he would just follow along. It has only been the last couple of years that I haven't ridden almost every day, and that was because of taking care of my mom who lived with me. And I have a knee problem that kept me from riding—and then sadly, inertia sort of sets in. Now I am spoiled. I just call Carlos and tell him to saddle my horse, and then of course, I have to go do it."

I understood all of that too. One of the pluses of moving to Arizona was that I could ride nearly every day as far as the weather was concerned, but I also found as I got older that inertia set in. It helped to have a riding friend. Once committed to a day of riding, I would do it.

Cynthia continued, "As I have gotten older, I cannot take the heat *at all*. One day I about passed out but luckily, I had my cell phone and called Carlos and he came down with the truck and got me. This time of year is perfect for me. These fall days are just right."

"Being 1,000 feet lower in elevation from Prescott makes it warmer too, but, of course, in the winter time it will be even better for you than for me," I said.

"I want to get back to riding. For years I rode virtually every day. I love training too, but I don't get on green horses anymore."

"Yes," I agreed, "we don't do that anymore."

"We don't bounce like we used to," she said.

"You trained horses for roping…?"

"Well, I barely can rope, but I trained them for working cattle. I started quite a few of them and trained more that I took off the track."

"You did raise some?"

"Yeah, I have one out here now that we raised. She is a pretty thing; she is about three now and is out of a Thoroughbred mare and a Paint stud, but she has no color, no spots. She has an odd disposition, but she is a working son-of-a gun.

"All the other colts I have raised are friendly. Within minutes they are on you like 'stink.' You are just pushing them away from you all the time. But with her, it always took two people to get hold of her. You had to corner her against a fence or behind her mother. Once you got your arms around her, she was fine. She is smart as a whip. She learned to lead and other stuff real quick, but she doesn't want to be messed with. She is her own woman.

"The other day I was coming home—she loves cookies—and my car and Carlos' look quite a bit alike. As soon as she saw that I was turning down my drive, she came running down toward me. Carlos doesn't give cookies so she wanted to be sure who it was."

Cynthia said that she had trained horses using a clicker. Many of

106

us animal people are familiar with dog clicker training, but I had not heard of using it with horses. I asked her to elaborate.

"Well, to start out you teach them to touch their nose to a target such as a small strange board. They do it because they are curious and want to investigate it. When they do, you click and give a reward such as a horse cookie—later that can be just a pat or praise. Soon you can move the board a distance or even throw it. I say 'target' and they walk over and touch their nose it, and come back to you for their treat.

"Once they know the click means they did good and they will get a treat, you start using it for other things, like sidepassing, opening or closing a gate. Two of those 'off-track' horses I got were bad at prancing instead of walking when I was headed home. I got both of them to walk on a slack rein by using the clicker. As soon as they took even one walking step, I would click and reward.

"I have one here who is a smart old cookie. He would start to prance, cock an ear and wait for the click and treat. He had that system down. When I said 'walk' if I didn't give a cookie, he would walk slower and slower. He also was the horse that when I threw the target and told him to go touch it, he'd look at me and I'd say, 'no that's not enough' then he would walk a few steps and stop and look at me again. You can see their wheels turning as they think. One of the horses was kinda bad to shy at things. When he did, I would say 'target', and he wouldn't touch it, but you could feel him relax and walk on by.

"One theory of training is that the reward system is a less harsh method, instead of using the spur to teach a sidepass. Eventually the horse does learn to move over with less spur pressure, but it is even easier with a reward system.

"Yeah," I said, "The reward the other way is in *not* being punished, but what fun is that? What is the name of that pretty little three-year-old you have out there?"

"Luna. She was born under a full moon and has a sort of half-moon marking on her face."

"Is she still hard to catch like she was when a baby?"

"I don't have any trouble catching her because I don't ride her." Cynthia chuckled. "But Carlos has a hard time with her. Slewpy, the Thoroughbred, is so different. He loves being with you. He doesn't care if you have cookies or not. I could stand with an arm over his neck all day and he would be as happy as a clam."

"Is he the one who pranced?"

"No, that was Irate. He was Three-Year-Old Arizona when he raced. He is mostly blind now, but he can still find that cookie wherever I hold it."

"You have some retirees along with the working horses?" I asked.

"Oh yes, we have a whole pasture of them. In the other pasture there are eight horses and maybe you can ride three of them."

"That sounds like me," I told her. "We moved from Indiana with five, and two mules are really ridable and one mare sort of, but they have a home for life. The two Tennessee Walking horses that I showed, I owe them. They did really good for me."

"I went to Tennessee one time and a man brought out a Tennessee Walking horse to show us. It had never had its tail or feet worked on."

"I know what you mean," I said. "You mean it wasn't a 'big lick' show horse where they 'sore' the front pasterns with chemicals, use chains around the ankles to make them do the 'big lick.' It is an ongoing battle between us 'sound horse' folks and those still wanting to train using chemicals. It is inhumane and I cannot fathom why people would want to do that. I wrote about it in my first book: *The Horse That Wouldn't Trot.* My goal was to write a fun book to read about my own horses, but also to expose that dark dirty secret."

Cynthia continued, "He was a pretty thing and sure could travel smooth and nice. Some people brought some here one time and wanted to show us how much faster they would walk. They were excellent on the flat, but surely not in the rocks."

"No, they are plantation horses, bred to walk on smooth ground down the crop rows," I agreed. "When I trail ride my walking horse mare, she looks off to the side at something and then stumbles over a rock or clod of dirt. I can just hear her say, '*Who put that there?*' She is a character, but what a show horse she was! All of my show horses were what we called 'plantation pleasure horses' and were not sored."

Cynthia said, "You know the Forest Service is now using some Missouri Fox Trotters, and I rode one of them once. We were helping a neighbor move some cattle onto the Forest Service lease. They had a Forest Service representative there and she was riding a Fox Trotter, and was letting others ride the horse and he did fine."

"A Fox Trotter has a little different type stride, it is shorter, not long like a walking horse, so I can see that it would work out better. One of my mules is a fox trotter. Her mamma was a fox-trotting mare."

Cynthia added, "It seems to me that when they selectively breed for any one special thing, they lose other things. Like cutting horses. They say if you cannot cut on them, there isn't anything else you can do with them because they have bred them to be tiny."

"Why are they tiny?"

"They think they are quicker. And then the riders are these big guys; I think it looks weird."

"I know! I have noticed that too. But I never really noticed that they were a smaller horse."

Cynthia wondered about my mules and how they were bred. I told her that they were gaited as I couldn't ride a trot because of my lower back. My favorite mule, Susie, was out of a Quarter Horse and sired by a gaited donkey. It was unusual that she would gait. One was out of a Tennessee Walking mare and the other out of a Fox Trotter mare.

"I grew up on a mule. Her name was Kate. We could do almost anything with her. I rode her and a strawberry roan Indian horse called Midget. He was a mean little sucker, and his mane came way down past his shoulders. He didn't like the human race very much, but he would do whatever you wanted. He wasn't a typical child's pony. My best horse died a couple years ago. Nobody else ever rode him, we were a real team. I think that is actually why I don't care so much if I ride now days because nothing matches up to him."

"He was your soul mate," I said.

Cynthia nodded in agreement. "He was the poster child for hot horses though, I can tell you that. He also was a Thoroughbred off the track and was three when I got him. I rode him right up until he died at 24. He was amazing. I never rode a horse that could run in the rocks like he could. He would run to turn cattle and when you turned to come back, you were afraid to *walk* over what he had just galloped through. He would watch ahead and look for little spaces to put his hooves, and shorten or lengthen his stride to hit those places."

"So, how many years ago was that?" I asked.

"Just a couple years ago. I would still be using him but he got bladder cancer of all things. Otherwise he probably could have gone on until he was 30! We had another mare that was born here and we still used her until she was 28. I turned her out then because she was so good at her jobs that people would pick her for working the cattle, but she was just too old to work that hard."

"That sure says something good about the Thoroughbreds," I said.

Cynthia agreed. "They're tough. I have had less problems with soundness than with the Quarter horses, because we have had both. I think their conformation is more correct or they couldn't run races. And their bone density is better and their feet are larger.

"Some years ago, Rex Ellsworth who owned Swaps, the race horse who won the 1955 Kentucky Derby and was one of the fastest horses ever—just recently his mile record was broken—got a bunch of Quarter horses and Thoroughbreds together to see how they stacked up against each other. None of the Quarter horses even made it to a race."

Interesting study for sure and very interesting that Cynthia favored Thoroughbreds for her ranch.

Cynthia had a photo album of her beautiful Longhorns, and my friend Pam and I were entranced. I dabble in acrylic art painting and on my 'bucket list' is painting a longhorn. I wondered if she would miss a photo or two if they just happened to get in my pocket. Since some of her older Longhorns are models for her sculpting and painting, those beautiful photos made a lot of sense.

Pam mentioned that the heads were shaped differently. Some had more of a dome and some more of a point.

"Yes," Cynthia said, "I always wanted to do a study to see if that meant something, but I never got around to it."

I said, "Yeah, you wonder if that 'little pointy head' saying really means something!"

"That is how I feel about the Angus cows—that they are ugly and dumb. People say, 'they will bring more money,' but I say that I don't care."

Of course, everyone has their favorite breed of anything, and Cynthia sure had hers where her cattle were concerned.

As we looked at her paintings, I picked out one that I had seen hanging in the Phippen Museum in Prescott. Cynthia said that those were some of the steers down by the creek. "I do a lot of them," she acknowledged.

"We can drive down there, they might come up and see us, but they will be terribly disappointed that I don't have any hay for them. They sure don't need any. I tell them they would do better at begging for food if they didn't wiggle like a bowl of Jell-o when they walked!

"The steer underneath your thumb, that red and white one, for his age he has some of the biggest horns of anything I have ever had. He is only three."

They were spectacular. I wondered how they manage to navigate trees, fences and other cows without spearing something.

"They know exactly where that tip is. And something interesting is that the bulls don't fight like the Angus do—because the Angus don't have horns and cannot hurt each other, at least not that way. But the Longhorns know that they can hurt each other, so they just avoid it at all costs. They can run down a line of fence posts and just lift their horns over every post and never hit one."

I found a picture of a young steer with his horns sticking straight out to the side. Cynthia explained, as babies that is how they grow. Later they start curving up, backwards or forward—however they desire to grow.

"Do you have a predator problem here?"

"Coyotes don't bother us too much, but I have lost a calf or two to a mountain lion. We had a strange deal happen awhile back. All the calves were in a bunch out in the middle of the flat. As far as you wanted to look in any direction, there were cows maybe a quarter of a mile away in a circle around those calves.

"One day we were riding through them and a dog spooked a calf and it bawled. *Instantly* every one of those cows came running to the calves. It was a big melee, dust flying, cows and calves bawling until each one of them had their own calf. Then they stopped like nothing had ever happened. About two days later a mountain lion was hit by a vehicle and killed and within 48 hours the cows had quit that. So those cows had a plan to protect their babies. Like I said, 'cows are smart!'"

We wanted to take Cynthia up on looking at her horses and cows, so we got in the pickup and headed to the barn and the horses. There we saw Luna the feisty, little seal-colored mare; Slewpy, the horse she now rides, and a couple other working horses. Then we headed to the creek to see the cows and the retired horses. Since I was sitting next to the door, my job was to open and close about six gates. Eventually we came to a most peaceful spot. Kirkland Creek, which runs year around and made this ranch very special, flowed between tree lined banks. Here was easy water for the animals and shade during the heat.

Then we spotted the cows and horses and just as quickly they saw us and came, looking for the hay that was not there.

"Oh, I feel so bad," Cynthia said, "I don't have anything for them."

Soon the horses were nearly climbing into the back of the truck and *were* sticking their heads in the window, searching Cynthia for treats.

"Look over there, I said, "what are those guys doing?" Two big boys were snorting and sticking their enormous horns through a fence. The bigger of the two was making boy talk: sort of a mixture of grunts and snorts.

"Those are the bulls. Each has his own herd. That big one is the old bull. He is threatening the younger one."

The old bull was impressive. I wanted to get a picture and hoped maybe I could paint him, but it did not turn out. A little later Cynthia pointed out the younger bull: he had left and was actually hiding behind some oak trees. We laughed at him, but darn, he was smart. Live to love another day.

Our time with Cynthia at the Rigden Ranch was another educational, fun-filled day. As I visit with these ranch women, I continue to marvel at their love of the land and their animals. This isn't just *a* way of life, it is *the* life.

Cynthia's art has been displayed in many galleries from coast to coast, in several well-known private collections and galleries. Her work is currently displayed in Trailside Galleries in Jackson, Wyoming, and in Scottsdale, Arizona, and at the Claggett-Rey Gallery in Vail, Colorado. The local Prescott Phippen Museum also frequently displays her work.

Cynthia passed away on June 5, 2019. On September 21, 2019, The Phippen Museum in Prescott, Arizona, held an induction ceremony for Cynthia. *The Rancher and Cowboy Hall of Fame* is a permanent exhibit that features biographical information, artifacts, photographs and memorabilia from notable Arizona ranchers and cowboys. In my opinion, there is no one more deserving, and I am honored and very glad that I was able to meet her and write this story.

SHELLY GODFREY
Yuno Ranch

Meeting gals to write about is a little like pulling a yarn string, it sort of unravels in its own time and way. Some of the ladies said, "But I am not a *ranch* lady." However, as I chatted with them, I realized they had stories to share and they are female, so in this book, they *are* ranch women. Shelly was introduced to me by another friend. None of us have big ranches, but we do have acres and animals and if you have those two things, you are bound to have interesting stories.

Most ranch folks have dogs; we do too, and I have to admit, they are not perfectly behaved. We got our new Doberman as a nine-week-old puppy, but along the way she developed anxiety. She is not comfortable with strangers coming in our home. As time goes on—minutes, hours, days (as in long term visitors) she makes up and is friendly. We live far from town and do not have a lot of visitors, but whether that is all of her problem is yet to be resolved.

I always need to admonish company to ignore Buttercup, to pet the other two overly friendly dogs, and she cannot stand it. Soon she will be right among them. It is strange how many people cannot do that, but Shelly did, to perfection. She crouched down, turned her body sideways—making herself smaller and non-threatening and started being mobbed by Arizona, the Rat Terrier, and Lady Blue, the Giant Schnauzer. Naturally, Buttercup couldn't stay away and soon was joining in with quick licks, darting away and then back for more. As we chatted, Buttercup lay down at our feet and went to sleep.

I remarked to Shelly that she did that just right and discovered that not only is she a dog lover, she works with therapy dogs. All three of her dogs are certified therapy dogs, all are rescues and two came from

United Animal Friends rescue in Prescott.

"What breed are they?"

"Bear is a Border Collie-Labrador mix and was my first therapy dog. I got him about five years ago. They need to be at least a year old to certify as a therapy dog. Sadie is a Catahoula-Aussie and probably my best therapy dog. I wanted to wait awhile until I was sure Bear was well into his training before I looked for another dog. Eventually I asked my dog trainer to help me find one, preferably an Aussie, because my favorite dog had been one.

"There is a story about Sadie. She was a stray and was found wandering along Copper Basin Road by a dog rescuer who lived in Yarnell but just happened to be in town driving down that road. No owner was found and eventually we got together. And then there is the little 'Nard'…"

"Whoa, a Nard? What breed is that, for heaven's sake?"

Shelly chuckled. "Nard stands for "Not a Real Dog" meaning in this case an adorable little mutt." His name is Ozzy, and we think he is a Westie-Bichon mix, and he has that wonderful soft hair that doesn't shed. I wanted him because some of the folks are blind and the tactile qualities of his hair are magnificent. I especially wanted a small hairy dog!"

"How did you get into therapy dog training and use?"

"I wanted to do this since our grandson was five and diagnosed with Hodgkin's Lymphoma. I was in the hospital visiting him one day and when I walked into his room, I saw this adorable little Papillon dog on his bed. Both my grandson and the dog were wearing sunglasses, and my grandson had the biggest grin on his face. I said to myself, 'OK, *I* am doing that!' It took many years before the dream could happen, but finally it did."

"Where do you take your dogs?" I asked.

"We go to nursing homes, retirement homes, and some critical care places. We are not allowed to go to Yavapai Hospital because they have a contract with Pet Partners only.

"My big black dog, Bear, has visited some Alzheimer patients. The nurses actually cried when they saw the response one patient had when he saw Bear. The nurse said this man had not responded or focused on anything. When I put the man's hand on Bear's back there was some body movement and eye contact with the dog, which was amazing.

"I have pretty much gotten out of taking my own dogs because I became a tester for therapy dogs. There wasn't anyone local to do this, and the dogs have to be tested to see if they will be able to do the job: stay calm, let strange people pet them, not be frightened of canes, wheelchairs, walkers, loud strange voices, or other dogs. Each dog and handler duo is tested separately; some do not make it, and it isn't always the animal! We take the duo to nursing homes and retirement home to see how they do. The dog becomes the 'bridge' between handler and person being visited. If someone just pops in a sick-room, the patient might not be receptive, but if the person says, 'Hi, would you like a dog visit today?' that can make a big difference in the reception."

I smiled. "That reminds me of an experience I had too. I know you have my dog book: *Dogs, Dogs and More Dogs.* Do you remember my story about Tiny the Miniature Poodle and Clyde? I took Tiny to visit Clyde in a nursing home after he had a stroke. He was one of my barn guys; even at 80 he was active and cleaned the horse stalls. I had recently adopted Tiny from the local animal shelter, and gave the little dog to him as a companion.

"At first when we visited Clyde, he clutched Tiny close to his chest as we took him in a wheelchair up and down the halls. Many other residents pointed and smiled at Tiny, but Clyde clutched him tighter. He wasn't going to share his precious dog.

"After a few visits, Clyde began to smile back and offer to let others pet Tiny. *Then* Clyde became famous! Tiny was actually a therapy dog!"

"I do remember that story," Shelly acknowledged. "It was a touching one. Isn't it wonderful to watch that? It can bring you to tears seeing what dogs can do."

She continued, "Another thing we try to determine is if the particular dog has 'high energy.' Not to jump around, but inner energy, and if they really enjoy meeting strange people. The energy they expend is phenomenal. People do not realize how hard it can be on them. I have had Bear come home after only 30 minutes of interaction and sleep for almost 24 hours. So not all dogs can be therapy dogs. Also, a dog that doesn't have the energy to visit a nursing home might be just wonderful in retirement and assisted homes."

I could relate. Years ago, my husband wanted me to work with his patients on their dietary and vitamin needs. I really poured my heart and soul into what I was saying, and when I was done, I was ready for a nap. Later I learned to pace myself, but to be 'up' and energetic does take energy.

"We also are connected with 'Gabriel's Angels' a group which works with 'at risk children,' children in foster care, group homes, or abused children. The kids in group homes are so inward that many times they will not relate or trust any adults, and once they are 18 they are put out into the world and expected to make it. By using a therapy dog, the kids open their hearts and later their minds to the dogs. Then they are more likely to relate to the dog handler, perhaps the only human they would trust. Gabriel's Angels goes to juvenile detention also."

I asked, "Do you visit the children in groups or one at a time? Who chooses the children you visit?"

"Usually we visit one at a time, and the people that are working with the children pick the ones we work with. You have to be able to commit to working with a child for at least six months because it takes a long time to overcome their trust issues. If that child can learn to trust just one adult, their chance of making it in the real world is 80 percent higher.

"My Sadie was the absolute best with children. Our first experience was with six three- and four-year-olds at a YMCA after-school program. If I had any reservations about how Sadie would respond, they quickly evaporated when I watched her disappear under a mound of little bodies all wanting to pet her. She was a natural."

I smiled. "Are these special needs children also?"

"Some come from difficult family situations, and these are the ones we want to reach. We teach them that these are living creatures."

"Yeah," I said, "please do not set them on fire!"

"Well, you know, we have heard horrific stories. One little girl said, 'Yeah, we used to have a dog and I would play with her, but she used to bark a lot, so my mom killed her,' and then just went on with the rest of the conversation as if it was nothing out of the ordinary. We have them listen to the dog's heartbeat, brush them, and they can also teach the dogs simple tricks. What we are doing is teaching that 'Life Matters.'

"When the dog and handler teams are graduated and certified, then they can pick where they want to go. The therapy dogs in our organization come with a three-million-dollar insurance policy when they visit a facility, so they feel more comfortable allowing us to come in. They know the dogs have been assessed, are up on their shots and that they come with insurance, instead of people just bringing in dogs off the streets. We give our teams a long list of facilities that just love to have us visit them and let them work out how and when to visit. It is a marvelous outreach to our community."

I like to ask questions about wildlife, especially snakes. Usually I get a story or two.

Shelly was no different. "Before we lived here permanently, we came to visit our lovely Arizona home. We were here one Labor Day weekend and when it was time to go home, my husband and my sister left with her little Shitsu dog in our pickup truck. I stayed here. A few hours later I got a phone call from Lance, my husband. 'You are never going to believe me when I tell you this story.' They were about ten miles east of the Hoover Dam on their way to Las Vegas. Traffic was heavy and they were going slowly. All of a sudden, a snake goes straight up the outside of the windshield and then over toward my sister in the passenger seat who is holding her little dog in a death grip, screaming. The snake disappears from sight. They cannot stop because there is a lot of traffic behind them. My sister is hysterical and tells Lance to turn off the air conditioning so the snake can't come in through the vents. It is 104 degrees outside. Finally they get to a turn off where Lance can stop the truck and look for the snake, but never found it again."

Do you know what kind of snake it was?" I asked.

"It was one of my Bull snakes. I just hated it—that was my first thought—that I had lost one of my Bull snakes, *not* that my husband and sister were terrorized by it! We had another Bull snake that we named Curious George because whenever there was activity around the house or barn, he would come and just look and watch us."

Bull snakes are interesting creatures, and much appreciated by ranchers and those who recognize their worth. They eat rodents and are harmless to humans. They sometimes are mistaken for rattlesnakes as their coloring is similar to the untrained eye and when threatened they can hiss and beat their tail on the ground which makes a rattle noise. Part of their defense is appearing as a rattler.

We have one on our property that shows up now and then, usually simply lying on a path or beside it. The other day I saw it in the road and stopped to "shoo" it off to the side. It very calmly decided to do just that. I guess we could call ours "Gentle Ben."

I asked her how they happened to move here; what was the attraction to the property?

"When we were looking for property in this area, we looked at 22 places! We were looking at another place close by and the real estate agent wanted to show us our present property, but said we couldn't go in as we didn't have an appointment. It was more or less a 'drive by'—or 'in' as we did drive down the driveway. It was more than our budget allowed, but I was ready to buy it right then; it just spoke to me."

Bear, Shelly, and Sadie

"So funny you say those words, because that is what so many ladies say about their property in Arizona, including us. Bob, who is like a son to Hal and me, and is the same age as our oldest daughter, lives with us, and he took me to ride down the Grand Canyon on the mules, which spearheaded our move to Arizona. He found several properties in the Prescott area, and I flew out with him to look at them. When I saw ours, I said the same thing, 'This is it!' It wasn't only that it had a beautiful view and was in a lovely setting, but 'it spoke to me' too."

Shelly continued, "I have to tell you more about getting our home because it was sort of a 'God Thing.'"

That perked up my ears because that theme has been common in the lives of other ranch gals I spoke to. I commented that I thought it was kind of spooky hearing that same theme repeated. I told her that it seemed we all are supposed to be here for a reason. God must want us here.

"OK, then," Shelly said, "I have to tell you a different story. This one is *MY* story. When you said we must be here for a reason, I want to tell you mine. Back in 2007 while we still lived in Las Vegas, I went in to the hospital for a simple hysterectomy. Mom came to take care of me and about four days after getting home, I was still in a lot of pain. I told my mom that I thought I really needed to go back to the hospital. In fact, maybe you better just call 9-1-1. I remember them coming, getting on the gurney, and then I woke up a month later."

I gasped. Say what?

"When I got to the hospital, they couldn't find anything wrong with me; I didn't even have a temperature. They thought I was just constipated. The ER doctor kept saying, 'She is too sick for this, there is something else going on.' He sent my CT scan to a friend of his. Meanwhile, I had a heart attack."

"While you were unconscious?"

"Oh, yeah, I knew nothing of all this. This is all third-party information. Just before they were going to give me an enema, the ER doctor's buddy called him back and told him that my bowel had been perforated and that I was septic everywhere. I had been septic for four days, and usually you last three before you die. They called in a surgeon and the doctor was a really sweet lady who told me later, 'Shelly, I thought you were going to be my first fatality.'

"But now we come to MY story. While I was unconscious for 30 days, I went to the Light and God was right there next to me. The first thing He told me was, 'Shelly, you believe rightly and you can come home.' That is a strange way of putting it, but those are the words I heard. When I was there in the Light, I had no memory of this world at all. I did have a sense of something horrendous and awful behind me. I said, 'Yes, I want to come home, I want to come home.'

"Then God said, 'But if it were My will that you stay where you are, knowing that I would protect you (from this unspeakable evil I felt), would you be willing to do that?' I don't know if it took me the whole three weeks I was on life support to answer, but I know that I did not answer right away. Finally, I said, 'Yes. If you would want me to stay, I would stay here.' And then I woke up."

"Wow. What a testimony and experience."

"I guess I had had another heart attack in the meantime, and they had given me a one in one hundred chance of living because I was just way too far gone. But I did survive. Medically I was not supposed to."

"What do you think this awful evil was you felt?"

"I believe it is where we will be if we don't believe in God."

"What do you believe your mission is now, here on earth?"

Shelly said, "Just to tell my story. It took me two years to heal

119

and understand it all. Folks began coming to me and telling what had happened to *them* while they were praying for *me*. It restored people's faith, it got others praying, and it got people believing."

"So, I said, "the fact you survived gave them faith that God does listen to prayer and does heal. Is that the idea?"

"*Exactly.* Because I shouldn't have lived. In fact, Pat, one of my good friends, is a pastor in Vegas and she has a counseling center. One of the women she counseled was a nurse in the hospital where I was. Pat just happened to mention that one of her friends was there in a coma.

"The nurse said that everyone in hospital knew of me because number one: I was still alive and shouldn't be, and two: there were people coming all the time and sitting in the waiting room and praying. People I didn't even know."

I wondered why that would be.

"Well because we had a very close-knit church and I was on prayer lists. They either came and prayed or prayed elsewhere, but I received many prayers. My friend Pat said to the nurse that she knew she couldn't divulge medical facts, but since I was her very best friend, could she say anything about my condition? All the nurse would say is, 'Pat, I am sorry, I'm sorry.'

"God also told both my husband, Lance, and my mom that I wasn't going to die. Anyway, after listening to all this and processing it for two years, I came to the realization that it really had nothing to do with me at all. It was just God working and He used me. My perk was that I got to talk to Him. And he just used me to get the message of faith out.

"I would talk and talk, almost stopping people on the street to tell them my experience, and I would get so angry when they said, 'oh it is just the drugs.' One day God told me, 'Look, it is none of your business how others take your story. That is MY business.'"

"What did God look like to you?" I wondered.

"I never saw Him. He was on my left and we were just standing in front of the light while He was talking to me."

"How did God talk to you? Did you hear an audible voice?"

"Yes, I did, and it was a male voice, not female. People have asked me that."

Shelly's story resonated with me on many levels. First, I do believe in "out of body experiences," believe you can talk to God, and believe we should share our experiences. It is fascinating how different folks relate to 'talking to God.' There are many ways divinity visits with us. Sometimes through rather unorthodox ways. For instance, would one think God would speak through a television program? I believe that happened to me. I had taken a fall from my mule, landed on my back and was in great pain. Fortunately, it happened in the riding arena of the barn and people were around. It was later determined that I had broken a lumbar vertebra, but it would heal on its own, in its time. However, it did hurt.

Three days after the fall, I was lying in bed watching television, feeling sorry for myself and crying. It wasn't about the back pain; it was about wondering if God wanted me to stop riding. I have had a long life with animals of many kinds, especially the equine variety which I do love ardently, and enjoy riding. I had experienced several mishaps in a relative short time, and I was 'spooked.' Was God trying to tell me something? Something I didn't want to hear?

The TV program was a Hallmark story, *Love Comes Softly* about a young pioneer woman whose husband had died suddenly. She remarried and one day was sobbing and asked her new husband why God had let her husband die. The man answered that God was like he was as a father to his own young daughter. He couldn't protect her from all pain, but he could be there for her as she went through it. *God* hadn't let her husband die.

I stopped crying and got still. Was God answering my question through a *television* show? I felt at peace, and as I looked back through my life with animals, I was reminded how many, *many* times I had been through mishaps and been protected. I knew in my heart, God had spoken, told me to dry my tears and get "on with the program."

"The reoccurring theme is that God does talk, direct and guide us in subtle ways as well as dramatic ones. Shelly, you had started telling me about getting your house. What was that story?"

"We saw it, it spoke to me, I just had the feeling we should live there, but it was out of our budget. We decided to make an offer anyway, and right away someone countered with a higher one, which was accepted, and it went into escrow. I was really crushed. To make a long story short, the real estate agent kept asking us what we thought about other properties he showed us, and I kept asking if 'our property' was out of escrow. He kept saying 'no' and I kept saying, 'well, I want to wait…. Pretty soon when he asked, I just said, 'Well, you know…'

"Another thing about the purchase was that I just wanted it so

121

bad. One day I heard God tell me in my mind that I just had to let it go. I was being too obsessive about it. I finally said, 'OK, I get it.' A few days after that the realtor called and said the property just fell out of escrow. We offered the full amount and the owner took it. My God Moment was that I wanted it too badly and had to let it go before He made it happen."

"What did you name your ranch?"

"Yuno Ranch! Just the other day we sold it after it had been on the market for some time. My husband and I felt that it was time to move on. It is bittersweet because we love this place so much, but we shall see what God has in store for us next. I am sure it will be exciting!"

I am sure it will be too.

VAUGHN COLLEEN SMITH
Twisted R Ranch

Vaughn, or VC as she likes to be called, is another neighbor who has land and animals—horses, cows, dogs and cats. When I drove by their ranch, I always looked for the big Angus bull that was in the front pasture. VC is an import from Alaska and rode her first horse when she was two.

She said her family went to Alaska during World War II. She was born there while it was still a territory, and remembered the celebration in 1958 when it became a state. Anchorage and Fairbanks were the two hubs then and she lived in Anchorage.

VC said, "I was the typical horse crazy little kid, but there were not any horses around. My father was from Minnesota and his dad had raised Belgium horses, so he had always been around horses, but in Alaska he was in construction, and no horses. My parents had been drawn to Alaska as the last frontier; they were very adventurous. My mother went up to Alaska to stay two weeks and stayed sixty-five years! She got off the boat and was simply enchanted. I, on the other hand, was not!

"I was born there, but knew from day one, I wanted to get out of there. It sounds terrible because I love my family, but I didn't like it."

I asked, "What was it? The cold, snow, short days?"

"All of that! Plus, I was a horse person with a passion and there was nothing there. I did end up having horses. My parents were super supportive and got me my first horse when I was fourteen, and I competed, but I always had the desire to do more—get more training and that wasn't available. My parents sent me all over—I even went to Europe twice.

"So about getting from Alaska to Prescott. When I was young, in

123

those days you couldn't do construction in Alaska in the winter. You worked like a mad man in the summer when the ground wasn't frozen, and that was from May to the first of October. For many years during the winter they went different places for two or three months, and Arizona was one of those. They went to a dude ranch which was on top of Camelback Mountain. Scottsdale was just a small street in 1954. It was there that I got to ride my first horse when I was nearly three years old. The dude ranch got me a pony that would follow the rest of the group when they went trail riding, and I rode with everyone. The following year I am now 'riding' a bit, controlling the reins myself, and I went somewhere I wasn't supposed to. I think it was a little golf course, and there were a couple of men playing golf. I rode along the edge of the course and one of the men came up to me and said, 'Aren't you a little young to be out here alone?' and I said, 'Oh *no*, I rode *last* year!'

I said, "That sounds like a lovely pony."

"Oh, yes, and I heartily recommend starting children on ponies. I think they get a bad rap. I have started lots of children on one. But you have to get a good one. So anyway, I always had Arizona in my mind, I think because I had loved coming here as a little kid. My parents had some really good friends in Anchorage, the Bittners, who had children about my age and every year they went to Arizona and went to 'the ranch.' Their mother was from Arizona, and it turned out their mother was *the* Elladean Hays of the Hays Ranch which is still there in Peeples Valley. I would always be so jealous that they got to go to a real ranch."

I said, "That is real Arizona aristocracy."

The Hays family and ranch are something of icons in Arizona ranching history. An ancestor, Boone Hays, Daniel Boone's grandson, drove cattle to California in 1849 and began the family ranching business. Elladean's father, Roy Hays, moved to Arizona in 1912 to start the Hays Cattle Company. Roy and Hazel had three children: Margaret, Elladean and John. Elladean married William Bittner, a contractor from Anchorage, Alaska. Margaret married Tom Rigden. An interesting item is that this story meshes into Cynthia Rigden's chapter in this book. I think Arizona history is fascinating because the old time ranches have roots that go way back into history, and many are still owned by the family.

VC continued, "Years later Elladean actually told me stories about her parents living in Arizona. One was when Arizona became a state—on statehood day—every bit of property that you had a deed to was yours, but all the rest became either state or federal land. On statehood day, the Hays family was the largest landowner in Arizona. So when those kids said they were going to the ranch…"

"You wanted to stow away!" I said.

"Right. It would take many years to get to Arizona to live. My husband was in the insurance business and was asked to move several times with his work, and when they asked him to move to California, he said he wasn't interested, but if *Arizona* ever became available, he would take that in a heartbeat. Well, in about six months they called and offered him a job in Scottsdale. About eleven years ago, we started looking for a place to settle where we could have my horses and cows for my husband. He was raised in North Dakota and his family had lots of land and cattle. One weekend we came up and looked around Prescott and found this property."

"So, the cows have always been your husband's love?"

"Yes, I knew nothing about cattle. Zero. After we got some fencing up around the property, he said he would like to get a couple cows. He was smart, and he managed to get some baby calves."

I said that I bet it was difficult because typically ranchers don't want to sell their calf crop, but apparently that year was in a drought and some ranches were selling off the babies.

"My husband picked out three calves and then I had to bottle feed them. That gets you hooked; cows start to look more interesting. Then I started learning about them, and enjoying their personalities. Because of my husband's cow background, he knew he could improve his little herd by using premium bulls in relative short order. He had done some artificial insemination when he lived in North Dakota. That is fun because you look at all these beautiful bulls in the catalog and just order who you want. He ordered some bull semen, which is frozen in special 'straws,' bought a special container to keep it in and went to Phoenix in his BMW to pick it up. The man who had it laughed himself silly when he saw the car. He said that he had put lots of semen in tanks in trucks and jalopies, but never in the back seat of a Beemer.

"It wasn't long before we figured out that using AI wasn't going to work for us because my husband had retired from insurance, but had another job and he traveled a lot. He wasn't always here when the cow needed to be bred. Originally when we got the cows, he had said that we were never, *never* going to have a bull on the property. We had gone to the Yavapai Cattle Growers fall sale which is quite the local event. He picked out the best heifer, who had actually won the Black Angus champion heifer award, and another couple heifers. When it came time to breed them, we took them back to the ranch that had bred and raised them to breed to one of their best bulls. We got some beautiful calves.

"That first year the champion heifer produced a bull calf which we still have. He is the big bull you see out front. The other nice thing about these cows and offspring is that they are super gentle. We raise them as kindly as we can, but still, genetics is genetics. Breeding matters. This is a twenty-four-hundred-pound bull that I can pet and groom. That cow has had two bull calves of super top quality and we kept both of them."

"What do you do with your cows? Do you sell beef?"

"Yes, we kept the females and castrate the bull calves and those we sell."

"How do you feed yours? You have fifteen acres and over thirty head of cattle. That again is different from the other ranches I have seen. Which makes these interviews fun. So much diversity."

"We feed alfalfa hay—a lot of it. We have started some small plots that we have planted in grass and irrigate. We can rotate graze these areas. It is amazing how well the grass grows and how long the cattle can graze in these irrigated areas. My husband found a butcher down by Wickenburg that he really likes and approves of. This man built his own butcher shop which is immaculate. We haul the animal down to him. He has a nice corral system so the cows can settle in for a couple of days, eat and relax so they are not frightened at the end. This is important to us because from the day these things are born, we live to serve them."

I said, "It is interesting to hear you say that because most of the other gals who raise beef say the same thing. One said, 'They have a good life; we take great care of them and on their last day, they take care of us.' They all want their cattle humanely dispatched at the end. I had the same issue raising family beef for us. I also found a good, close butcher to send mine to. I tried to assure a friend that my beef was humanely butchered. She said that was an oxymoron. I definitely disagree."

"What I feel like is they are on the earth for a short time, so I want every minute they are here to be as cow friendly and nice as possible, and I want to show them respect. We do vaccinate and deworm; we don't use growth hormones or feed a lot of grain. We have discovered that many people do not only want their beef to be wholesome, but they want 'happy beef!' They want to know that their animal had a happy life. I had a woman call from California and tell me, 'I am going to eat beef, but it bothers me that I don't know if that animal lived a happy life.' Those are the kind of customers we have and they keep coming back.

"I have pulled calves; when my husband is out of town, it is my job. This year I had one which was breech. I called the vet, but he was two hours away. It wasn't her first calf, and she was a real tame cow so that made it easier to pull. Talking about genetics and why we are so proud of our gentle stock, here is a story about our big bull. We don't halter break the cattle, but we do pet and groom them. My mother who lives with us much of the year—the other four months she stays with my brother in Alaska—grooms the bull through the fence. My husband was gone again and the bull injured his eye. It was swollen, weeping and starting to turn white.

"I called Rudy and he said to call the vet. But the problem was that the squeeze chute that we can use to hold the animals for vet care was on the other side of the property from where the bull was. At this point the bull was full grown, probably weighing a ton, and he doesn't have to do anything he doesn't *want* to. That could be quite a deal because I would have to move all the cattle as he isn't going to leave them. It was at the end of the day. I call, but of course, there is no vet available. Rudy said if I could put in some eye ointment that I had for the horses, that would probably take care of it, but how?

"He was so big he hardly fit in the head chute and how to get him there? I felt so bad. I couldn't let him lose his eye. I got the ointment, a small tub for some grain and went out to him in the field. I thought I am either going to die, get trampled, or it will be OK. I just walked out there, and put the grain pan down. I stayed on the side he could see and petted him, then moved to his bad eye and petted him. Then I peeled his eyelid back and put in the ointment. In the morning I did the same thing. I did that twice a day for three days—and it healed perfectly. The only reason I could do that was because he was so gentle and nice. The funny thing is at the end of the three days—and this ointment doesn't sting or anything—he was like, 'I don't think so' and would turn his head away."

I said, "That story reminds me of my feral kitties I got for the barn last year. I kept them in the house for a month just so they would not be totally wild, but they were not tame like a house cat. One day the little female showed up with a swollen and runny eye. Not good in cats.

She wasn't tame, I couldn't pick her up, but now she meowed and stayed still. She let me medicate those eyes—showing up twice a day for her treatments—for about *ten* days! And she was good about it. Anyone with cats knows that is unusual. Then she disappeared again. Next time I saw her, her eyes were fine. Animals are such fascinating creatures!"

VC nodded, and I continued with the interview. "Tell me about your life with the horses."

"Horses have been my passion my whole life. I was so fortunate that my parents supported me and helped me work with the best trainers in the country. People would ask me how I got to work with so and so who was a top-level trainer and my answer was that from the time I was a little kid, any horse person that I asked to help me, did. They were always wonderful to me and I got exceptional opportunities that way. For centuries, in Europe, there have been outstanding horsemen and teachers. It is relatively new here in our country. It started with the military, and then the Olympics were an offshoot of that, and when our country started competing, basically we were sent packing. The European horses were so much better and better trained. We had to get a whole new outlook on riding and training horses. In order to teach riding classes in Germany, you have to be certified, take a test, and have credentials. At that time, I wanted to be more than a 'child rider' and become a trainer; we didn't have much in America.

"I think we had two colleges that had some kind of equestrian program that were just beginning, and I asked what it would take to be accepted. The answer was: a certain amount of dollars a semester, and you are welcome to come. Then I applied to a couple of big equestrian schools in France and Germany and both of them sent me back a letter saying basically: Are you kidding? No, you can't come here. We are a training level school for our highest-level riders. So one place I can pay to go and they will give me a diploma, and the other place is rejecting me. I want to go to the place where I am being rejected because the standard of learning will be way higher than here. Then I spent a year trying to figure out how to get into one of those schools. One I had looked at was the French National Horse Riding School of Saumur. Another was The German National Riding School which is in Warendorf, a little town in West Germany."

"How old were you then?" I asked.

"About sixteen, a junior in high school. I was fortunate in that my grandmother, my mother's mother, had emigrated as a child from

Germany. When I was a senior in high school, she wrote a letter for me to the head of the German school. She said: My granddaughter wants to come to your school, and here are her credentials. Which actually were nothing noteworthy by European standards. The German gentleman responded saying that I could come for a two week seminar and 'we will see how she does.' He gave me a date which was within thirty days from when the letter was sent that I needed to be there. I did not speak a word of German. I was not prepared to go then; I was thinking months or a year from then and I would take some German lessons. I took the opportunity and went."

I said, "That could be a story in itself. How in heck did you communicate?"

"My dad literally took a three by five inch card and wrote the address of the school on it, went to the bank with me, ordered some Deutsche Marks, bought me a ticket to the closest city and said, 'Good luck. You are going to be fine, and don't do anything stupid.'"

"So you landed in the airport in Germany and then what?"

"I say, 'Train, train?' And eventually someone tells me how to get to the train station. I just held out some money in my hand, and they took what they needed and gave me a ticket. I made it all the way to that little town of Warendorf but by now it is 5:30 in the afternoon and of course, I don't know where the school is. I ask someone and through gestures I finally locate the place, walking along with my suitcase. When I get there, it is closed for the day, but a lady is there scrubbing the front steps.

"She says something that I take to mean the office is closed. I show her my little card and say 'I am from Alaska.' And she says, 'Ohhhhh, Fraulein Alaska!' And starts pointing down the street saying, '*Emshoff, Emshoff.*' I went down the street and it turned out to be a little pub. I walked in and since it was evening there were a lot of farmers sitting around the bar having a beer. I walk up to the bar and show the waitress my little card and she says, 'Oh, Fraulein Alaska!'

"It turned out that since I couldn't stay in the barracks with about thirty men, they had made arrangements for me to stay at the Emshoff. The next day I went down to the stable. No one would speak one word of English to me. I took my lessons in German."

"How in the world could you do that?" I was amazed.

"A lot of the lessons were in drill team formation, and the horses were all young 'sort of broke' stallions. The lessons were in a riding hall with a platform at the end for the instructor. You had to keep two horse lengths between you and the horse in front of you while you did the maneuvers that the instructor called out. If you messed up, or if the horse bucked or jumped up or something else stupid, you went to the end of the line. This went on through the whole hour-long lesson, and of course I didn't understand the instructions, so I ended up at the end of the line all the time. The school had a contract with the Emshoff to serve dinner to the people from the school—the thirty men—and me! They were all laughing and talking, and drinking beer, and of course, I didn't understand a word. But what I did quickly learn was that this one particular lesson that took place after lunch—whoever ended up at the end then had to buy a round of beer for everyone. For the first couple of weeks, I was broke.

"I had to write a letter home, because in those days you couldn't call. What happened was that you would call the operator and say you wanted to talk to the Smith family in Alaska, and the operator had to call other operators to connect—it was a big deal and very expensive, so you didn't call unless it was an emergency. A letter took a week to get there and another to get back to Germany. I couldn't say I needed money to buy beer—lots of beer!

"What was funny was the Japanese Olympic Team sent a rider who was going to be there for a month. He spoke German, but the first day he was there he had some kind of difficulty and he ended up at the end of the line and I was so thrilled! Eventually I got better and didn't always end up at the end of the line. So that is how they got me going, but the first couple of weeks, they did give me private lessons."

"How long did you end up staying there?"

"It was supposed to be a couple of weeks, but then they just said I could stay, so I stayed for five and a half months. Then I went home to visit my family and then went back to Germany the second year."

"Are you taking German lessons during this time?"

"By then, if you live in a place where they do not speak *any* English to you, you learn. I spoke German terribly and they all laughed at me, but they knew what I was saying."

"Do you do dressage now? That was the type of lessons you were taking, right? Compete at all? What is your favorite horse?"

"Yes, I have and I do dressage and jumping—compete and give lessons. I have several different breeds, but my favorite is the Thoroughbred."

"Why?"

"I think they are very smart, very sensitive, light and easy to train. They are remarkably giving. I love them. I was a licensed jockey for a while and I rode in California on the training tracks. I used to like to buy racehorses and make them into sport horses. Some people say 'Oh, a racehorse—they are more difficult'—but I don't find that. They have had a lot of training, been to a racetrack and seen every kind of machinery, lots of noise, so to them it is 'old hat.' I don't care what the breed the horse is—I just want to do what that horse is *good* at. Years ago, people would bring me a horse and say, "I would like this horse to be a western pleasure horse,' for instance. You work with it for a couple of days and you know it doesn't want to be that, but it could excel in something else."

"Do you still hook up the trailer and go across the country like you used to?"

"Not anymore; I haven't done that in probably five years, but occasionally I do go to Tucson, California, and Santa Fe. At one time I did have customers that showed, and showed and showed, and we did that, but that is a different deal. I don't do that now—because I've got *cows*!" We laughed.

VC with Diesel and Wyatt

"Do you have any wildlife stories? Do you have a coyote problem?"

"We used to, in that they would come right up the door almost. And that is why we have those two white dogs. They are Colorado

131

Mountain dogs and they are sixty percent Pyrenees and forty percent Anatolian Sheppard. They are bred to watch and protect livestock. One day I saw a coyote come on the property and the dogs took after it and rolled it around and the next thing the coyote was out of here."

"Do they stay out all the time?"

"No, they sleep in the bedroom, but can get out when they want; they patrol the property, and the coyotes in this neck of the woods know it. Once in a while I see some coyote scat at the end of the driveway, and if they are in the house in the evening and hear a coyote, they bark and I let them out. I feel good about that because we have little calves. The mother cows will protect their calves, but once in a while one rolls under the fence and then the cow cannot help it."

"How about snakes? Any stories about them?"

"Not really. I have not seen a rattlesnake here, but we do have gopher snakes, which I love. Maybe part of the reason we don't see many snakes at all, is because of the cows and we do keep the grass and weeds mowed so they cannot hide. Plus, our property is a flat fifteen acres, wide open, no big rocks for them to hide in. We do have the gopher snakes, and I would take as many of them as I could get. One day the neighbor came down the driveway in his four-wheeler with a snake in a sack. He said, 'There is a big snake in the bag; I know you want it, otherwise I would kill it.' We took it over where I had seen a gopher hole and let it out and he whisked down the hole as fast as he could go.

I said, "We never saw any rattlesnakes until this year, and we have been here five summers by now. This year we saw three. The last one was the scariest as Bob, my son, and I were riding the mules on a cow path. Bob was in front and passed by the snake who was coiled and hissing. He didn't notice it. I think because it didn't make any noise until he passed by. I called out, 'Snake!' and Bob stopped, but when he did, that made me stop right beside it! It was not a happy snake, but thankfully didn't do anything and we went by."

"I did have a large gopher snake here this summer; it came out of the bushes while I was cleaning the horse pen. All of a sudden, I noticed that the horse was looking at something, but walking away from whatever it was. I went to look and saw the snake, but instead of going to look at it, she was slowly walking away. I went in the pen, the snakes sees me and goes into the next pen. It was really cute; every horse I had moved *away*—just looked but moved away. So I don't know if we have snakes move through when we are not around, but luckily, no bad stories to tell. I did see a green Mohave rattlesnake one day by our mailboxes and I killed that one. Those are wicked mean."

"How did you do that?" I asked, because you don't want to get close to those snakes, even to kill them. A gun might be a good choice.

"I ran it over with the car—back and forth—several times and smashed him."

Yes, that would work!

VC looked at the clock and said it was time to feed her two baby calves a bottle, so we went out to the pen and gave them their milk.

"How did this happen?" I asked.

"This one the mother wouldn't accept. It was a hard birth and the cow's first calf. She had it around 4 a.m. and she was out with the herd. She was tossing the baby up in the air away from her. It is just easier for me to bottle feed in these cases than try to deal with the mothers. The other one is from one of our good cows, but she has a fat teat that makes it hard for the new born babies to grab and nurse. It was during the monsoon season and was pouring down rain, so I just took him to the nursery. It is just as easy to feed two as one!"

Next, I got a tour of the cows and the gentle giant bull that had allowed VC to doctor his eye. Every animal seemed very pleased with their lives, and I would agree that when their time came to fill someone's freezer, it would be with "happy beef."

LAUREL WALKER DENTON
Bar U Bar Ranch

I met Laurel through several other local ranch gals. We go by the Bar U Bar if we go south toward Phoenix via Tonto Road. Laurel said she likes to start her story by sharing her family history because she is a true native Arizonian.

"My mother, Idamay S. Walker (Sissie), came to Walnut Grove when she was five years old in about 1925. Hers is a story of privilege as she came from the Swift Meat Packing family from Chicago. Her mother, also named Idamay, married James Minotto who was an Italian Count. He immigrated to America with his father, came through Ellis Island, and their marriage which was arranged, was a very social affair and in all the newspapers. They had two children, one of which was my mother.

"She was raised in Chicago in a huge house, and never went to public school a day in her life. However, when she was five, they came to this area to Walnut Grove to visit friends."

"Where is Walnut Grove?" I asked, as there are a lot of small towns hidden in the hills and valleys around here.

"Walnut Grove is right past Kirkland on the way to Yarnell. There's a road that turns off to the left; there is a ranch there called The Diamond 2. My grandparents bought part of that ranch and named it the Z Triangle. They built a huge adobe house which is still there. There was a fireplace in every room, maid's quarters, and a swimming pool. This was very unusual for that time. This is where my mother was raised. She had tutors and spoke three languages fluently—French, German and English. Her name, Idamay, was the same as her mother's, so she became known as Sissie.

134

"The Minottos did not run cattle on the ranch, but every summer they held weekly rodeos with lots of singing and dancing. There were many famous guests who visited the Z Triangle, such as Will Rogers, Clark Gable, Tom Mix and Gregory Peck. I remember my mom telling me how she used to hide behind a door and watch all the dancing.

"My father was also from the Chicago area; his parents were immigrants from Scotland and they headed west as well. Eventually they settled in Phoenix, but my father, whose name was George S. Walker (Sonny), and who would have been around six or seven years old then, was very strong and athletic. His father took him around the country as the 'World's Strongest Boy.'

"Eventually, he became a renowned boxer. When Joe Louis was ranked fifth, Sonny was ranked a close eighth. He joined the Marines the same day as the attack on Pearl Harbor. His unit was the first to be deployed at Guadalcanal.

"He probably met my mother at the race track, as he broke Thoroughbred colts for the well-known horse trainer, 'Doc' Pardee at the Arizona Biltmore. That is important because this is where the opportunities to love and be with horses came about in my life. Not only was it 'in the genes' but the background of race horses and later breeding our own famous racing Quarter Horses, formed my early years. Sissie and Sonny were married in Quantico, Virginia, as my dad was in the service. The following October my older sister, Carol, was born.

"After the war, Sissie and Sonny returned to Arizona to start their life together. When they found the Bar U Bar Ranch, they knew immediately that was where they wanted to live, but it was expensive and they had no money. Vic Swanson who was the president of the Valley National Bank in Prescott made them the loan using my mother's pearl necklace as collateral. They were proud of the fact they repaid the loan in only ten years."

"What kind of cattle did your parents start with?" I asked.

"The ranch had cattle when they bought it, but they were not top quality. They bought some excellent bulls from Long Meadow Ranch and began to build up their herd. They also started buying top notch horses.

"I remember the big snow storm of 1967 when I was twelve. The snow started about December 12 and piled up well over four feet high. I had been home from school for about a week because our dirt road to the ranch was impassable. Dad would head out, riding one horse and leading another so he could switch when they got tired, to check on the cows. One of the men who worked at the Bagdad mine made it to the ranch with his road grader and got the road cleared for most of the ranchers.

"As soon as we got our road cleared, we all loaded up in the Dodge Power Wagon and headed to town for supplies, but we had problems getting home because of the drifting snow. The cows got into the bladed road and couldn't get back out because the snow was piled so high, so food and water had to be carried to them. Arizona Game and Fish dropped hay in spots for the deer and antelope, but the antelope wouldn't eat it and hundreds were found dead after the snow melted.

"Mother and Dad were also expert trackers and learned that art out of necessity for finding a wild cow or a lost calf. They also found lost people. I think it was 1965, at the end of October deer season, when a man walked into headquarters. He had been camping with his thirteen-year-old son and twenty-year-old nephew and they had gotten separated. There was a storm coming in; it had already started to snow.

"Setting out with CB radios, Dad and my sister, Carol, rode out on horseback. About dark they found the boys' tracks, but the storm was getting worse and covering the tracks with snow. I remember it well because it was the first time I had been left alone. I was ten and my sister was twenty. It was my job to call the Sheriff's office if needed. Just before daybreak, Dad and Carol found the boys, very, very cold and wet but unhurt.

"I called the Sheriff's office and a helicopter was sent for them. Mom drove the dad to Prescott to meet them. The father vowed that he owed his son's life to the Walkers. He owned an auto painting shop in Glendale and insisted that he paint our horse van and big truck."

****

Laurel was the only one of my gals that told childhood stories of growing up on the home ranch. In fact, only a handful of them have been born locally. Laurel is a horsewoman through and through. As she continued her story the "how and why" that came about becomes clear. When I was four I informed my mystified city parents that *we* should move to the country and raise horses. When I was married and thirty-years-old, I got that chance, but Laurel lived my childhood dream.

Laurel continued, "From the time I was born, horses played a big

136

part in my life. Both my dad and mother knew good horseflesh. Mother had won ribbons in Illinois as a young child, and Dad had been a jockey until he got too heavy to ride the race horses. It wasn't too long in their married life before they both wanted to get some race horses. The Quarter Horse breed was still very young, and Arizona is known for being the birth of Quarter Horse racing and the Walkers were in on that from the beginning.

"In 1948, Dad heard about a mare that was unbeaten in the match racing circuit around Arizona and New Mexico. She was owned by the Zuni Indian tribe and he and my mother went to Raymah and purchased her. She was a little bay mare foaled in 1934 named Old Mae West. They bred her to Leo, a foundation Quarter Horse sire. She, along with another mare, Red Cent, became the foundation of the Bar U Bar's legacy of breeding champion race horses.

"In the 1960s, the Prescott Quarter Horse show was one of the most prestigious and largest in the country. I was six or maybe even younger and remember those days as being very exciting and busy. Many of our horses, both young babies and older horses, were shown in the conformation classes, but Mother and Carol did show in some of the performance events. Red Cent who was an old mare by now was taken along to babysit me all day during the show. I spent hours in her stall grooming, braiding her tail and mane and wrapping and unwrapping her legs. Mother never needed to worry about me.

"My parents started raising race horses and that is where my horse influence came in. They were so beautiful that we showed them and about this time, when I was seven, I wanted to show. The 4-H horse program was growing and my parents could see that the race horses were too much for me and the ranch horses were not good enough to compete at that higher level, so they bought me my own horse.

"He was a ten-year-old gelding that already had AQHA points in halter, trail, reining, and pleasure and I started showing. My sister, Carol, who also grew up on the ranch and was also horse crazy and an excellent horsewoman, did not get into showing like I did for two reasons: When I was young my parents weren't working as hard. Carol is eleven years older than I am, and at that time everyone worked the ranch. Second, AQHA had no classes for youth riders then as it was still in its infancy.

"From the age of ten until now, thank the Lord, I have been on the road showing horses. The cattle were very much a part of the early ranch and paid for the horse hobby and the great horses we had. In 1972, my father was losing his eyesight from macular degeneration. At that time my parents sold off the major portion of the ranch and kept the north end of the ranch where we live today. The 'Mullens Field' area, as it is called, is perfect for riding and training Quarter horses. I feel honored to live on part of the original ranch which in the beginning was range land. My sister, Carol, and her husband, Ray Belmore, live on another part of the original ranch and they raise horses and mules. Some of Carol's mules' bloodlines can be traced back to old Red Cent.

"Now the ranch is seventy-five percent horses. We have some cattle—some Herefords for beef and to work the horses with, and a few Longhorn cows that are pretty worthless—just to look at.

"One of the problems of training horses to work cattle is that the cows used to train the horses 'don't last very long.' They will quit working."

I said, "Yes, I remember Kim saying that, which is why they lease out some of their Corriente cattle for that purpose. They are tougher. The heavier cattle will stop and stand looking at you like, 'I'm done doing that!'"

"Right," Laurel said. "The Corriente are very good for working cows. When I was young, I went to Skull Valley School and then Prescott High School. My mother always said she didn't plan things very well because of the eleven year difference in my sister's and my age. When Carol was a senior, I was starting first grade which means she drove us to the bus for twenty-three years!"

"That is a lot of difference between sisters," I said. "There are five years between me and my sister and it does make a difference."

"Yes, Carol complained that I was always getting into her perfume and lipstick! As you know, she lives right down the road on another part of the original ranch. My hope is to stay here for the rest of my days."

"Did you have an issue with the Doce Fire? I know it was burning on Granite Mountain, which is right over there at the back of this property. Did it have an impact on you other than to make you nervous?"

Laurel nodded. "Yes, it did make me nervous. We had our rigs hooked up, and the volunteer fire and Williamson Valley Fire had their trucks stationed here. We have a bulldozed area around our back, so I wasn't real worried. It was burning fast and hot, but it was going away from us. Because of Facebook we could keep the others here informed. After it crested the top of the mountain and started down the other side, it was eerily quiet at the ranch.

"The second night we finally got some sleep, but about 2 in the morning we heard this noise that sounded like gun shots. We got up and saw that the mountain had kicked back up in some spots. It was like the devil himself had come back with a huge fire here and another one there. It was strange that it didn't finish the first time through."

"Yeah, what was left to burn?"

"I guess the first time it was burning so fast it skipped over some brush."

I am sure both of us hope we shall never see another wildfire in close proximity.

****

Laurel said, "Since you have had horses, you know that stories about them are not always happy, but as a child growing up on the ranch, it taught me the circle of life. Some are good and happy such as having baby foals, but some are sad as when you lose a favorite horse to colic, for instance.

"I have an interesting recent story about a mare that was pregnant with twins. Because twins in horses is a bad thing, the vets can usually find that out by ultrasound and can 'pinch' one out, so the mare only carries one foal. We were still doing the race horse breeding, and I had a big, beautiful, grey mare that I had bred down in Phoenix. The vet ultrasounded her at thirteen days, found a heartbeat, and said they would redo it in thirty days, and then I could bring her home.

"They did and found two embryos, but they said, 'That is not a problem, we will just pinch one out at forty-five days.' At that time, they said they couldn't get at it, so they would wait until seventy-five days, and they will turn and grow and then we can pinch one off. At seventy-five days they still couldn't do it, so I brought her home. They said to have my vet check her after another twenty days and go from there. They thought in the next twenty days one would die.

"In all my life with the horses, this is the first time I have ever had this happen. In twenty days, my vet came out and found she still had twins. He said that we would have to abort her. That was fine with me because I don't ever want to go through the twin thing."

I said I sure understood that. In my breeding days, I had three sets of twins, all with the same agonizing results: perhaps one lived for a few minutes, long enough to make it heartbreaking when it died, and the other fetus was much smaller, did not have hair and definitely was not viable at birth. Then the mare didn't pass the afterbirth correctly, requiring a vet's aid. A very bad deal. I have read about successful twinning, but it is extraordinarily rare.

Laurel continued, "He said to bring her in and we will keep her over night and abort the foals because it is rather traumatic. She looked beautiful, big, fat and looked pregnant—you know how they look—she was three months pregnant by now. I picked her up the next morning and she looked like she had lost two hundred and fifty pounds, and she had the most God-awful look on her face.

"I brought her home, and she did nothing but run and scream in her pasture for a solid week. I couldn't believe it, and neither could Barry, my husband. And that's an animal. I said to myself, 'People need to see this.' I have had mares naturally abort a fetus and it didn't affect them like this. Something to think about.

"Everything that I have done and every place that I have gone has been connected with horses. In 4-H I learned to talk to people, but it was about horses. Now I work with students who are older people. They have successful business lives, have more money, have the time now and want to learn to ride horses. Some have a hard time meshing with the horse—getting a higher level of horsemanship.

"It's funny because women want to nurture, but a horse is always asking for guidance and for someone to be the boss. I enjoy seeing interaction between women and horses because it is special."

"So, back up a little," I said. "You were raised with horses, started in 4-H and then began to show with your parents, then what happened?"

"I started showing Quarter Horses actively in 1965 when I was ten. We went all over the country—Wyoming, Oregon, California, and all the way to Columbus, Ohio, to the Quarter Horse Congress. My dad had a horse van that he designed that held eight horses. There weren't any 'horse vans' on the road at that time, so we were 'before our time.' My mom and I followed in the car with three dogs.

"I was having a great deal of success. I was showing a horse named Irish Buzz which was the original horse they got me, also Skip Scamp who became a world champion. I was also showing some of the race horses either after they came off the track or before they started racing."

"Showing them in halter?" I asked.

"Yes, and riding them. Western pleasure, horsemanship, did some barrel racing and some reining. I also did over-fence classes—so I've done a little bit of everything. I showed extensively locally and all over the country until I was eighteen and got out of the youth activity division. The friends that I made through the horses are still my friends today.

"When I was nineteen, I went to the World Championship Show in Oklahoma City. Now I was showing in the professional division and I won the Aged Gelding Class with Skip Scamp when he was eight years old. I just loved that horse; he was such a big part of my life. He is buried here on the ranch. It is a wonderful thing when you have the opportunity to do that. Not every horse earns that, but it is nice to be able to offer it when they are."

I nodded. "It certainly is. My special retired show horse and breeding stallion of twenty-six years is now in my office in a beautiful box. He passed over this February at twenty-eight, and the opportunity was offered to have him cremated, which I did. I understand that totally. His name is Praise Hallelujah, and he was a Tennessee Walking Horse."

Laurel continued. "A part of my life was involved with race horses. I have many wonderful memories of running horses. I loved the race track. In those days it was a wholesome, good environment. The horses that I was around were treated very, very well.

"One thing the race track taught me was that the desire to learn and to excel is in nearly every horse. It is your job to find it. They love the routine, getting better, and getting stronger. Right now, I am working hard training my horses to again go to the World Championship Show."

"What classes will you be showing in?"

"Working Cow Horse, which is a two-portion class. The first part is a reined portion which is sliding stops, spins, figure eights, and then they turn a cow into the arena. It is not a timed event. You get time to work the cow in the end of the arena so you can get a feel for it—what it might do. How fast will it be, does it look somewhat trainable—then you take it down the fence.

"You run it down the fence, staying on its hip, all the way down to the end, then you turn it once in each direction, and then you bring it to the center of the arena and run it in a circle in each direction. This is all done at a high rate of speed—depending on the cow. If it is done right, it is the most spectacular event."

141

"Showing is what I have done all my life, but you never get to the point where you say that you are as good as you can get. The quality, athleticism, and intelligence of the horses I am riding today is just so incredible. And that is what has made it so amazing for me—the horse.

"When my parents were raising horses, they were beautiful, athletic and had good minds. And they did *everything*—ran on the track, halter, western pleasure, and had some cow sense. Then folks began to specialize in the breeding. Such as Doc Bar who had great cow sense—and so then a person will breed their mare to him."

Laurel and Sylish NXS

"Explain 'cow sense'. What is it and where did it come from?"

"Well, the Quarter Horse is a compilation of different breeds. It started with the Spanish Barb when the vaqueros came from Spain and brought their horses with them. It has some mustang blood, and some Thoroughbred. Many of the army remount horses had Thoroughbred blood, and later many of these horses were given to the people so they could breed good horses for their use.

"The Thoroughbred influence is the speed. The Spanish horses were working cattle for centuries before they came here, and the stamina comes from the mustangs. In early cattle days it was very important to have a horse with cow sense, stamina and speed for the long cattle drives of that era.

"Three Bars was a sprinter, but Doc Bar, one of his grandsons, whose dam was also a race horse, couldn't outrun me! So, they showed him in halter and later sent him to a really good stock horse trainer. That trainer told them Doc Bar was really talented—he wanted to watch a cow. Then people started bringing mares to Doc Bar that were not racing stock. They were good strong, athletic foundation mares, and as they say, 'The rest is history.' He revolutionized the cutting horse industry."

Yes, history made. From the AQHA: "The key to Doc Bar's success, as summed up by Charlie Ward, manager of the Jensen's ranch, "is that he's so consistent in his type. His colts are all uniform and possess a lot of sense. They're easy to train, have a lot of natural ability and every one of them is 'cowy.' Doc Bar died in 1992 at thirty-six, and was inducted into the AQHA Hall of Fame in 1993."

There are three true American horse breeds that began along a similar vein. The Quarter Horse is one and Justin Morgan who was a tough little bay horse in New England became the father of the Morgan horse and the father of the Tennessee Walking Horse is considered to be Allan. Allan was born in 1886 and was bred to be a racing trotter as that was the rage then. However, Allen, like Doc Bar who wouldn't race, refused to trot; he paced. For most of his life, Allen was the horse no one wanted. But after many years when he was an old horse, it was found that breeding Allan to the local smooth-gaited Tennessee pacing mares produced an easy gaited horse, eventually called the Tennessee Walking Horse.

Laurel continued with her story, "Now we have Quarter Horses that are specialized—they excel in their fields. Every time I think I have a great horse, another one comes along that amazes me. Every horse affects my life. I am so lucky that I get to do what I do here. I have wonderful clients who actually *pay* me to get on a horse and do what I love.

"Every single horse that is here gets turned out, I don't care if it is snowing or raining, they get out. I don't keep them in stalls, I think it is so important for a horse to be a horse. I have three arenas, but I don't work every horse each day in an arena. Some days we lope across the fields, we go through the trees, or we gather cattle. That is my training philosophy—keep the horses happy and wanting to work. I do not drill, drill, drill on anything.

"Six years ago, AQHA started 'Ranch Riding.' That is the best thing AQHA has done in modern time because it is a 'natural horse.' Natural movement, natural head and tail carriage—a horse that has purpose—walks somewhere. The horse has a nice trot—an extended stride and an extended lope. This has been a great thing for me because it is what I have been preaching my whole life."

"Are these rail classes or working classes?"

"It is an individual pattern work class. There might be thirteen maneuvers in the pattern. Some are set patterns and the judge can make up some others. It is wonderful for people who are trying to learn horsemanship. And the thing that makes me the absolute happiest is that it is great for the horses because it is that horse's natural movement.

"I have several client horses that I show in both the Working Cow Horse and the Ranch Riding. Up until about fifteen years ago, I always had my own horses and showed them exclusively. Then I started taking in some client horses, which I hope has been good for all of us. I know it has been for me."

"Do you show the client's horses for them?"

"Yes, but I also have some amateur riders who show their own horses as well. I have one lady who recently retired and has two high-end, lovely horses with me. One is for me and one for her to show. She has been working very hard and she will show next year and she will be competitive.

"These horses are very smart. They figure out the difference between the classes. The Working Cow Horse class is very, very fast and it is strenuous. Their hearts tend to pound when they know that class is coming. So you put a different bridle on them for that class and use another one for the Ranch Riding where you are doing a quieter ride."

"You are right," I said. "When I began breeding my stallions, I read that you should always use a different piece of gear for that and never use it for anything else, and you know what? It worked—they are very intelligent. My boys always knew when they were going to visit a mare."

Laurel said, "I just read a book, *American Pharaoh*. Bob Baffert and I were kids together. He was raised in Nogales, New Mexico, and his family raced horses, so we saw each other when we were young kids. Anyway, it was just interesting reading this book. The horse had won the Triple Crown, and they decided to run him in Saratoga at the Travers. That race is called 'the graveyard of champions' because so many have gotten beaten there.

"American Pharaoh had already cemented his place in history, but Baffert said that he just wanted the people to see the horse and enjoy him. Two or three days before the race they worked him on the track and he worked *way* too fast. Baffert said he would never forgive himself. What happened was there is a pony horse that lives with American Pharaoh, his name is Smokey and he is a beautiful buckskin Quarter Horse. Smokey always went out with American Pharaoh when it was race day. He took him to the paddock and to the track.

"That day Baffert had said to the boys to take Smokey out with American Pharaoh because everyone would want to take pictures of the two of them. American Pharaoh naturally thought he was going to race. So you talk about how *smart* they are!"

****

I changed tracks again. "Do you have any wildlife stories to share? Has a bear ever come visit you?"

"My mother was an amazing woman in that she came from a life of privilege but when she came to this ranch with my father, she worked harder than any woman on earth. She rode every day with my father, and they would be gone fifteen hours a day. She roped cattle with the best of them. When I came along she wasn't doing as much of that anymore.

"One day in October while it was deer season, we were coming home from school. On the road back to the old ranch there is a spring beside the road. I was probably seven years old at the time. We saw a doe lying on her belly right at the water's edge. We could tell something was wrong. My mother stopped the car and we got out; as we walked up closer, she put her head under the water. As a kid I couldn't believe this.

"Mother said, 'Okay, here is the deal. Something is wrong, she is hurt, and she is trying to hide; she is not trying to kill herself. But this is really bad.' So, she walked back to the car and reached into the glove compartment and got her .38 out of the glove compartment. She walked back down to the deer that by this time had her head under the water again. My mother pulled the deer's head out of the water and shot her.

145

"She said, 'Now I want you to know, that's your job—when you see an animal suffer, it is your job to take care of it.' And I will *never* forget that. To this day, I don't care what it is—whether it is the mouse the cats won't kill, or something else, I take care of it.

"One of the most interesting wild creatures that we had for a while when I was young was a Red Tail Hawk. He had a broken leg and we kept him in a cage and fed him. He got gentle and we fed him hamburger, which now they say you shouldn't do because it doesn't have the hair and bones for a more complete diet."

I asked, "Did you have to have the leg splinted?"

"No, it healed on its own. What he couldn't do was run to take off. As he got better, he sat on the stone wall and watched everything. As he got even better, he stayed out all day and finally all night too.

"Eventually we started catching gophers for him, and he was such a special creature—he knew when we went outside with the shotgun that we were going to shoot something for him. If it was a bird, he'd watch and when the bird fell, he ran to it and stood over it 'mantling' (spreading wings and tail over a kill to hide it from other predators).

"Soon we saw him every other day, later once a week. He would come and sit on the arena fence while we were riding. Sometimes he would fly and land on your head while you were walking around. It was a huge growth experience for me because he was a wild animal yet he accepted the whole care thing, but when he was healed, he left."

"So, it was more of a rehab thing," I said. "You didn't try to tame him."

Laurel laughed. "Well, I tried, but it didn't happen. Everybody here on this ranch gets along. I'd love to have chickens but my dog kills the chickens. I don't want animals in cages; I don't want a chicken pen. If they don't get along, they are gone, except for my dog!"

"Do you have grasshoppers this year? And is there anything to do about them?" I asked. They are the grossest things I have come across out here. They appear late summer and dot the roadways, especially where there are sunflowers, a specialty of their diet. Plains Lubber grasshoppers are large and I have seen enough of them, but apparently, they go with the territory. Nothing much seems to eat them and they litter the roads where they get run over and then are eaten by other grasshoppers.

"Yes, yes we do. The grasshoppers really aren't very bad this year. They are worse in dry years. I think it was 1995 that we had a horrible drought and it had been dry before that year. So the end of August here come these grasshoppers, and you can't believe what they did to the grass that was left. They ate it down to bare dirt, like in the arena. They ate the fruit trees or anything with green on it down to the twigs.

"I watered my green grass lawn because they didn't like the wet, and then they climbed up the walls of the house—it was like a horror movie! The one thing that worked to check their invasion was a bran mixture 'grasshopper spore.' But it was terribly expensive so there really is not much you can do especially on a large scale.

"We have never seen a bear, but a couple years back we had a mountain lion (cougar) get a yearling calf. You know it is a cougar because they bury their kill. They dig a semi hole and cover the kill with branches and leaves. I have never feared them as I knew they were more afraid of me, but I don't live in California where the people have moved in on cougar territory."

"How about snakes? Most gals have a story or two about them."

"Well, yes. Here is a story for you. The Smoki Club which was started by several of the Prescott store owners many, many years ago, decided that on the first Saturday in August, they were going to re-enact an Indian ceremonial dance at the Yavapai Fairgrounds as part of Prescott Frontier Days—the Smoki Snake Dance. The proceeds would go to the Chamber of Commerce to benefit the community. They dressed up as Indians and one of the dances was a snake dance and so they needed about twenty-five bull snakes. But they had to be about six feet long. So at the start of the summer I could not wait to find snakes for the Smoki people! If you found a snake they could use, you got a free ticket and for some reason, that was very important to me. This probably went on for about ten years from the time I was six until sixteen.

"I don't care where we were, if we saw a snake, I had to catch it, put it in a gunny sack and then take it to town where it would be measured. My dad helped me too, but my mom hated snakes. Bull snakes are very interesting. They can mimic a rattle snake by coiling and shaking their tail, but the noise comes from their *mouth.*"

We were sitting in Laurel's kitchen for our chat and all around the tops of her upper kitchen cabinets were many identical bronze horse models. I commented on them and she said they were 'All Around Youth' trophies she had won. They were patterned after the bronze statue that local artist George Phippen had been commissioned to make of Wimpy—the first registered Quarter Horse.

Laurel said that she hadn't displayed her trophies for many years but her husband, Barry, told her she should get them out and enjoy them. She said that each one meant something to her, but she didn't want to put it out to say 'This is something I have done.'

My personal thought is that she should display them all and be proud of what she has accomplished throughout the years.

We talked about mules. Her sister, Carol, has mules and we agreed mules are *not* horses with long ears. I wrote a book, *Mules, Mules and More Mules*, about my experiences with them and how they are more like dogs than horses, and how they need to bond with you, among other things for it to work well.

"Here is my mule story," Laurel continued. "Barry and I went to Mule Days in Bishop, California. Barry loves mules and enjoys walking through the barns. In a small pen were three mini mules. One was just the cutest little red dun mule you ever saw and I wanted him. The price was $1,500.00 and the lady was sitting nearby. I said that the price was too high, and she said, 'What would you pay?'

"That should have been my first cue. To make a long story short, we paid $1,000.00 for this mule. Carol was there with her rig and she hauled him home. He came out of the trailer snorting fire. He was broke to lead but wasn't gentle. He tolerated people—period. I had him for five years. Taught him to pack and showed him in the rodeo parade.

"We had a lovely young lady working for us and she just loved Matthew, the mini mule. When she left, Barry told her to 'Take her little ass with her,' and she did. The mule is probably twenty now and lives in Phoenix.

"You probably saw the mule in our pasture as you came in? He is with an old Belgium horse. We bought him when I married Barry; he was probably ten years old, his name was Ted, and he was beautiful. He came with a wagon and one day we had some people here and had gone all around the ranch with Ted pulling that wagon. As we were going up a hill, of all things, one of the shafts broke. I put on the brake and told Ted to 'Whoa.' Barry jumped out and got Ted loose. A piece of the broken shaft was sticking into his ribs. I'll tell you Ted earned his place here *forever* at that very moment.

"The old Quarter Horse that was in retirement with Ted died and Carol gave me the mule, Rosa, to keep Ted company. The other retired horse in that field is one that was a wonderful horse owned by a client that I used to show. We decided to sell him, trade up and move on. The new people had him about two years and something apparently happened when his stifle was injected because he became lame. So his show career was over; the vet said he would probably always be in pain and they should put him down.

"I know all this because of Facebook. They were trying to give him away and I just didn't want that to happen. Who knows what might happen to him? He had a show record, and someone might try to show him anyway. I offered to take him this March. We have been doing some light trail riding, moving some cattle, keeping him in shape and he *stays* turned out. Now you wouldn't know there is anything wrong with him."

"So you have a sort of a rescue too." I chuckled.

"I seem to, but not intentionally."

"Well we won't advertise that," I said.

As we were wrapping up our talk, Laurel said, "I am just so happy that I am still able to compete at the level I am and help other women who want to learn. I tell anyone that will listen that I am the luckiest person in the world because of this ranch. I don't know what I would do with myself if I didn't get up every morning and get on a horse!"

CHERYL SEARER
Tenaja Oaks Ranch

Cheryl is a neighbor in our community. Since she has rescued dogs and rides endurance, I thought she would be an interesting interview. For those of you who may not know what endurance riding is, simply put— endurance riding tests a horse's fitness and stamina and a rider's horsemanship skills. It is a timed ride traversing a marked cross-country trail consisting of 50 to 100 miles in one day. The courses are usually challenging with hills, water, rocks, sand and maybe wildlife.

The American Endurance Ride Conference (AERC) is the regulating body for North America. As well as the long rides, the AERC also has a Limited Distance (LD) program. These rides are 25 to 35 miles in length. Time allowed for the 25 miles is six hours; time for 50 is 12 hours and the 100 mile must be done in 24. This includes the time spent in the veterinarian checks called "holds." There is no age requirement, and several older folks have participated.

Horses must pass a pre-ride vet check for soundness and during the "holds" the horses must lower their pulse to a specific heart rate (60 to 68) before they are checked by the veterinarian to be sure they are fit to continue, otherwise they are pulled from the event. Every precaution is taken to ensure the safety and health of the horses as this can be a strenuous sport.

A ride begins as a group when the trail is opened at a specific time to riders in that mileage division. They are free to go at their own pace as long as they finish within the allotted time-frame. They also may run, jog or walk along beside their mount. Endurance is the key.

Any breed of equine is allowed, but I already knew Cheryl's breed was the Arabian. I had loved that breed since as a child I had read all the "Black Stallion" stories by Walter Farley. And of course, when I finally was able to have a horse when I was fifteen, an Arabian was my dream horse. What I got was Smokey, an older draft horse a neighbor had, but that is a story for a different day…

"So, Cheryl," I began, "have you always had horses? Were you one of the lucky gals who grew up with them from early age, and where did you grow up?"

"Well, I grew up in Pennsylvania and I had been around horses since I was little, but my parents wouldn't let me have one, so when I was sixteen, I got a job as a life guard. My uncle had Standardbreds which he raced behind a sulky, and I was over there frequently. With my money I bought a 17.1 hand Thoroughbred steeplechaser. I had a horse before I had a car."

I said, "That does not sound like a beginner horse to me. He was huge! And what exactly is a steeplechaser?"

"It is a horse which competes over obstacles in a course, like water, hedges, jumps and ditches. Like the Three-day-eventer courses. I did jumping with him for a while; it was a lot of fun and excitement and maybe I got my inspiration to be an endurance rider from that.

"In my junior year of high school, I went to a boarding school called 'Greer.' They specialized in teaching horsemanship and a lot of jumping. Then I went to college and got out of horses for a while. When I met Dan, my husband, we bought an old farmhouse in Pennsylvania; it would remind one of the farm on 'Green Acres.' There we had two horses and acreage, but a move to Texas required selling the horses, so I was again horseless. We lived in a house in a cul-de-sac and that was culture shock. I hated Texas! We were there three years before moving to California.

"I had never had Arabian horses before. They had been Quarter horses and Thoroughbreds. But when we moved to Temecula, there was a local rancher who had Arabians and he wanted someone to exercise them and live on the property. And that is when I fell in love with the Arabian horse.

This person had the Khemosabi bloodline, and was raising babies. I got to play with the young horses. (Khemosabi is a national treasure in the Arabian world.)

"There was a gelding in the pasture; he wasn't a Khemosabi bred horse, but I asked about riding him and was told, 'You are welcome to ride him!' Well, this horse could buck so hard that his tail would hit my head. And that explained why no one was riding him!

"This lady who was a horse trainer would drive past while I was working with this horse. I am sure she thought I really needed some help. She was the president of the Arabian horse club in Temecula which I later joined. She became my trainer and I began showing him. He was real pretty: a bay with four white socks and a white diamond on his forehead; in fact, his name was Diamond. He was a lot of work, but I won a lot with him.

"My trainer and later friend, Margaret, had a four-year-old grey mare named Miss Ellie. As a kid, I always wanted a grey horse. I kept bugging Dan that I wanted this horse. He kept saying, 'no' but then he surprised me on our tenth-year anniversary with this mare. I showed her for years, but eventually I got bored riding in the arena. I went out on the trails with her, which is not usually done because if you have a nice show horse, you don't typically do something that might get it hurt or blemished.

"I was looking for a saddle and met another neighbor who asked me if I had ever ridden endurance. I hadn't but she offered me one of her horses to give it a try. I did a 30-mile with her and got 'Best Condition' which is even better than winning (finishing first) because you got all good vet scores at the 'holds.' The goal is to have the horse in good enough condition to run again the next day.

"When I know a vet check point is coming up, I get off and walk as well as loosen my girth, and I have never had any problems. The 25-mile races are a good place to start young horses, and you are not supposed to really 'race.' It is a good way to actually train the horse for endurance riding. The horse learns how to eat and drink while on the trail. You carry a little card that shows how your horse is scored at the holds. A rest stop for the long races is an hour; the short ones just thirty minutes."

I asked if it was hard on the horse to stop, eat and drink and then resume racing and how much do they eat? I could envision colic, bloat and who knew what else happening.

"They eat a lot, and it isn't hard because you are not really running, mostly trotting and some cantering if the footing is nice, to use different muscles. At least that is the way I do it. Also as I ride, I let the horse stop and graze for a few minutes and drink. There is usually natural water such as a creek, or the ride manager puts out water along the way. Sometimes there are gates to open; some ride managers are better than others in marking the trails. I have done a lot of the same ones and it is funny, my horse will remember the rides and where to go.

"There is a ride in San Diego that I have probably done for fifteen years. Last year they changed the course and my mare was just livid! She kept saying, 'We are not going the right way!' And my friend's horse was the same way. I think they have GPS in their brains."

I had to agree. My mule can pick her way along in the Prescott National Forest better than I when we are off the paths. But mules have a sense of humor and they get bored, so Susie might just as easily try to find a "new one." So far, I have thwarted her each time she tries it.

"Tell me about the Tevis Cup Race. You did that. Even non-eventing people have probably heard about Tevis."

"Yes, I did it in 1999. The Tevis Race is the hardest one in the country. It is held once a year from Truckee, CA, to Auburn, CA—one hundred miles. It is in the high Sierras and usually only half of the first-time-riders finish. The horse I rode was Megellon. He just recently passed away, a month from his thirtieth birthday.

"Since I got bored showing Ellie, the grey mare Dan got me, and started trail riding her and then rode endurance on a friend's horse, I was hooked. I had bred Ellie, so I couldn't compete with her. My friend, Margaret, told me about a five-year-old horse that was a half-brother to Ellie. She said she had sold this horse to a seventy-year-old man and the horse was too much for him. She wondered if I would like to take him and just put some trail miles on him.

"I brought him home; he was the complete opposite of Ellie. He was chestnut, she was grey; he was little, she was almost 16 hands—big for an Arab. He had a *lot* of energy and she was low-key. I had even done sheriff posse work with her. He tried to dump me so many times, but I guess I was more stubborn than he was. About three months later the horse owner's wife called me and wanted me to buy the horse, or he would go to a sale. So, I did. By then I knew he was going to be a great horse. This was Megellon.

"He took to the trail like he had been born to it. He was little, but the more hills he had to climb, the happier he was. That is one reason we did really well in Tevis— there are a *lot* of hills. Nothing was ever hard for him. He is like a little mountain goat. I competed on Megellon for years.

"Eventually, I decided I needed another horse. Several did not work out."

I asked her what it was she looked for in an endurance horse.

"I like a real 'forward' horse. A lot of people don't."

"That is exactly what I do not want at this point in my life. Slow and steady works for me now days," I said, "but even for riding endurance some folks don't want a forward moving horse? Forward to me means wanting to go, run. How does having a quieter horse work for endurance?"

"The thing with endurance is that you can go at your own speed, you just have to finish within the allotted time frame. So if you want to go faster or slower you can do that.

"There is another type of competition called NATRAC that is no longer than twenty-five miles and has obstacles to traverse which are judged, like how a horse crosses water, climbs the hills, over logs, that kind of thing. Those are a lot slower."

"Why do you like Arabians for competition? I know you fell in love with them and have them, but what is it about them you love?"

"They are very sure-footed and tougher. They are smart and do take care of themselves—most of them anyway. They can handle the heat and go without water a little longer. And they really have a personality."

"So that actually does go back to their desert heritage, doesn't it?" I said, thinking about movies with beautiful Arabian steeds flashing across the blazing desert and then sharing the owner's tent. They were bred for utility, brains and companionship, no doubt about that in my mind. I had always loved them too.

"Yeah, they really want 'to be in your pocket.' As an endurance rider you really get to know your horse. How he thinks and feels physically—if he is a little 'off' or feels great. You really become close to them spending so much time together."

"What other horses have you had that are, or were special to you?"

"I bought Silver. He was two and I liked his bloodlines because he had racing blood. His sire had the fastest racing record on the track at that time. He became available and I went to see him. He was still a stud and was big. I bought him on the spot and took him home.

"We had five acres for the horses, and I put him in the pasture and then couldn't catch him for two days! I called my vet to come geld him, and Mike gets out of his vet truck; Silver gets a whiff of that 'vet smell,' pushes me out of the way and takes off. We catch him, put him down in the pasture, do the surgery and he was up in twenty minutes and running. Mike said, 'He is going to be a tough son-of-a-gun, and he was.

"The only thing I would do differently—and this I learned as I went along—he had a club foot. (A foot that grows straighter than the other foot, so they are not matched). I had a lot of lameness issue with him and why I cannot ride him today.

"You still have Silver? How old is he now? You really do have a geriatric farm don't you!"

"He is nineteen. He was tough and I know he could have done Tevis, but with his foot issues we could never keep him sound. It was sad because he loved endurance; he was a horse that never got tired. Sometimes things just don't work out like you would like.

"Here is a story from my Tevis ride. The biggest thing in endurance, just like in showing horses, is having help—a crew. In this ride there are three stops your crew can come to and help you. I think there are five stops altogether. Dan, my husband, and two girlfriends were my crew. I came in at 67 miles and we had my living-quarters trailer there, so I could take a shower. That makes a world of difference. I am getting ready to leave and it is about 7:30 in the evening and starting to get dark. Dan asks me, 'How are you going to see?'

"We put Glow Sticks on the breast collar of the saddle, which shines the light toward the ground. The horses can see really well in the dark, and you have to be careful not to interrupt their natural ability. Tevis is held during a full moon, but the problem is you are in the trees much of the time, so you still cannot see well. And there are a lot of drop-offs; some people have actually fallen over. I think what happens is they get nervous and overcompensate and lean and throw the horse off balance."

"Yeah, I know when my son and I rode the mules down the Grand Canyon several years ago, one of the things you were *not* to do was lean away from the drop- offs. Just trust your mule. But that can be hard when you see how scary it is. Please describe Tevis a little more. We know it is 100 miles, and in California. What else?"

"The elevation starts at 7,000 and climbs to 12,000 feet, so there is a lot of elevation change. First off, the trail gradually drops nine miles to the Truckee River. They actually lower the water level for the race. When I went through my feet got wet because Megellon was so little.

155

The trail goes through Squaw Valley and then goes up to Emigrant Pass, a climb of about 2,500 vertical feet in four and a half miles to an elevation of 8,750 feet. Then the ride goes west and eventually reaches the old town of Auburn."

I checked the internet for more information and this is why you would *not* find me doing this race: "The Tevis Cup Ride follows a rugged portion of the Western States Trail which stretches from Salt Lake City, Utah, to Sacramento, California. Much of this historic route passes along narrow mountain trails through remote and rugged wilderness territory. Much of this territory is accessible only on foot, horseback, or helicopter. Due to the remoteness and inaccessibility of the trail, Tevis differs substantially from other organized endurance rides. The mountains, although beautiful, are relentless in their challenge and unforgiving to the ill-prepared."

I said, "All the famous pictures of Tevis that I see are horses scrambling up a nearly vertical rock formation. What about that?"

"I didn't do the rock. The reason was that when I got close to it people were lined up waiting to do it and Megellon had no interest in waiting. He was ready to go! So I went around. You don't have to do it, and I wanted to complete the ride and get the special belt buckle that is awarded. It is really pretty.

"One of the biggest things is you go down these canyons and it can be over 100 degrees down there—with humidity. I had trained him to let me walk beside him going down, and then I rode him back up. A lot of people will 'tail' their horse—hang onto the tail and let the horse pull them up, but Megellon was so good on hills I rode him up. To him it was really easy.

"I usually rode by myself, but every now and then I would catch up with some other riders and chat for just a few minutes, but because you are on a time restraint, you can't screw around. There are places where you have to just walk, so you can't make much time there. In places where I could trot, I did. There is a place on top of one of the higher elevations where they get a lot of snow and there are bogs. There were people in front of me getting stuck in the bogs. They will pull a shoe or the horse gets lame. A lot of people stopped, but I just kept going on. Megellon did fine. Maybe because he is small. Like I said, Tevis was easy for him."

"Did you just do it once?"

"Yes, I wanted to do it on Silver, but that didn't ever work out because of his foot problems. It is also very expensive to do. Entry fee is $500.00; you have to pay for your crew to stay overnight, gas, and food. I wanted to do it year before last because it was the 60th anniversary of Tevis and I was going to be 60. I wanted to do it on my mare, but she was battling with stomach ulcers. I wouldn't go unless I was sure of my horse's health. That means more to me. Some people do go and they are not prepared, and they get pulled from the race."

"Have you ever had any scary experiences while riding or traveling?" I asked.

"Well, just last year coming back for riding the North Rim of the Grand Canyon with Dan, a front tire blew on the truck while we were coming down hill. Dan was driving and thank goodness the truck was a stick shift because he could shift it down. We were swaying. The living-quarters trailer is heavy and it was pushing us even more. When we finally got stopped, the whole tire was off; we were on the rim!

"Now we are headed downhill, and Dan is trying to get the spare on, that was challenging. The tires were not old either. I was sure happy Dan was along on that trip and it was not me and a girlfriend.

"Another thing that happens, but never to me, is that people get lost on the trail, they miss a ribbon or something. Then the ride manager has to go out on ATVs to find them. Horses get loose and they usually find their way back to the base camp, or their rider will find them. People can get hurt.

"There was an incident at the Grand Canyon years ago where this gal got hurt, and the helicopter came down to rescue her, and it crashed with everyone on. They were fine, but talk about scary. I think maybe she ran into a tree."

"What happened to the horse?" Leave it to me to ask that question. From Lassie on to Bambi, the animals always came first for me.

"The horse was fine. Tevis is the hardest ride on the horses, usually because of falls. Sometimes they make it, sometimes they don't. But I have never heard of any people dying doing Tevis."

"OK, you have Megellon and Silver. Any other horses?"

"I have Verdytk, my other grey. He came from the same breeder as Silver— racing bloodlines. He is the same age as Silver and when he was first offered to me, I did not want two three-year-olds. Later when he was five, I got him. He was a little pistol. He was still a stud because of his good bloodlines, and not really broke. He took to the trail like he had done it forever. He is my 'Decade Horse.' That is a big honor because he has done endurance for ten years. At least a fifty-mile once a year and he is a 'top ten' meaning he always finished in the top ten placings. Silver would have also, but I missed a year with him because of lameness. Verdytk is the one I do the cows with. I never thought he would like cows, but he loves them."

Cheryl and Verdytk

"OK, this will be a good segue to talking about your life here on Las Vegas Ranch Estates and the free-range cows that are pastured here. In the past you have shared some interesting stories about the cows and wildlife with me. You and Dan were the first to build here. This is a relatively new subdivision in the Williamson Valley area and there are not a lot of homes here yet, so we do live in the middle of a 'cow pasture!'"

For those who may not know, Arizona is a "fence out" state, meaning if you don't want animals on your property, it is your responsibility to keep them out. There are a lot of free-range cattle in Arizona. Our development wants the cattle; they keep the vegetation grazed, which helps prevent possible fires getting out of hand. Many other developments do not. I personally just love cows and enjoy having them as neighbors.

But that was not the case when we first moved here before our barn was built, and the area around the house was fenced. Cows then peeked in the windows and licked the glass, pooped in inappropriate places and ate the hay put out for the horses if they could reach it. Eventually the barn was built, and the hay could be stored there instead of in the garage, but we did not yet have the big garage door installed. One evening when I went down to check the horses before bed, I discovered the herd of Black Angus happily eating my lovely alfalfa hay that was stacked in the barn.

Bob quickly came down, parked the truck and placed several metal fence panels in front of the door, but the cows had learned we had food. They would regularly check it out, but never got back in. Believe me, the fence to protect the house and barn area became a priority. As new homes are built on the ranch, the cows, which are curious creatures by nature, always inspect each and every one.

"Cheryl, our home is in a more wooded area, and we don't see the cows as much as you do as you are closer to the open grazing areas. I remember your telling us some funny cow stories."

Cheryl smiled. "We had a bull in here with the cows, named Oscar. Before we were fenced in, he would make his rounds about the house. Our bathroom has a lot of glass so we can enjoy the wildness of our lot. One morning I am taking a shower and I felt like someone was watching me. I peeked out of the shower and there is Oscar licking the window and peering in. I told Dan that he had some competition.

"The horses were fenced in their area and they had a stock tank with water. There are several watering tanks and ground tanks (water holes) around the ranch area, but once the cows discovered our tank, they broke through the fence to drink it. The first time that happened, Dan was not home and I could not get them out. That is when I met the rancher who had to come and get them.

"After that we decided the easiest thing would be to just put out a water tank for the cows and keep it filled. Appeasement works. They were friendly and I could actually touch some of them. Even the bulls are nice."

In Indiana we had a small herd of beef cows for our own use, but they were hand raised and very tame. Even though I do like cows, I admit to having some trepidation about riding on the ranch trails with cattle here and there. Susie, my mule, is out of a Quarter horse mother and a donkey sire. She has some 'cow sense' and was never afraid of them on our farm; in fact, I had to be sure and keep Susie out of the cow pasture as she would chase them.

I had to get assurances from Cheryl and others that these cows were used to horse riders and would be no problem. One other very lovely mule we had in Indiana I sold before we moved partly because he had a 'cow phobia.' A previous owner had ridden into a pasture with cows 'just to see what would happen,' and the cows, being the inquisitive beasts they are, came running up to see what 'it' was. The mule turned tail and bolted out of the area. Samson never forgot, even hated the smell of my cows on my hands. Since we never got him completely over that, and we knew we would be living and riding among cows, he had to find another home.

Still I was concerned. Would *these* cows chase us? One day Bob and I were riding in the pasture and came upon the herd of cows and babies. I had seen some before when riding alone, and Susie was fine; the cows just stood as I rode by. I assured Bob we would be just fine and proceeded to bravely walk through the herd. A mamma cow bellowed to her calf that was lying under a tree, the calf got up and the herd decided to move, but the problem was they were all moving *behind* us!

Keeping my cool and tightening my reins a smidge, we proceeded on with the cows quietly trailing behind. I came to the conclusion they thought we were going to feed them and followed us to the dirt water tank.

"How many water tanks do you now have for the cattle?"

"We have four 100-gallon tanks, and they get pissed if they are empty. They knock them around and make lots of noise. We dump our horse manure from the pens down in a back area and they just love lying down there. When I go to dump if they are there, I have to weave in and out of them because they won't get up.

"Before we moved here my horses had not seen cows before. Dan and I have always helped the rancher move the cattle for the spring and fall works. Dan's horse is a Quarter horse and is good. Silver is OK so long as he is pushing the cows, but if they turn around, he is out of there. Verdytk is good, he will even push the calves with his nose.

"Here is the latest cow story; it happened just a few weeks ago. Around 8 o'clock at night Dan and I are getting ready to watch a movie on TV, and two motorcycles come down the driveway. Dan goes out to our gate and they are two neighbors from down the road a bit. One of the men said, 'Hey, there is a little calf out here in the middle of the road and it is acting kinda sick.'

"We get in the truck and drive up and here is this little calf just

160

walking down the road. He walked right up to us. We stood there thinking we would hear the mother, but didn't. The calf looked pretty dehydrated, so we called Bill, the rancher's dad, who lives closer and who had helped put these particular cows in here. He said, 'I don't think that there shouldn't be any babies in there,' but we were looking at one.

"Dan came back to the house and got a blanket; I sat down on it and the calf lay right down on my lap, right along the road. When Bill got there, he still couldn't figure out why there was a calf here. We loaded him in the back of the pick-up, blanket and all, and Dan and I drove over to the ranch which is adjacent to this development. Carol, Bill's wife, had calf bottles and stuff. I told her that my vet had always told me if you have a sick calf or colt, get electrolytes in them. I had picked up two bottles of Gatorade and took them with me. We put that in the calf bottle and he drank them right down. Immediately he looked better.

"The next day the search was on to find his mother. The rancher, Dan and I, and some others took ATVs and horses to look. The first cow we came to had a dried-up udder, so we kept looking, but later came back to her and decided she must be the momma. They caught her, trailered her to the calf and she began licking the baby, so it was hers, but she had no milk. So "Gatorade" became a bottle-fed baby. In a few months he would be able to be turned out with the other cows."

I lamented to Cheryl that I hardly ever saw wildlife around our place. Maybe because we have two large noisy dogs, but Cheryl has three, so who knows. Anyway, I was envious of her tales.

"The other day I looked out the window and saw a bobcat standing along the edge of one of the tanks. I usually keep the water level high so any critters can drink and not fall in. Half an hour later there were deer down there."

I asked if there were more horse and riding stories.

"Yeah, so I still do endurance, have been since 1996. I had a nice mare, Firrari, who I had been racing, and before I had her, my friend, Kim, had raced her. She had done Tevis, and Kim said she was the best 100-mile horse she ever had. She offered her to me, and at that time I just had Verdytk to ride and he was getting older so I was in the market for another competitive horse.

"Firrari is a lot of horse. When I got her, I never knew anything about equine ulcers, now I know more than I ever wanted to. I had trouble getting weight on her, finally had her scoped and they found ulcers in her gut, hind gut and her stomach. She is not a nervous horse, and she is fun to ride, not spooky, knows her job, but I think she internalized all her stress.

"Some days were good and some bad. Some days I would only get to ten miles and she would quit on me. Just stop and all she would do was walk. My friend, Barb, who I ride with, had a gelding that she said I could ride if I wanted to. She said, 'He is a forward horse and I don't like him.' We traded Firrari for Tucker. Now Firrari just gets to be a pasture mate and that should be super for her."

"How are you getting along with Tucker?"

"In March I did two twenty-five-miles on him; the next was one in Wickenburg, Arizona. That was a disaster. It was put on by people new to the endurance world of riding. It was on the Boyd Ranch, and to get to it you had a seven-mile dirt road that was pretty interesting. The actual riding trail was so rocky you couldn't trot on it; it took three hours to do one mile. My friend and I pulled our horses because we wouldn't be able to finish in time and it was hard on the horses, and they got frustrated.

"There was this one hill that was solid rock, straight up. I asked Barb if this was a joke! Hardly anyone finished. What was weird was that right beside the awful rocky path was a nice jeep trail. They could have put us on that."

"Well, like you said, they were new to endurance. Like putting on horse shows, you live and learn. Some friends and I did that for four years. It was a learning experience even though I had been showing for years. These folks probably just wanted to make it challenging."

"I don't mind challenging, but I don't want to get hurt either, or my horse hurt. I didn't finish that one. In May we went to Kanab. That is a tough ride. Lots of up and down and deep sand. There is this one hill called 'The Hill of Death.' I was in front of my friend and her horse. I got off to lead Tucker down because it is so steep—straight down dirt and it was kinda slippery. I started walking down, slipped, and went down on my butt. Tucker was beside me and *he* was on his butt. We went sliding down this hill, side by side. He looked at me like, '*What* are we doin'? Fortunately, he was another horse that loved hills.

"Near San Diego is another ride in Descanso I plan to do this weekend. This is put on by a lady who really treats us riders well. She has been doing it for about fifteen years and she is very organized. She has popsicles for us at the vet check, she feeds us like it's a smorgasbord.

She has melons, donuts—it is wonderful. It is supposed to be very hot this year."

"Do you carry water for yourself?"

"Oh yeah. I carry water, electrolytes, horse electrolytes, food, and extra grain for the horse."

"How long have you been riding endurance?"

"For twenty years. It has changed a lot over time. I have done three rides back to back; some people have done five. I don't know if I could do that now. Sometimes I will take Verdytk and do a twenty-five. That's kinda nice because you are done by noon. Then you can sit around and chat with old and new friends. When you do longer multi-days, you are done at four in the afternoon, and by the time you eat, take care of the horse and sleep, you don't have much time to chat."

I thanked Cheryl for her time and story and decided that moseying around the Prescott National Forest and ranch trails on my trusty, careful and slow mule, Susie, was just fine for me.

DARICE WHYTE AND TIA

After I wrote Cheryl's story, I became more interested in the Tevis Cup Ride. It just so happened that the 2016 Tevis Ride happened shortly thereafter and posted on Facebook were several personal accounts which told in rather wonderful detail that person's experience. After getting permission to tell these stories as they recounted them, I shared them in this chapter. I certainly am in awe of the riders and am even happier to ride my quiet mule on local paths. These women have guts! Or are nuts!

Written by Darice

When I was a preteen, I remember reading an Arabian magazine that talked about this 100-mile ride that was called The Tevis Cup. I thought, wouldn't that be a fun thing to do. When you're a kid you have no concept of the idea; it just seems like a fun thing to do. Turns out when you're an adult you don't either!

My name is Darice Whyte, an almost senior citizen, from Manitoba, Canada. I grew up riding horses and had an Arab gelding until I was about twenty.

Unfortunately life got in the way and, for many years, there wasn't time or money for horses. I would watch people riding and I would think: I wish I could be doing that too. Thirty years went by and in 2007 I bought a little grey mare called Beau Tia Maria from my sister. Tia is half Crabbett breeding, half Egyptian and 100 percent attitude. She was exactly what a person who hasn't ridden for thirty years needed! (Not) She had one month of training, and I hadn't ridden much, if anything, in thirty years. To say it was a horrible mistake would

164

be an understatement.

Within six weeks of owning her I took a bad fall. As I lay there in the dirt I thought, *WOW* this hurts way more when you're old. I then thought, OK, get up and get back on that horse. Only that wasn't happening. I had to wait for an ambulance and was carted out of the field.

The end result was two broken bones in my neck. I had three doctors tell me I should have died in that field or at minimum been paralyzed from the neck down. Well I dodged that bullet by the skin of my teeth.

My family wasn't keen on me riding Tia so I decided I should take riding lessons and get a horse with much more training. Enter Tia's full sister who had *two* months of training. Practically bomb proof! LOL.

I got my balanced riding seat back and continued to ride more and more. And there was Tia—just standing there taking up space in my pasture. Mocking me. So, me being me, I couldn't handle that. Here's a perfectly good horse that needed a job so I started taking lessons on her. I went from: I'll never ride Tia again to I'll never ride her outside an enclosed ring to I'll never ride her off the property to I'll never ride her by myself to galloping her down the trails by myself with a huge smile plastered on my face.

Tia and I started in endurance in 2011 and we haven't looked back. She seems to be a natural at it. She pulses down well at the vet checks and is an extremely hardy horse. She's all of 14.1 hands tall on a good day but I never let that fool me as I'm very aware of what she is capable of doing. She is an extremely easy keeper and runs towards being fat. I've had numerous vets remark on how she's not the body type they usually see doing endurance so we began calling her "Phat Tia." "Phat but Phit." The only issues she's had have mostly been of my doing. Saddle fit and girth issues have been a struggle; however, with the help of others more knowledgeable in the sport, we have managed to solve those problems. I seldom shoe her as she has naturally great feet.

Of my horses I knew that Tia was the one that could do Tevis. I'm pretty sure the others I own would have fainted at the thought.

The original plan was to go to Tevis in 2015; however, it just didn't work out and I had to make some adjustments to what I was doing with her. There was no point in taking Tia to Tevis if I didn't believe she was in the best shape she could possibly be, especially coming the distance we would be travelling. (The trip took four days each way). I got the issues sorted out and we were on the road for 2016.

I was heading to Tevis with fellow Canadians Wendy Carnegie and Tracy Vollman who were also going to ride, and Dianne Borger and Lola Seince who would crew the ride for me. A few friends asked me to keep them updated on our journey so I kept a bit of a diary of our trip that I posted on Facebook daily to update how things were going.

And this is my Tevis ride story:

Saturday July 23rd. Tevis Cup race day!!!! This is going to be a long one. After a rather chilly night trying to sleep in the horse trailer, we were up at 3:30 a.m. to get the horses ready to start the ride. The area is extremely dry and the amount of dust 168 or so horses creates is choking. I'm not sure of the official count but there were a lot. I know the ride number was down from previous years. All sorts of equines take part in this ride. At least two mules, Fox Trotters, Standardbreds, Appaloosas, etc., but obviously Arabians have the greatest representation.

I was shocked at how calm Tia was. Usually with a group of revved up horses Tia would be the ring leader; however, she stood calmly waiting at the start. Good girl, don't waste your energy as you'll need it. Trust me on this one.

The dust was ridiculously thick! Tia was coughing from all the dust and I had dust in places I didn't know existed. It is a mass start; however, pen 1 is started first. Pen 1 is for those who are vying for the win. That wasn't me! I was quite content to settle for last place if it meant a finish.

I was riding with my friend, Wendy. We ride together a lot on endurance rides. Our horses complement each other and will push and pull each other which is ideal for endurance. Wendy and I also have the same concept about our horses and that their welfare comes ahead of all else so it's a win-win. The first vet gate was sheer pandemonium! Horses, riders, volunteers, scribes and vets everywhere. I somehow managed to get myself separated from Wendy. I have to say I totally panicked. I couldn't see her anywhere and I thought she had been right behind me. I walked to the 'out timer' and asked if rider #22 had gone through. She said yes. I thought well that's weird that she would have left without me. I thought I'd better haul butt to catch up to her. I got to the next vet gate and no Wendy. Well, Wendy was rider #24 not 22. I know that often you will end up riding these things alone BUT I wasn't expecting that at mile

36. AND our plan was to stick together as much as possible if we could.

Wendy said she saw me leave and the look of panic on my face so she chased to catch up to me. OK, all was good again. After the initial vet gate, the horses really start to spread out, thank goodness. The craziness gets spread out; however, it is hard to settle in on a ride like this. So big, don't know the area and I've never ridden a point to point ride so that means I had to keep my vet card. Oh joy. How not to lose that when totally sleep deprived and a bit freaked out by it all. For those of you that know me, calm has never been a word used to describe ME. I have a lot of "squirrel moments." I did manage to not lose my card but it was one grubby mess by the end of the ride.

We decided there was no way we were giving up the photo op at Cougar Rock. We both ride sure footed mares and we were confident they could do it. The thought is you get the picture at Cougar Rock or you get the buckle, which is given to those who finish. I hoped that this was a myth but the lure of the picture was just too much to pass up. Up and over we went and continued on our way. I hoped that the pictures would make me look tall, slim, and younger.

We headed into the canyons. This was the area I was dreading as the heat was supposed to be ridiculous. The cooling vest I bought was wonderful and saved me. Money very well spent. OK, the canyons! Who knew there were three of them? I guess I should have read up on that. They were brutal. Down, down, and down some more but let's throw in a ton of switchbacks just to make it interesting. I was so glad I worked with Tia in trotting down hills as well as going up. Once you get down the canyon then you get the joy of climbing back up the other side again with more switchbacks just for fun!! And three of them for your riding enjoyment. Ick! I can live without riding another canyon. Or at least no time soon.

They have vet gates after the canyons and that's where a lot of riders get pulled. The heat, the climb and the descent take their toll on the horses and some riders. When we stopped at Forest Hills for our hold I thought I should think about changing clothes. I read where someone suggested changing your underwear. I sat down and went to take off my half chaps and I didn't have the energy to unzip them. So unless I put my underwear on top of my riding pants it wasn't happening.

If someone tells you that you can ride Tevis without a light or glow sticks, well, they are just dirty rotten liars. The full moon does you diddly dot squat of good when you're riding through the trees. As we didn't want to get lost in the dark we would join up with a rider with a light if possible. If they were moving out we would stick with them; if not, we moved ahead in the dark hoping we wouldn't lose our way or fall off a cliff.

At about mile 78 disaster struck. I had been following a horse for quite a few miles when he suddenly balked and we got too close. He kicked out with both hind feet and caught me in the face. Off I came and smack onto the gravel road. I got back up quickly, as this is *Tevis* after all. Mustn't tarry as you need to be constantly moving or you're out. Only one problem—my nose is bleeding profusely. Like "Call in the Red Cross as I'm giving a donation bleeding." I had nothing to use to stop the bleeding so Wendy gave me her bandana. My motto is: Unless you need an ambulance get back on that horse—and I did. My husband would have said to me, "You've been hurt worse." He's very compassionate.

My knee was also injured in the fall, making it hard to get back onto Tia so Wendy had to come to my aid to get me back in the saddle. What I found out later is Tia spun away from the kick and started to go down the embankment. Tia's athletic ability saved her from tumbling probably to her death. (They didn't tell me this little gem until after the ride but maybe just as well).

I wasn't sure if Tia was harmed and couldn't help but think (as my nose continued to flow like Mount Vesuvius) what a shame it would be if we got pulled so close to the finish. And yes, that happens all the time.

I got the vet that I had seen a couple of times and he assured me that Tia was fine. I asked him to tell me if he thought my nose was broken. Vet, Doctor—whoever is handy. He didn't, but found me some ibuprofen and we were off. Nose still bleeding but at least slowing.

One section of trail is crossing a river where they use glow sticks to mark the route and you stay between the markers. We were told that the river would be 1 1/2 feet deep there. Well liar, liar pants on fire!! Imagine my surprise when the water was up to Tia's belly and now I had soaked shoes and socks. Squish, squish down the trail we went. At the vet check at mile 94 I could tell Tia was tired, but we were almost home. She vetted in well and we were in the home stretch. Once the horses get close to home, they really pick up the pace as they know they are going home. As we had a cushion on our time, we kept them to a walk for most of the way in.

We were very happy to see our crew at the finish line and know we had at least made it within the time allowed. We came in to the stadium and did our victory lap. I'm not going to lie. I cried. I was seriously tired having spent so much time in the saddle and relieved that I was done with just the final vet check to pass. Horses do get pulled at the finish and I hoped after everything I'd been through, I wouldn't be a casualty of this.

Tia vetted in very well. I believe a lot of A's, but I don't have her final vet card. Wendy trotted her out for me as by now both my knees were totally useless. The trot out wasn't stellar but enough to get us the green light and our completion. I hugged the vet, cried some more and said a prayer of thanks.

Darice and Tia

I was surprised that I handled most of the ride well. I drank constantly, coped with the heat, and didn't have a crash (well the one on the ground) or hallucinate. I guess some people do. I was a bit motion sick but that started after the fall so not sure if I would have had that or not if I hadn't fallen.

And once again was glad I had a helmet on my head. My knees ached though. One of my legs is seriously larger than the other from my fall. It will require icing and maybe some Bute.

The volunteers at this ride are second to none. Dianne R. brought us a cooler with ice to soak our cooling vests, another lady lent us her headlight so we could see down the trail in the dark. They would offer you food, fill your water bottles, sponge your horse, saddle your horse, hold your horse while you ran to the loo (which sometimes was behind a downed tree) all with kindness, interest in your well-being and wishing you a great ride as you headed off down the trail again.

We were never aiming to win or to top 20. We just wanted to complete and get the buckle. Beginners luck? Maybe, but I will cherish that buckle anyway.

This was an amazing experience that I will treasure until the day I die. I have no doubt that I will still have some of that Tevis dust up my nose when that day comes.

A Note from Wendy:

I rode with Darice all day and we planned and trained together leading up to Tevis. While Darice strolled to buffet tables at each check point I frantically cooled my horse as she is half Morgan. At one stop a volunteer chased me with a peeled banana so I would eat something while taking care of my horse. Darice never told me about all the food...she doesn't eat much ever, and I eat tons...so it never struck her as important. I didn't realize until the lower quarry that there was food! I actually said to Darice, "Look at all the food!" To which she replied, "It was like that at every stop." Live and learn. Next time I am going to make sure I get in on that!

Darice is my neighbor, for some reference, and we have been riding together for years. Darice keeps saying her age will stop her some day and I say it never will—just like I never let having young children stop me (2 years ago I ran 50s and had to breastfeed a new born at every vet check). I am lucky to know and ride with Darice!

ANDREA TAYLOR
General Manager
(retired)
FLYING E RANCH
WICKENBURG, ARIZONA

Andrea was suggested to me by Bev Pettit, the photographer. We tried several times to get together, but it never worked out. Finally, it did and she came to me instead of my having to go to Wickenburg. The trip from Prescott to Wickenburg and the other small towns south of Prescott, require going down Yarnell Hill. It is a rather tortuous drive, steep with many curves—definitely not one of my favorite trips, so when "Ande" said she was coming up for a lunch date with friends in Prescott, and would I like to have her come to my house, I was ecstatic. Indeed I would! And I was eager to hear about living on and running a Dude Ranch.

Ande dove right in telling about her roots, so I had to ask her to repeat it, because I said, "What you just shared about your dad losing many of his animals to a storm, is part of the western life. See, people in the East and Midwest don't understand how different it is here. I think that is part of the reason I wanted to write this book. I have been fascinated in many respects, and somewhat dismayed in others.

"And some people think differently out here, but I am not going to go into that too much because it opens up a can of worms that a lot of people who read my books don't agree with such as animals are not treated like they would like to see them treated. But the ranch ladies that I interviewed, and who make their living raising cattle for human consumption, *love* their cows and it comes out in their stories. That just rang a bell with me, because that is how I feel, and felt about my own

171

cattle in Indiana when I raised a few for our freezer meat.

"Anyway, how did you end-up here?"

"Sure, I was born to a ranch family in Greybull, Wyoming. My dad and mom decided we would move to a warmer climate, and that time we moved to Scottsdale, Arizona. We were only there a few months as my dad was a rancher, before he looked into a ranch about forty-five miles east of Raton, New Mexico, so we were in the middle of nowhere. My brother and I grew up on that ranch. My dad raised registered Hereford and registered Angus cattle. I have very few memories of being there on that ranch."

"How old were you, do you think?"

"Well I was probably a year old when we moved there, and four and a half when we left. There are parts of the ranch I remember and a few experiences—like during a bad storm an old cow came walking through the door into our house! You have to remember the land was so flat, there was no natural shelter, no protection and a lot of blizzards came through there—lots of wind, snow and freezing rain.

"My brother got a colt one year that was born in March, and Dad promised me that I would get the next horse that was born. That horse turned out to be from a mare that was bred to go on the race track. My granddad and Dad both were on the race horse circuit. Dad said that I couldn't have that horse, but Mom said, 'You made that little girl a promise, and you need to keep it.' So I got this buckskin Thoroughbred colt, and that was pretty much my first horse."

"How old were you then?"

"I probably was four, so I couldn't ride him right away; meanwhile we had a blizzard, and parts of the herds were killed—frozen to death. Dad said he didn't want to go through that again. He sold the rest of the cattle, and we moved close to Morristown, Arizona, out towards the Castle Hot Springs Resort. He purchased a small airplane and became a cattle broker. He bought young cattle and finished them at a feedlot—which is where Sun City is today—and then sold them."

"Did you get to bring your race horse from New Mexico?"

"Yes, my horse, Smokey, and my brother's horse, Frosty, came with us. We couldn't ride them because they were too young, so I had a little Shetland pony that my dad got for me. It is never kind to get a child a Shetland pony. But you do learn to ride. Those ponies are very cute, but notoriously mean and stubborn. But I could saddle and ride him. My brother and I practiced to show in the local gymkhanas. I can remember before we got our arena fenced, my pony would just take off across the desert with me, knock me off, run under trees. I was only five, but I *did* learn to ride!

"I remember my brother got a really nice, little black mare, and my Shetland pony went everywhere with that mare. We went nearly every weekend to a competitive event. When I was eight, my dad put me on the half-broke thoroughbred that he had given me. I got bucked off several times, and I would cry. My dad said, 'If you stay on top, you won't get hurt!' So that is pretty much how I learned to ride. I kept Smokey all through grade school and high school."

"Tell me about your donkey."

"I don't know where we got him, but I remember he pulled a cart. One time my brother and I were in the cart, I was driving and got too close to a pole and flipped the cart. My brother was so upset that I might have hurt the donkey; he wasn't worried about me, just the donkey. This donkey would break the gate open and let the horses out and go to our neighbor's place which was about four miles away. So, my dad said we would just keep the donkey on the outside of the corral, and then he broke the gate getting back in with the horses! We finally traded the donkey and cart for a Norwegian Elk Hound dog. I never saw the donkey again, but he was very lovable.

"My mom and dad divorced when I was eight, which was kinda devastating. Dad went in his direction and Mom, my brother and I stayed on the acreage which was three hundred and sixty acres. We didn't run cattle on it, but our neighbors had cattle on their ranch and we were able to go help them with the roundups. I went to a little two room school house. As I said, we were near the Castle Hot Springs Resort which was very popular in the '30s, '40s and '50s.

"It was a guest ranch and many famous people went there—the Eisenhowers, Hoover, JFK. It was a place after World War II for people with tuberculosis to go as there were three hot springs pools. While my brother and I were going to the local Wickenburg gymkhanas, I got acquainted with Wendy Wellik, whose parents, George and Vi, owned the Flying E Dude Ranch, and we became friends through the saddle club."

I said, "Then the ranch was a dude ranch back when you were a child?"

"Yes, the ranch was started back in 1948, and the Welliks came as guests one year and eventually bought it. How my story fits into this is that Wendy and I became great friends, and at my first 'dudeo'—which is a rodeo for dudes—the photographer took pictures of my brother and me, my mother purchased some, and one was to be a Christmas present for my grandparents. They were large 17 inch x 15 inch pictures and very nice."

"How old were you then?"

"Six or seven. I was not on my big horse at that time; I was still riding the Shetland pony. It would have been the 1960-time frame. So how that ties in, is that all through high school Wendy and I developed a very close friendship. I spent a lot of time out at the Flying E with her, so her mother, Vi, knew who I was. For my wedding, Wendy was my maid of honor and her mother, Vi, gave me my wedding shower, and I was the matron of honor for her wedding.

"I met my husband, Steve Taylor, in high school, and his dad was a professional polo player so horses were in the family. We would meet at a certain place by riding our horses, and then we rode the hills together, and that was our date, then we both went back home. Steve had a draft number, so he enlisted in the Air Force in 1971. We'd been married for six months and I was nineteen when he left. One day Vi Wellik saw me at the post office in Wickenburg and she said, 'What are you doing?' I said Steve just got shipped out to Viet Nam, and I am moving back to be with my mother in Wickenburg. She asked me if I wanted to work at the Flying E as a server. So, I worked that season on the ranch—and thirty years later I came back as the General Manager."

"Wow," I said, "but what happened in those thirty years?"

"My husband was career Air Force almost twenty-three years, so we traveled a lot. My horse went with Steve's dad who had some acreage in Kansas. Smokey passed away at age thirty-six, so he was a very strong horse. When we visited, I would saddle and ride him. Once I lost him, I never had another horse of my own. When I ended up going to the Flying E as manager, I was able to go back to riding horses again, work some cattle and enjoy the western way of life with horses. From 2004 to present 2017, I have been the manager.

"My Cinderella story is from that very first 'dudeo' at the Flying E, I eventually went to being the General Manager. And that picture of me and my pony from that day now hangs over the fireplace here at my residence, which was the Welliks' personal home. Dude ranches were very much 'the thing' when I went to high school. I think Wickenburg was the 'Dude capital of the world.' There were seven dude ranches then, they were quite popular in the '60s. Now there are only two."

Jane Gibb was another ranch lady I had hoped to interview, but since she and her husband were only in our area part of the year—in winter, I had a hard time connecting with her, but I knew she was in the same general area as Ande was. "What does Jane do?" I asked. "Don't they have some kind of horse riding business too?"

"Jane and Gibb Kerr have both worked for me as wranglers at the Flying E. Gibb's mother used to have a riding stable in Tucson and Gibb used to work for her. He is a wonderful horse trainer—he just loves his horses. He and Jane now own a remuda of horses and he has been supplying horses to the Flying E for about eight years. This year I leased forty horses from him. They also take riders out themselves as a business. In the summer they run a stable out of Park City, Utah; it works out good, in the summer they are there and in the winter they come south to Wickenburg to do the same thing."

"Do they move horses back and forth? Or do they have horses in both places?"

"They move them. We will get the same horses back year after year. When some retire, then we will get new ones."

"It gets hot in Wickenburg; it is lower elevation more like Phoenix."

"Do you work year around?"

"No, we open November first through April thirty. During the summer we run a cattle operation because the Flying E has a cattle business as well as the hospitality business. So that was the other kicker that I was able to get back into the saddle and do some ranch work like I used to as a child. I feel very, very fortunate that I was able to go back to my home area, my roots, and do what I love.

"A short time ago we rescued a dog that had been thrown out on the road in Whitman, which is close to Surprise. A lady saw the dog and stopped and told the man that his dog was outside his truck. He said that he was throwing her out, hoping someone would pick her up. The lady said that she would take the dog. She took her home, but unfortunately, she had two small children and two other dogs, and the puppy was six weeks old. Supposedly the mother was a boxer and the father a German Shepherd. This lady worked with the wife of our cattle foreman at the Flying E.

"Steve, my husband, and I had tried to adopt a Golden Retriever because when we got to the ranch there were two Goldens there, and as a breed, they are just nice docile dogs for a ranch environment. But every one we tried to adopt was an older dog, and it just wasn't working. Either they were runners or they just didn't work out. In one case the husband gave us a dog and when his wife came home from work—she was a nurse and stayed for a few days at a stretch in a condo—and discovered her husband had given her dog away and she was far from pleased, so we gave it back. How that *marriage* worked out we never heard.

"So, Bobbie Culp, the wife of our cattle foreman, called me saying she had this little puppy that was just a sweetheart, and were we looking for a puppy? She brought the puppy over, and she has had nothing but love and cuddling. The guests love her and she has been absolutely amazing because she has always been nurtured around guests, when a car pulls up, she doesn't run up barking, she runs up expecting love and petting."

"Tell me what a usual day is like at the ranch for you, and what kind of people you meet."

"The ranch started in 1948, and our guest clientele are 65 percent return customers. It is almost like going to Grandma's house. I was fortunate to have worked for Vi, and I understood how she wanted the ranch run. Vi passed away in 2004 and her husband, earlier. The ranch is in the Wellik Foundation and the board oversees the ranch. My day is long because that is what I want it to be. A typical day at the ranch is breakfast is from 7:30 to 9. A ride goes out from 9:30 to 11:30, lunch is at 12:30, and the afternoon ride is from 2 to 4. Happy hour is at 5:30 and dinner is at 6:30. Our guests typically come for an average of three to five days."

"Do your guests go on each ride, or pick one?"

"We have both. Some are very avid riders who want to go every single ride, and families who go in the morning and then enjoy the pool in the afternoon. We offer team penning with the cows and the horses, we have barn dancing in the historical Oregon type barn. Our events are all around the weather. We have a Christmas morning ride—weather permitting. The 'dudeos' have gone away. Our horses are not trained to neck rein as needed in working cattle, we don't want them to run—we want them as quiet as they can be for safe trail riding.

"The team penning is fun and safe. We bring in a group of fifteen to twenty heifers to the arena and divide into teams so there are three to a team with one wrangler. They sort out three cows and bring them down the arena and put them in a pen, so they get the idea of ranch work in a very safe and structured way. In that way we try to keep the Wellik's idea of preserving the West for many to enjoy. For instance, not many people are able to see the stars like we can see them here, or enjoy the wide-open spaces and the quietness of nature. Also what we provide is a chance for families to enjoy something this wonderful *together.*

"One of my favorite things is seeing corporate people come in requesting to do everything—they are so busy in their minds they think they have to do everything we have: ride, go to town, play tennis, and they cannot relax—but after two days they are very relaxed. There is something about being on the back of a slow walking horse that quietly sways you back and forth while you see such beautiful scenery, and that calms them down. There is nothing you can get to—you *have* to relax!

"I have considered being here a wonderful privilege. You get tired—it isn't easy—it is long days, hard work and you have to be happy all the time! I would say that in my thirteen years of working there, *maybe* two handfuls of guests, were those that we were happy when they got in the car to go home. You bring the guests to your side of life. If they come and they are very demanding—perhaps they are gluten free, lactose intolerant or they need 'this, this and this', after the second day they are happily working with my cook for their meals.

"What a joy it is to meet people from all over the world. Our farthest came from Australia, several Europeans, a lot from New York and California because they want to experience something a cruise ship or Disney Land doesn't provide—something quiet and relaxing. We are on a great corridor for visitors to Arizona. They land in Phoenix, drive north to us and then more north to Sedona and the Grand Canyon. We have made lasting friendships. My husband and I consider it more like inviting people to our home than a business. Our head wrangler has been with us for twenty-eight years, our cattle foreman for thirty-two years, the head housekeeper for twenty years, and this shows the dedication to the Flying E and that they love their work."

"How do you do meals if you have thirty plus guests?"

"I have phenomenal cooks. Our breakfasts are made to order, except we don't do fancy stuff like crepes, we just do ordinary good cooking: ham, potatoes, eggs, pancakes. Lunch is usually a buffet. We have one entrée, for instance: bacon, lettuce, tomato sandwiches with French fries or potato salad, and a cookie bar."

"So that is what they eat unless they have a special diet that they

177

have gone over with the cook beforehand? There are no choices."

"Exactly, so you don't decide off a menu. It is just like if you went to your grandmother's house for lunch. Dinner is a family sit-down. If we happen to have a large number, we usually have a buffet, like prime rib, baked potatoes. My cooks know we have a certain number of people to cook for, and if we have special needs like a vegetarian plate, they know that ahead of time."

"Gee, it makes me want to go!" I said. We both laughed. But I was serious, sort of. What a pleasure it would be to go there with the visiting granddaughters and family!

"When I got here at the Flying E, I was not exactly qualified for the job as my education had been in physical education for students. And being in the military, we moved every couple of years, so having a 'real' career, was out of the question. I grew up around horses, my dad was a cattleman, and I knew I loved to *eat* food and I love a clean room. I had worked in a construction office for twelve years, and in construction, you see everything, including labor disputes. When I got here, I realized I had a little experience in all of those, but not a lot in any of them."

I said, "A lot of what you do is dealing with people, so you really did have some life experiences doing that."

"Yes, and that is the hardest thing and making this experience *fun* for them. And our advertisement is by guests telling their friends how amazing it was for them. And this experience is not for everyone. It tends to cater to those individuals who are outgoing, athletic, and adventurous people.

"To finish up my 'Cinderella' story,' part of the management package for running the Flying E Ranch was to live in the Wellik home which sits on a hill overlooking the ranch. There is a beautiful, beautiful stone fireplace in the main room and I have hung that picture of me and my pony, Surprise—for obvious reasons, over that fireplace—that was taken so many years ago at one of the dudeos.

"So I now say, 'I live in the house on the hill, and my portrait hangs over the fireplace', and I feel like this is my mansion and that was my destiny, and if nothing else happens to me in my entire life, the opportunity that has been *here* has been simply amazing!"

"Well, I think Vi is very happy that you are here carrying on her dream to have folks experience the West!" I affirmed.

Ande said, "I had another childhood saddle club friend, who when I was offered this job said, 'Ande, Vi would be so proud.' And that has always stuck with me. Vi never knew I was at the Flying E…"

"Oh, I think she knows you are there!" I said.

"One year I lost a cook—my first year. First years are never easy no matter what. My cook had walked off the job, and I thought, 'Oh, man, how am I ever going to find another cook' and all of sudden a lady drives up in a truck and says, 'I'd like to fill out an application.' I said, 'What do you do?' and she said, 'I am a cook.' I didn't end up hiring her, but I think that was my signal that it all would work out."

"Why did you lose the cook?"

"Irritation. He just was not happy with what he was doing, he was my secondary cook and he had been very unprofessional with the head cook, and she had a little bit of a break-down."

"Well," I said, "they do surely have to get along."

"So, I hired another head cook, and he didn't want to work with him either and drove off in the middle of the night. I walked into the kitchen and said, 'What did you do to this one?' and he just lost it, said, 'I am out of here' and left. I have learned a lot about people and employees. In every experience you grow."

"How long have you had the cook, or cooks that you have now?"

"That goes back and forth like a ping pong ball."

"Do you think that is one of the harder jobs?"

"Definitely! I don't know if it's because they have to have everything together so quickly, or the stress of the job. For instance, you can make gravy one hundred times and then when you have forty people in house, the gravy doesn't turn out—I don't know. That is why I am not a cook! But that has been the most difficult challenge."

"Do you have more men than women cooks?"

"That is a very interesting question. I ponder on that all the time. In the '70s and '80s there was always a lady in the kitchen cooking, and the guys were always in the corral. Now you are seeing girls in the corral and the guys as cooks. I actually prefer to have at least one guy cook because you have to load the supply truck—there is a lot of manual labor involved. We do a lot of grilling, cookouts, and the food has to be transported outside, so I like a guy, but I also love the fact that there is a woman's touch. This year I had two male cooks and it wasn't as easy as when I had the guy and the girl."

"I had some turnover this year, but I was due because I had had five really great years. You know, they all work together day in and day out for six months; it is sort of like working with your brother or sister, and there are bound to be some squabbles. But I have been very blessed with a loyal team from Vi's era to help me."

"Do you ever have anything to do with the horses, or animals?"

"Not usually, because my job is to be sure all runs smoothly, but one year there was a group of nine kids, all related, that wanted to go on a ride together, so I trailed that ride with the wrangler. I was totally, totally impressed with my wrangler. The kids were not paying attention, they were giggling and talking and not paying attention. He stopped the ride and said, 'OK, this is serious, I want you to have a good time, but when you are on the back of a twelve-hundred-pound animal, you need to be serious and be aware of your surroundings. I don't want to scare you, but you cannot be goofing off on horses.'

"As far as the animals are concerned, we have been very fortunate. There have been things happen that we think, 'Man how did *that* happen?' But I work with very experienced wranglers; all have been through horse certification classes."

"How many riders go on a ride and with how many wranglers?"

"No more than eight with one wrangler, and usually we limit them to five or six. And that also depends on whether it is a 'walk ride', or a 'lope ride.' We put less on a lope ride unless the riders are experienced. A lope ride is faster, going at a gallop, as most folks would say, so that requires much more experience."

I nodded. That made sense.

Andrea said, "You asked about stories with the rides or the animals. What I find interesting is when we sit down to dinner and people will talk about what happened, like, 'Oh, yeah, my hat fell off and it spooked five horses,' or 'We saw a rattlesnake and the wrangler's horse jumped to the side and my horse spun around three times.' I don't hear those stories! But we have a 'dude string' of horses which are very well trained—you never know with an animal—but we depend on that horse doing its job, and we don't have a lot of craziness.

"On the other hand, when you are out working the cattle during the 'off season,' more can happen. The other day we were branding and the guy threw the loop, it went over and through the calf and ended up in front of his horse and the horse stepped into the loop. That could have been real serious. I had two guys on horses and three of us on the ground. I was alarmed, but three of those guys yelled, 'Loop' and the guy on the horse knew exactly what had happened. That is cowboy 101. It is the language they all use, and that is the fun part when you get with people like that!

"Then we had one calf that was roped and went running for the gate, broke the gate, and the guy just threw the rope down and basically said, 'see ya.' So that is what I get by hiring experienced people. Of course, you could sit at what we call the 'wrangler round table' and they have stories."

"Oh I bet! Wouldn't a recorder set to run capture some fantastic ones? I sure would love to hear those."

"Yes, as long as you are *not* the ranch manager! You don't really *want* to hear *those* stories!"

I asked if the Flying E had restrictions on the riders as to weight or other issues, like the Grand Canyon mule rides do. Theirs is a limit of two hundred pounds going down and up, and two hundred and twenty-five doing the flat 'rim ride.'

"We say two hundred and fifty, but we had a gentleman come with a group who was a running back for the New England Patriots and he was two hundred and eighty pounds. But he was athletic. And yes, there are times when the wranglers just have to say, 'No, sorry we cannot take you.' One of the things we do is have a mounting block for the riders to get on. But we say, this is NOT for you, it is for the horse because having a horse mounted perhaps four hundred times a season with many people trying to pull themselves up onto the horse would be horrible for the horse's back. My call is: we can get you on and we can get you off, but if something happens out on the ride, you probably couldn't get down or back up. And that is a liability thing too.

I asked about the rates.

"We charge $330.00 a night for two people in our lodge rooms, the food is included; the horseback riding is $50.00 a ride, and we request a two or three night stay. We try to be competitive to Disney Land, or skiing. I think dude ranching adventures are actually an economical family get-away."

I told Ande that I was using a picture of Jane Kerr taken by Bev Pettit for my cover. She had already told me that Jane and her husband, Gibb, had worked as wranglers for her, and then started their own business of dude riding.

"Jane actually came from a very interesting background," Ande said. "She used to be a competitive ice skater! She fell into this way of life—she wasn't raised around horses, and now she absolutely loves it. I can't think of a more beautiful picture for your cover."

"Oh, I know. I saw that in the group of pictures Bev sent me to look at and instantly knew that was the one. Talk about 'Western eye candy'!"

"Yes, she is very photogenic and sweet, but she is tough too."

I said, "Jane was on my list of gals to talk with, but things kept happening and I never got to visit with her. Maybe when she comes back in the fall I can try again, but in the meantime, I appreciate your sharing these tidbits with us about the Western lady on the cover of this book."

Andrea and Steve

Andrea retired from the Flying E on September 1, 2017. She and her husband, Steve, felt it was time for an easier trail and wanted to do some traveling while they are still healthy and able to enjoy life together.

CAROLYN HARRIS
Van Dickson Ranch

Writing about these Western gals was a little bit like following a trail of bread crumbs. Chatting with one many times led to another lady who agreed to share her story, and that is how I met Carolyn. At this particular time in Arizona, it was monsoon time and some of the gals lived on dirt roads with consequent mud and possible flash flooding. That would make a difference when I wanted to travel but Carolyn's ranch is on a paved road and relatively close. Pulling into the ranch we went under a railroad trestle that was ten feet wide, but sure looked much narrower. Both Nadine and I agreed we wouldn't care to pull a horse trailer through it—but many have, as it turned out.

It was natural to start our conversation about the weather. I had asked Carolyn if we would need to cross any washes to get to her—which we did not, but she had a story about a wash.

"We sold our neighbor, Sondra, the lot up the hill, and she has to cross that big wash to get in and out. I have watched her cross it up to her knees in water. She sends her dog first, and then she walks across to her car which is parked on the other side. One time she went away and asked us to feed her horses. I went down to feed them but the water was roaring—there was *no* way to get across. The next morning it had slowed down a little bit and I said to my husband, 'Paul, Sondra's horses haven't been fed for a day, what can we do?'

"We drove the truck down the wash and backed it up to the edge; I tied two snap straps together and fastened one end onto Paul's waist. My thought was if he got swept downstream, I would get in the car and jerk him out! He did make it across and fed the horses, but he told me that a couple of times his feet did get swept out from under him. These washes are not to be underestimated."

I asked Carolyn the usual questions about her earlier life and how she ended up here.

"I was born in Michigan and Paul is from Texas, but I had been in California since I was four. I met Paul in Palm Springs, California; he was a polo player and a business man, and I had a motor home sales company, and dabbled in real estate. I was forty-nine and met Paul on a supposedly real estate deal. I thought he was very boring and he thought I was very prissy. We had both been widowed at about the same time, ten years earlier, and we both were horse people, so we made a riding date.

"I pulled up in my trailer, unloaded my 16-hand-tall Trakehner dressage horse, put the saddle on, jumped up, and he looked at me and thought, 'Wow, look at her, she isn't prissy after all.' Then I looked at him. He was on his Thoroughbred polo pony that was doing everything she could to dump him, and I thought, 'Look at that guy ride!' And that is how we got together."

"What exactly brought you to Skull Valley?"

"We came to Prescott first, looked for a place to board the horses and saw an ad for Juniper Wells Ranch, in Skull Valley. The joke was that Paul was trying to drag me back to Texas, but this was as far as I would go. Paul started looking for 'dirt,' and found this ranch. He immediately fell in love with it—trestle and all."

"So, tell me about that trestle. Do you take your horse trailers through it?"

"Yes, and here is a picture of a forty-seven-foot tour bus that came through. He just pulled his mirrors in and drove through."

Nadine and I were both suitably impressed. Yikes.

"Paul was told the property was already sold, which it wasn't, but some people had been trying to buy it for a mobile home park. But the mobile homes couldn't get through the trestle, so that saved the day."

I said, "That surely would have been awful—to think of this beauty as a mobile home park."

"When Paul brought me out to see this place, he said, 'Carolyn, get out the checkbook, this is *the place*—and I said, 'Squalor Holler.' It was a mess. He had vision that I did not. Where the polo field is now, it was covered with brush. The house was dilapidated and half the size that it is now. Here is a picture of the original homestead ranch house."

I had to agree it looked nothing at all like the beauty it had become.

Carolyn continued, "When we purchased this property, we spent eight months remodeling and enlarging the house. While some workers were in the crawl space above the kitchen removing the old ceiling, they heard a rattling and hissing sound. They came rushing down the ladder so fast they almost fell. Paul and Alex, our number one fellow, went up the ladder and killed a huge rattlesnake who had taken up residence in the attic.

"Here is a turkey story for you. At one time we had some Rio Grande turkeys from Texas but they gradually got eaten by coyotes except for one. 'Tom' went across the road and joined a wild turkey flock. We saw him now and then. One day I asked George, the neighbor, if he had seen Tom lately, he said no, but that there were a lot of wild turkeys with Tom's black feathers, so Tom had been busy. It was said that wild turkeys and domestic ones don't mate, but don't guess that is true."

"Tell me a little about the house and the Van Dicksons and polo."

"The house was built about 1895. The homestead deed we have showed the property homesteaded to James Van Dickson in 1906, and the deed was signed by Teddy Roosevelt's secretary. The ranch is six hundred acres and situated along Skull Valley Creek, but it used to be bigger. James Van Dickson was the son of John Dickson who came to Prescott and Skull Valley in the 1860s with the Walker Party. John may have been one of the people who referred to this beautiful valley as Skull Valley because of the pile of skulls they found here from ancient battles between the Yavapai and Apache people. Young James became known as Van Dickson. Van was a rancher and a world-class rodeo champion and was friends with and was in movies as a cowboy with Tom Mix. Van raised polo ponies and leased them to Will Rogers. When my husband, Paul, saw that field out there covered with brush and thought that it would make a super polo field, little did we know that it had been one almost 100 years ago."

"I didn't know Will Rogers played polo."

"Oh yeah, there is a Will Rogers Polo field in Los Angeles. Will Rogers would come here on the train which stopped in Skull Valley then, and look at the horses Van Dickson had. He leased those he wanted and took them to California. When the horses were through with polo they came back here and became ranch horses. Remember the black mare, Cover Girl, I showed you that was so wild and nearly unmanageable

186

when she was young? Well, now she is a child's horse. Polo kinda makes nice horses once they are finished playing. If I ever lope her on the polo field, she does get excited, but I can ride her all over on the miles of rough trails we have.

"Years ago, I had a granddaughter of Seattle Slew that I rode on our trails. I was coming down a steep mountain trail with some kids and adults on borrowed horses. The horse ahead of me was going too fast. I said, 'Hey, slow down, I'm on a green horse,' and just then my mare which was jigging around, got her foot caught in between some rocks. When she yanked her foot out, her whole body jumped and I was thrust off her back onto my back on a pile of boulders. After I was through screaming, I thought, 'This could be serious!' I was told later that the mare almost fell on top of me. I have since ridden that trail, but I have never gone down it again, just up.

"Someone went for help and I walked all the rest of the way down—about a quarter of a mile—holding onto Paul's belt with someone else behind me. I got in bed and said to Paul, 'I think I've got some pain pills in the bathroom. I planned on going to the doctor the next week, but my neighbor who is a nurse said, 'Paul, you get the ambulance.' It turned out I had two broken vertebra and a cracked sacrum.

"What is amazing is, my doctor said, 'Carolyn, if you can get the balloon kyphoplasty, do it.' That is a procedure that uses a balloon and bone cement to stabilize the fracture. I was healed as soon as that cement hardened, but had to recover from the surgery. However, it took the sacrum six weeks to heal and I had to be in a wheelchair. I learned to enjoy golf on the television in those days. I don't have any pain at all and if I am careful, I can lift eighty pounds.

"I just saw my doctor a few months ago and he thought that I might have osteoporosis because I have small bones. It turned out that I was normal for my age. I am sure the reason is because of something that happened forty years ago. I had fingernails that were soft like cloth. I tried many things but nothing helped. Then I heard about silica and it worked so I started taking it religiously. But the story gets better. Paul's polo mare got navicular disease in her foot and Dr. Martin, who owns Cave Creek Veterinary Hospital, and also plays polo, prescribed silica powder. I gave her a cup of silica with syrup every day because she hated the taste, for six weeks. And she got well."

That is pretty amazing, as navicular disease is a chronic

degenerative condition of a small bone in the foot and can be the end of a horse's career.

Carolyn continued, "About six months ago I was on a big 16.2-hand grey mare on the polo field…"

"You play polo also?" I asked.

"No, I am too smart. I can actually hit the ball pretty good, but not interested in playing. I was following Paul on the grey mare. He was hitting the polo ball and my mare was watching it. Then Paul started to trot and the next thing I knew, I was on the ground. My mare threw a huge buck, and you know when you are just walking, you are pretty relaxed, so it caught me off guard. Paul said, 'You need to get back on that horse,' and I said, 'You will *never* get me back on that horse!' I had x-rays but I did not break anything this time. I later talked to the vet who gave the silica to our horse and told him I had also been taking it when Matilda bucked me off. He was astounded and asked me to bring out the bottle so he could take a picture of it and tell his wife about it. I share these stories because I am certain silica has been very beneficial for me and I enjoy spreading the word!"

"When did the polo field become a *real* polo field?"

"About 2001. The Skull Valley Polo club just had its thirteenth annual tournament. A couple years after we got the polo field finished, a friend died and I inherited the golf clubs. We started using the polo field as a hitting range. Paul decided that golf was a lot cheaper than polo and we went golfing together for a while. Then he played with some really good golfers and never played after that. He said, 'Why can I hit a ball straight when I am on a horse running forty miles an hour, and can't hit that little golf ball looking up at me?'"

I laughed. "Tell me a little about how you got started doing weddings here. It is such a beautiful spot."

"We have done parties for historical societies, The Westerners, and then someone asked if they could get married here. We rented some chairs and it was a lot of fun. Plus, Paul got to feed the people. He grew up smoking brisket and he *loves* to cook for people. Now we smoke tri-tip and have a staff of three who do the cooking, but he still supervises."

"This is a crazy year for the monsoon rains. How do you cope with the weather? Do you book during the rainy season?"

"No, we take July off. In six years of doing weddings here, only one time did we get some serious rain. Every bride has been able to get married down on the grass except for one. Interestingly at this wedding the CEO of Papa Johns was a guest. The bride and her father were by the front door of this house, everybody else was down in the wedding area, when it started to pour. Everybody came up to the house and got under the overhang. I had 72 people sheltered there and I wondered what I was going to do. So, I opened the doors and said, 'Everyone in the house.' The minister had his back to the open doors and started the ceremony. I still have goosebumps when I think of that day. It turned out to be a beautiful wedding. Then, all the electricity went out!

"About six months before that, one night I sat straight up in bed and said, 'Paul, what are we going to do if the electricity in Skull Valley goes out during a wedding?' and then I went back to sleep. That week we bought three generators."

I asked her if they raised cows.

"We do, they are longhorns and we hope their calves go to homes as 'yard furniture,' but if they end up as beef, that is all right too."

"Since you have six hundred acres for them to roam on, are they wild?"

"Oh no, the other day they got through the fence and I pretty much just shooed them back home. We got them from Cynthia Rigden. You told me you have met Cynthia."

Carolyn showed us some pictures of weddings held there and mentioned how bright and numerous the stars are here in Arizona. I had to agree. I told her that in Indiana we had a lovely 75-acre horse farm, but because we were close to towns—and had so many cloudy days and nights—we are always amazed at how beautiful the night sky is here.

Carolyn said, "Not every night is serene for star watching. One night the barn caught on fire. We had decided to build bathrooms in the barn for the polo players and visitors. We hired someone to stain the wood, and he put his stain rags in a plastic trash can, and left. It was 1 a.m. on February 14, 2013. I had just watched *Gone with the Wind* on TV before I went to sleep. Paul jumped up and said, 'The barn's on fire.' I looked out the window and thought it was a dream like *Gone with the Wind*! My dreams are so realistic; Paul had to convince me it *wasn't* a dream.

"I threw a bathrobe on and ran out. By then there were two fire trucks already there, and we never heard them come in to the ranch."

"How did the fire department know you had a fire, since you didn't call them?"

"A young man who had been a volunteer fireman was coming

home from Prescott, and coming down the big hill, he could see the glow and he called it in. We ran out to the barn—we don't keep horses in barn stalls, so there were none locked in, but there was one big Thoroughbred horse that was in a pen attached to the barn so he could go in and out of it. He was frantic. The halters had all burned up, so I took the sash off of my robe and went up to Pete and said, 'Come on baby, let me get you out of here.' I never imagined he was going to stop running around, but he did and put his head down so I could get him and lead him to safety.

"Another funny thing happened a couple of days after the fire. We had a pair of ravens who lived near, and they were flying over the ashes—you could hear them wondering: What happened to the barn? Where is it?"

I asked if she had any funny stories to tell about the ravens, because they steal Nadine's chicken eggs; she did not, but we laughed, and Nadine said, "Yes, we have watched them; they sit on the fence and wait for the hen to leave the coop after she lays and then they swoop in and get it. We have seen them fly out with an egg in their beaks. We are planning on covering the coop area with netting. They are very smart birds."

Carolyn continued. "Paul and I have helped Cynthia Rigden with round up. One time we went over I had this mare that was quiet at home, but more excited away. I told Paul that I wanted to stay close to him because then she would be quiet. When we got there Cynthia told Paul to go one way and for me to go with her. The mare behaved fairly well until we went over to where Paul was working. Right away she started fussing and pawing the ground and then she ran backwards. I figured she was going to back into the barb wire fence, and that would teach her a lesson. Instead she went straight up into the air and then over backwards! I thought that she was going to roll over onto me, but the saddle stopped her and she went the other way. I needed stitches on my head and limped for a while, but was otherwise OK. Daisy May found a new home and learned to keep her front feet on the ground.

"Another fun horse story is the time Paul was looking for a new polo pony, about 1998. He usually raised his own, but this time wanted to get a 'made one.' He had tried out a lot and eventually came to William Devane's (the actor) ranch near Indio, California. He got on a mare, and boy, she was perfect. He came off the field with a big grin on his face. The lady representing the horse said, 'Let me tell you her name. It is Surprise. She is a half Arab.' Now, no respectable polo player would play a half Arab.

"The lady explained that one of Devane's Arabian stallions got loose one night and evidently bred a mare through the pipe panel stall. They didn't even know the mare had been bred until they went to saddle her up one day and found this little filly in her stall. I saw William Devane a few years ago and told him that I had a mare of his named Surprise. He remembered her as 'just the prettiest little filly.' We named her Dahlia and still have her; she is 29 now. Paul played polo with her for about four years and made me promise to tell no one that she was half Arabian!

Carolyn and Dahlia

"One day I went into the pasture and my mare that I used for dressage had a broken front leg, probably because some horse kicked her. We had to euthanize her and Paul told me to take Dahlia for my dressage horse. The first time I asked her to canter without the tie down on—all polo ponies have tie downs on, they use it for balance and for turning but also to keep their heads out of the players' faces—her head came up and I thought we were going to fall down.

"With the help of a local dressage teacher, we taught her to not do that and I started showing her. I found that if the test was simple, she lost interest and didn't do well, but if it were hard, she paid attention and was great. Then she came up with ringbone and I mostly just trail rode her. One day coming down a hill from a trail ride she started drifting to the left. I let her go and she went under the trestle and ended up in the dressage ring up on the hill and walked around it. You can't tell me she didn't like dressage. Then we taught her to pull our Doctor's Buggy, and now her job is to show off for weddings when she's not yard furniture.

"Here is one more story for you. One day I was at the front door and heard this odd 'screaming' sound. I looked up at the railroad track that is a couple hundred feet from the front of the house and there was a doe and two fawns—on the tracks. The fawn in the back was the one screaming because there was a coyote right on its heels. My heart was in my mouth and I was sure the fawn was going to be killed. The doe spun around and went after that coyote, and the last I could see, the coyote was running as fast as he could go with his tail between his legs!"

That was a good one to end the conversation with—and we all agreed, you gotta love mothers!

ELLA MCCRACKEN
Gold Bar Ranch

Ella was referred by another gal, and unlike a few of the other 'real ranch women' I had been told about, she agreed to talk with me. I was finding out that some were reticent or even shy about sharing their lives. Ella grew up in Arizona, so she was a superb "find." We sat around her kitchen table snacking on delicious cheese, which it turned out, she made at the creamery just down the road.

"Tell me a little about your life growing up in Arizona as a child," I said.

"I have lived on the Gold Bar Ranch for thirty-five years, but I grew up in Crown King. It is an old mining town and now it has a lot of summer homes, and is pretty crowded. When I grew up there were a few homes, an old mercantile grocery and hardware store, a saloon, a one-room country school and the post office. It is a tourist attraction now and has been there for probably one hundred years. The railroad used to go through the area to pick up ore—there were actually a bunch of different mines up there.

"My dad was the teacher at the little school when I went to it, as well as my three brothers. My dad was the most awesome dad in the world. He also worked for the forest service in the look-out towers in Horse Thief Basin. I lived with my grandmother who had twelve children and seven grew up in Crown King. They were cowboys, military men, miners, worked at the Crown King Post Office and the forest service, and my dad was a teacher."

"So you have deep Arizona roots!"

"Yes, my grandmother is Ella Tewksbury who married a Tewksbury descendent of the Tewksbury and Graham rivalry here in

Arizona. There were several books written about the feud."

Well, I had to Google that! There is a book: "Arizona's Dark and Bloody Ground" with this description:

> The Pleasant Valley vendetta that swept through the Tonto Basin country in central Arizona during the latter 1880's was one of the most sanguinary and bitter range feuds the old West ever knew. Its ferocity and hatreds were rivaled only by the bloody battles and assassinations of the Lincoln County war in New Mexico ten years before, but it is doubtful, even with all its terrorism, if the number killed there equaled the casualties of Pleasant Valley. Both were born of blood feuds, and both were fought in defiance of the law of the land until they burned themselves out after most of the participants has either been killed or had grown weary of strife. Even the well-known Hatfield-McCoy feud that held the West Virginia and Kentucky mountains under a reign of terror for almost twenty years did not surpass the lifelong hatred born of the Pleasant Valley war...

Ella continued, "I got my first horse when I was six and started shooting when I was eight."

"Why were you shooting? I guess it just a normal thing to do out here—hunt and what not?"

"Well, we mostly did target practice. My dad was a real stickler about shooting. I have always had guns since I was small. So anyway, I spent a lot of time with my dad up in the towers looking for fires. My dad was the coolest dad. I always sat in his lap; he wasn't one of those 'untouchable dads.' He was real funny, he was a pretty 'raw guy,' but never cruel. He'd spank us kids, but then come in and apologize and read us a book. He hated spanking us."

"So he was the teacher in the one-room-school. How many kids, how many grades, and after that where did you go to school?"

"It went up to eighth grade and in the whole school there were probably six to twelve kids, depending on the year. Then we went to school in Yarnell. My mom and dad got divorced when I was six; my mom lived down in Phoenix but I spent all the summers and weekends up with my dad after that, staying with my grandmother."

I said, "I am confused, how did you go to the country school and live in Phoenix?"

"I went to summer school with my dad, and that's a bitch, right? Every single summer going to school! My brothers did also, if they wanted to come; however, I *always* wanted to come."

I asked, "Why did you have to go to summer school?"

"I was dyslexic and the teachers always thought if I had more schooling, they could fix it. That did not happen. I figured out how to work with it on my own.

"My brothers and I always fought like banshees, so it wasn't as much fun if they came with me. When I was there, I slept with my grandmother, Ella Tewksbury, and talk about old western women, she was 'the bomb.' She raised twelve kids in Crown King and she said the only time my granddad was home was when he hung his pants on the bedpost. He worked in some of the mines and he was gone all the time, so she augmented the money by having dances, doing laundry, and feeding some of the miners. My dad would go around and pick up cigarette butts and re-roll them and sell them. She was a real entrepreneur."

"I suppose she was a real 'pistol packin' mamma.'"

"She was. She was just the most beautiful woman. Next to her bed she had two jars: one was for her 'chew' and the other for her teeth. The bottom drawer of her dresser was filled with pennies. She gave me five pennies a day to go down to the general store to get some candy and ice cream. Then I could ride my horse and go meet my dad somewhere, go to Horse Thief Basin, take a peanut butter and jelly sandwich, take a nap, go swimming, fishing—back then it wasn't a scary thing to let your kids go off and do stuff alone.

"Granny was a real character. Her super power was making something out of nothing. She kept watermelon in the well house so it would be ice cold for us. Her pies were legendary; they were made from the apples in the old orchard. We also picked prickly pear fruit and wild blackberries for jam. Her kitchen by today's standard would be really old fashioned with a baker's box for flour in her cabinet and a surface to make those famous pies.

"We had an outhouse outside and a honey pot in the pantry. Years later I took it after finding it under the porch. She taught me to take a stick and put it down in the outhouse potty and wiggle it about before sitting down, then to put a cup of lye, I think it was, down it. The stick trick was for spiders and such! Granny would set up my bath in the kitchen in a galvanized tub. From there I could see into the back yard where there was a stone wall. One day there was a mountain lion looking down at me like I was soup. I called Granny and she got her boys after it the next day. However, even though they were great hunters and trackers, they did not find it.

"I caught my first fish at Horse Thief Basin with my dad. It became a tradition with me. Granny let me keep them in a horse trough until the raccoons ate them. I cried. One day Dad and Granny were sitting on the front porch shooting the breeze when I came riding hells bells past them in the creek, showing off, and a branch from a tree scooped me off my horse. My dad was upset, but Granny said, 'Just rub a little dirt in it. She's OK.'

"Granny loved to quilt and had a big quilting frame in the living room that would pull up to the ceiling when she wasn't using it—that was my dad's invention. She would use material from any old thing. Her quilts always reminded me of 'the coat of many colors.' When the weather was warm enough, I would sleep out on the front porch and listen to the band at the bar and hear my dad and cousins and granny hootin' and hollering, stomping feet and the pool table balls clacking together. I couldn't wait until I got old enough to do that. Years later there I am at that same bar—hootin' and a hollering!"

I laughed and encouraged her to continue.

"My mother was also a real powerful woman. She went back to school and graduated from Northern Arizona University. She belonged to Mensa, she was a scientist, and she traveled all over the world and met with other scientists. She was totally a 'kick ass woman.'"

"Did you follow your mother and go to college?"

"I did, I went to one in Phoenix, and later to one in Prescott, and during that time I stayed with my dad in Wilhoit and helped him on the little farm."

"Did you study anything in particular?"

"Nursing."

"Are you a nurse?"

"No. But after I graduated from Prescott, I went up to Flagstaff to NAU to finish my nursing. I had money for the first semester, but didn't have a house or apartment so I camped out by myself with my dog, Ruby, in the back of my truck—or under my truck. I found a spot on state land, next to a water hole—which is kinda frowned upon. The forest service rangers would come out once a week and check on me—and have a couple beers. I lived there four months, went to school, cocktailed at night and got enough money to get an apartment. I did that for three years, and then I met Mike, got pregnant, and it changed my life. Then Mike bought this ranch with his family and we moved here together.

"Lillie, my daughter, was really never in the picture of my future, because I wasn't supposed to be able to have children. She was a real miracle baby—they said I would never have another, and I didn't. I had her when I was in my early thirties. At that moment in time, Mike wasn't interested in getting married, so I decided to leave the ranch, took Lillie who was three months old, and moved to Hawaii. I worked for my brother, Greg, and ran a wood shop in Honolulu. That is where I became a master woodworker, using exotic hardwoods and making furniture. Next I got a job working for the Navy exchanges and traveled the world."

"Lillie sort of grew up 'on the run,' didn't she?"

"Yes, but every summer we both came back here to the ranch. When Lillie was six, she flew back to the ranch by herself for visits. After ten years I came back to Prescott and bought a house; Mike and I started dating again and got married. Mike does guided hunts and is gone three months out of the year. I run the ranch. This ranch used to be huge when we bought it thirty-five years ago. We went in with his parents and two sisters, but we lived here in this house. When Mike's dad, Jack, died fifteen years later the ranch was divided and some was sold, but we kept Gold Bar Ranch and the cattle. However, now we only have about forty-five head of cattle, and we used to have over three hundred. That is all the two of us can manage now that we are older.

"When we were younger, Lillie rode, all the kids in the neighborhood rode, but now I am sixty and want to do other things. We sell our beef as grass fed to customers, but for my own I feed some home-grown corn to finish them. We like that taste better, you get a little marbling that way."

"Tell a little about your other ranch venture."

"Up until 2000, we were all cattle, but then we decided to diversify and turn our little 'cowboy cabin' into a guest house with a campground which included the lake. This helped augment our income."

"When you were a cattle operation, did you have cowboys here all the time?"

"Yes, and we got more during the spring and fall works. However, as Lillie got older, she had a bunch of guy friends, but she was always very 'prim and proper,' and the guys were always very respectful. They made really good cow hands for us, and Lillie was an awesome cow hand too. Lillie had a Paint horse that was a dynamite barrel racer, and I had a horse named King, who was very photogenic."

"He was a Quarter Horse, I imagine?"

"No, he was an Arab! I never thought I would *ever* have an Arabian. However, I wanted the Paint horse for Lillie and I had to take the Arab also because they were a pair and inseparable. I had no use for Arabs."

I laughed. "Right, most people don't unless they love the breed!"

"And I did not love them; however, once I started riding him, it felt like skating. He was such an athlete. I ended up doing some endurance riding. I loved it. I thought it was crazy fun. He liked cows and would do anything I asked of him. He was seven when I got him and I had him until he was twenty-three when he choked and died. That just about killed me. We were of one mind—when I was on his back, we were *one*. He could go up and down the mountains, jump obstacles in the path like it was nothing."

"Could you use him for roping, cattle sorting and such?"

"Cattle work, yes, but I did not rope. He was amazing, but when I came out on him, people were like: *What the heck, an Arab*?"

I said, "Another gal I talked with, and you might know her—Carolyn Harris—said they also had a part Arab that her husband played polo on, but he swore her to secrecy that his horse had Arabian blood!"

Ella chuckled. "Yes, I know them. You know, after he died, I never wanted another horse of 'my own.' He was so stinkin' cute—it looked like he had mascara on. He was a big horse too—maybe sixteen hands."

I asked her what they did for vet care since they are really quite far from towns.

"I do all my own. I have a chest of drawers in the back room that is filled top to bottom with sutures, medicine, shots, and bandages. I did everything except two semesters for my nursing degree, but I learned a lot and you know out here, insurance is not good and so health care is expensive. I doctor everything that I can, human and animal."

"How about snakes?"

"For a horse snake bite, which is usually on the nose area, first thing I do is stick a piece of hose up their nose so it won't swell shut. Then I give a shot of Benadryl, some cortisone, antibiotic, a pain killer. I have only ever had one case of snake bite, but colic is another story. When you have lots of horses, you are sure to have colic now and then.

"How about the cows? Do they pretty much stay out of trouble?"

"We have uterine prolapses which is when the uterus falls out, we have had several of those. Our vet showed me how to deal with that."

"That is a *physical* chore!" I said.

"Yes, it is and you have to get them in a squeeze chute, give them a shot to relax the pelvic area, then you wash off the uterus really good and then you shove it back in and stitch it closed enough to keep it in and give antibiotics. Another time I came home and Mike said, 'We got a cow out here and the baby is hanging out.' We couldn't get her up to get her in the squeeze chute, so I said that I would pull the calf, and told Mike to distract her. I started pulling on the calf's legs and the cow jumped up. Mike ran behind the bushes—that cow had big horns too— and I started running and the cow was chasing me. I could feel her breath on the back of my neck, and I thought to myself, *I wonder how bad this is going to hurt.*

"Mike was yelling at me, '*Turn, turn!*' I heard him yelling and I was scared to death, so I figured, what could happen that was worse than this, so I did—and the cow went straight! Cows do that, normally they keep going straight. I ran into the barn and was just shaking. Mike was out there laughing his head off. I said, 'What is so funny?' He said, 'You hurt?' I said, 'No.' He said, 'Then it was funny!'

"One spring we were over at the Smoke Tree Ranch, which was part of the original Gold Bar, doing a huge round up branding the calves. I was manning the gate and Lillie, who was fifteen then, and the boys were supposed to be looking for more cows and calves, but the boys got excited about something and left Lillie. I saw Lillie all alone in this big open area, and all of a sudden, she ran her horse over to a spot and picked up eight cows and their calves, all by herself. She pushed them against the fence line, down to the road and all the way back to the holding area. The boys, meantime, found nothing. When Lillie came back her hat was torn up, she had a black eye because she took her horse through some brush and a tree limb got her because she was in the heat of chasing a cow. But you know, she looked so satisfied! I was really proud of her."

"What did you do in between the spring and fall works?"

"I had a huge garden, chickens, Mike's hunting dogs to feed, goats to feed, tons of canning. We have lots of fruit trees. Asian pears are one of my favorites. These trees are really old, but they are so delicious and they get big. They are a cross between a pear and an apple and are crisp like the apple, but have the flavor of a beautiful pear. We have a lake that is gravity fed by the Hassayampa River by a two-mile-long ditch that goes along cliffs that was dug by the CCC boys about ninety years ago. It is an engineering marvel. Then it goes underground across the ranch and into the pond. However, it gets very dirty and a part needs cleaning every day. Twice a year we clean out the whole thing, which takes about two weeks to finish. The bridge on our road goes over the Hassayampa River, which means 'the river that flows upside down' because parts of it disappear underground in places and pops up again in others.

"The headwaters are in Prescott, and when it rains up there, it might be dry down here, and you really have to watch out because of the flash floods. We have been cutting wood down in a completely dry river bed and see a little trickle start to come and yell at everyone: 'Out of the river!' It gives you a thrill seeing it go on by—it's primal. We will sit down and have a beer and watch it—it is just mesmerizing. Sometimes I like to take Wwoofers down to see the river when it is just running a little--have you ever heard of 'Wwoofers?' It is an acronym for 'Worldwide opportunities on organic farms' and they come from all over the world. We don't get many Americans, mostly from Europe, Australia, China, and New Zealand. They come and learn how to work on a ranch. The American interns we have had do not like to work, and that is sad.

"They will help us with whatever we are doing while they are here: animals, gardening, fence building, they helped us build that outdoor kitchen over there. It is a 'hands on thing,' though; you have to work with them. So it is actually double the work for you. You don't pay them, it is volunteer, but you feed and house them. I have been doing it for six years, and you don't always get *more* work done and things are always breaking, plus it costs about $1000.00 a month to feed them. You more or less give over your life to them while they are here. We do it because these kids need to know where their food comes from—from the beginning to the end. They help brand and butcher, plant and harvest the garden and can the produce. They learn how to be self-sufficient and how to use tools. A lot of these kids have never used a hammer or shovel."

I said, "It is too bad they *don't* come from *our* country!"

"You know what? The Americans don't like to work, and ranching is hard work. I am very specific who I let come. For instance, they have to speak enough English that I can understand them, I need to know if they have medical issues, take medication—because we are at least an hour from town. I don't care if they do, I have had handicapped people before; I just need to know. These kids stay from one to three months and they become part of the Gold Bar Ranch family. We keep in touch on Facebook and other ways. I have a group coming next week."

"Do you ever have returning Wwoofers? Are they mainly teenagers?"

"Yes, I do. I have a couple of Israeli guys who have come three times. The people can be from eighteen to forty-five. I have had some that were my age. It is the coolest program ever. These young people eventually will rule the world and by golly, I want them to understand about life."

I said, "Maybe a good way to put it would be that it is a labor of love on your part, to help the world."

"Yes, my motto is: Sweep your own corner. I may not be able to do a lot politically, but in Walnut Grove, I can do this."

Ella said, "I have another motto: 'If you don't have a dog, use a cat.' It means you can do anything you want to. If something doesn't work, try something else. One of my favorite places is Home Depot. I love buying wood and stuff like that for my many projects. I take my paper in and ask for help in finding what I need. 'Oh no, we don't have anything like that.' So I will go to another person and maybe I will go through five people but eventually I will find that person who says, 'Oh, I know what you need, let me think…' But it is persistence; you have to be your own advocate in life."

I said, "Tell me about the creamery. When I first contacted you, we had to schedule around your work there."

"Oh, the creamery! This asiago cheese that we are snacking on came from the creamery. Two years ago, my girlfriend and her husband came over for dinner and she said, 'Ella, you are so good at running things, how would you like to manage our creamery?' They had just built it and it is state of the art. With all the things I was already doing, I was almost overwhelmed as it was. That night I lay in bed and thought about it all night and wondered how I could make it work.

"At that time since 2000, I was doing ranch trail rides four days a week that was part of the campground-bed and breakfast thing, and I did summer camps for kids. One month was for inner city kids, which was free, and one month where I got paid. They learned how to ride, how to ride bareback, and how to care for horses. It was a lot of work and mental stress too, because you had a lot of responsibility. I thought: you know, I am tired of being on a horse and doing this. So I quit and started working at the creamery and it is my *love*."

I said, "Well, I am trying to figure out where you get the milk!"

"She has Jersey dairy cows, and a beautiful milking barn."

I asked, "Can we see that? Do you make butter also?"

"Yes, I would love to show it to you on the way out. Before we were licensed and could sell cheese, I made butter, yogurt, ice cream and all that stuff, but now we just make the cheese because that is what they want to concentrate on."

I said, "We had Jersey cows when I was growing up in Pennsylvania, and that is where I learned to love butter on *everything*! Where do they sell the cheese?"

"At Farmer's Markets, wine tasting places, and restaurants. What I love about the creamery is that I am there all by myself. It is my gig. I work on Mondays and Thursdays."

"Can you tell us how you make cheese?"

"Sure. The milk goes into a cooling vat as the cows are being milked. It collects for three days until there is enough to make cheese. Then I pump it into my cooking vat, heat it to a certain degree, then I add my culture, let it sit for thirty minutes, then add the rennet and let that sit for anther thirty minutes. Next I cut the curds that were formed and stir it. As I stir, I heat it—and this is the difficult part because you really have to pay attention.

"It changes depending on the type of cheese, but for twenty minutes I heat it up to a certain degree, and for each minute the heat goes up a certain degree. Then it stirs at that top degree for fifteen minutes, and then for ten minutes, you have to go up to another required degree. Next it sits for twenty minutes, then you scoop out the curds and put them in your containers and then you press it for twenty minutes, flip it and press again for twenty minutes.

"With the asiago I then press it for two hours, flip and then press again for two hours. Then it sits out at room temperature for two days, and then it goes into the brine where it also sits for two days. While in the brine I flip it every other day, and from there it goes into the cheese cave to age."

"Wow, that is quite a process. How long does it age?"

"As long as you want. Cheese will keep aging. This asiago we are eating aged for three months."

I asked if she had ever been stranded between the numerous washes that cross her road. Another gal who I planned on interviewing had cancelled because she said heavy rain was expected and we could get stuck there.

"Sure, all the time! But the thing is, you stop at a wash, then someone else stops, then another person, so then you got yourself a party."

"How long can it take for the water to go down enough to cross?"

"From an hour to maybe two. But someone usually has beer, or sandwiches, or *cheese* so it is really fun, like a little neighborhood party. Once we had a margarita kit in a suitcase—no ice though, we had to rough it!"

I said, "Fun so long as there is no emergency."

"If there is an emergency, the hospital sends the helicopter. You had asked earlier about animals getting hurt here on the ranch, here is a story. All the horses were down at the lake pasture, running around chasing each other, swimming and having a good time. Mike was down there working and saw one of the horses run into a branch and cut an artery on her face. The blood was just spurting out, so he took off his shirt and wrapped it around her face and used his belt to hold it on. He comes with the horse up to the house just covered with blood, and he yells, 'It's not me, it's the horse.'

"I gathered up all my medical stuff and we got a halter on the mare, put something over her face to calm her. (If horses cannot see, they are usually quieter.) I gave her some Banamine for pain, injected some Lanacane into the cut area, shaved it some, cauterized it and sewed it up. And she let me do all that. The Lanacane numbed it, and she couldn't see what I was doing so she was OK, but that kind of stuff happens all the time."

"Any human injuries you had to deal with?"

"Sure, I have done people before. I had a farrier who was shoeing a horse and got his hand ripped by a nail, I got to sew him up. I just love sewing people up."

Nadine and I had driven by several of the older ranches along

Ella's road, which had been purchased by Rex Maughn, and became part of the Maughn Ranch. If there were no family members who wanted to continue on with ranching, ranches would be sold, some perhaps for subdivisions like the ones Nadine and I live in, or by someone with enough money to buy them and keep as ranches. Among other things, Rex Maughn is the CEO and founder of Forever Living Products which nearly all contain aloe, and he is known as a philanthropist who has given millions for several causes. I wondered if Ella knew him and asked her to tell a bit about him.

Ella and Lillie

"Our friends, Amy and Don, are the managers for Maughn Ranches in this area. On each one of these ranches Rex owns, he has his own house, which is cleaned every week. His favorite is the TK Bar. It is beautiful. He and his wife, Ruth, are just the best people ever. He buys up these ranches, but he doesn't turn them into golf courses, he keeps them as they are and I love that! He is just a regular guy; he comes by when I am all grubby and working in the garden, leans on the fence and asks, 'What's goin' on in the neighborhood?' And we will chat. He is awesome. He was a huge help in rebuilding Yarnell after the fire."

I said, "Speaking of that fire, how close were you?"

"We had to evacuate. As the crow flies, we were pretty close, and the fire was traveling pretty fast. We got the horses and cows out— they all went various places, and got our important stuff out, but we stayed here because people from Yarnell had to have some place to go with their animals. We closed the ranch down for a month and a half, and had 'Yarnell refugees' I want to call them, here. They stayed in the Bed and Breakfast cottage, camped wherever they wanted to, and had the animals in the pens. They really left Yarnell with nothing, just themselves and their animals.

"My daughters, who worked in town, would call each day and ask what I needed and they would bring it to us. Safeway and Fry grocery stores donated food, Costco donated animal supplies. It was amazing how everybody pitched in. What I wanted to say about Rex Maughn is that he doesn't broadcast the stuff he does for people but he helped people rebuild their homes and gave an enormous amount of money for the rebuilding of Yarnell."

I asked if Rex raised cattle on all of his ranches.

"Yes, and he hires a lot of people which is also good for the community. We are glad to see the ranch land remaining as ranches."

In closing Ella's story, I think that one of the things she said explains it all, not only for her but for all the other gals also: "You know, the thing I really love about living our here is that every day is different. You can plan your day, but you never know what will happen. When I go out to feed my chickens in the morning and see the ranch, I say to myself how much I love being here—I *love* my ranch and my life!"

EVE BLUMENFELD
And
EARS LOOKING AT YOU

I saw Eve's Facebook entry about her Tevis ride and had to find out more because she rode a mule! "Ears" was one of two mule entries in 2016, and I was sure it would be a fascinating story. Here is what Eve told me about herself, Ears, and the Tevis Cup ride:

I am fifty-six and I have lived in some great places: Berkeley, Tahoe, Boulder Colorado, Sacramento (not so great), and now I reside in Loomis, California, which is within riding distance to Folsom Lake and *Tevis*. That is important because when I decided to do the Tevis ride, I could actually condition my animal on some of the actual trails. I have always been athletic. In high school I was a gymnast, and then I took up skiing because I lived in Tahoe. I also was a cyclist, a runner, rode mountain bikes, and well, you get the idea.

In 2013, I was let go from my job after fourteen years and it took me a year to get another one. In the meantime, I "got a wild hair," and thought how cool it would be to trail run and ride a horse. (Ride and Tie—two people share one horse. One rides and the other runs. Then the rider ties up the horse and the runner comes to that horse, gets on and rides to the next stop and ties up the horse.) One problem: last time I rode a horse I was about seven.

I rode four races; however, in all but one I ran past my horse! They all looked the same to me. Needless to say, I did not make the best partner, but I could *run*. For my birthday in 2013, the woman who let me ride her horse in a Ride and Tie race let me ride that horse in my very first 50-mile endurance ride. Afterwards I couldn't walk for days, but I

206

was hooked. I met a whole new group of people and that year I went to Tevis and watched the riders come in to finish, and thought, "I want to do that someday."

I still had no job, but told my friend to find me a horse. In January, 2014, Tux Red Baron came into my life. He was a 14.1 hand, seven-year-old Arabian. I really didn't know much about horses, but I asked a lot of questions, read a lot and treated my horse like one of my dogs: family. On one of my LD rides (limited distance: 25-35 miles), I met a man on a mule, Roger Downey. That whole season I kept running into Roger who was on a different mule each time. That year Tux and I ranked sixth in LD for the west coast and first in BC (Best condition).

The next year I bought a house so I could have Tux right outside my window. We moved up to 50-mile races and did five in 2015. I still saw Roger, and now and then rode with him, but he stayed in LD races and had other people condition his mules for longer races. I found out he did Tevis every year if he could.

We became friends and I would call him up and let him know what races I would be in, and he always met me with a mule, mostly one named Jody, who is a real sweetheart. In 2015 I crewed for one of my girlfriends at Tevis, and that made me really want to ride it. That same year Roger came off his mule at Tevis and was airlifted out. He broke six ribs and punctured a lung, and because he doesn't wear a helmet—a concussion too.

I told him he could never ride Tevis alone again, and he called me on it and said I had to ride it with him. Well, that was great, but my horse was too young and I wanted to do more 50s with him first. Plus he was facing surgery on an old splint bone injury. So Roger said he would give me one of his mules. Now that was funny because I had only been riding horses for barely two seasons and he wants me on a mule!

For your information, Arabian riders can be a little snobby—like "Does your mule kick?" I would be rich if I had a dollar for every time someone asked me that. Roger, on the other hand, would ask, "Does your *horse* kick?"

So last October I met Roger for a ride and he brought Ears Looking At You. Shit, he was *big*—15.3 hands big and I could barely get on him. We rode a few times together, and one day when he was dropping me off, he started getting Ears out of the trailer. I said, "What are you doing?" and he said, "Well, if you are going to ride him, you will want him at your house."

Ears had recently come off the race track. He has thoroughbred blood in his mule veins. I love watching mules or horses race; they are just beautiful, but I wish they did not get the abuse or discarded if they don't do well. But that is another story. It took time to bond with Ears; at first, I didn't even think he liked me at all. I hate it when people say mules are stubborn. When you get to know them, you realize they are just very smart and more into self-preservation. They are careful and don't want to get hurt. This quality would make Ears a fabulous partner for my big adventure of riding Tevis.

I freaked out and called JoDe Collins who kept all of Roger's mules and she said to keep Ears and Tux separate as sometimes when mules play, they will mount a horse and squish goes Tux. So, I set up separate corrals, but it turned out that Tux could tell Ears what to do and they got along fine. In fact, too fine.

I could take Ears out on a ride and leave Tux, but couldn't take Tux and leave Ears. You should see my gate slightly bent—okay, a *lot* bent. So I decided to pony Ears off Tux so I could start to condition Tux, and then took Ears out alone on hard rides to condition for Tevis. Going into 2016, I had the help of JoDe Collins who is a donkey and mule expert. We would chat almost every day on what to do, what races to push and what to take it easy.

Roger went with me on each one, and we did six rides including Cooley Ranch. They offer fifty miles on Saturday and fifty on Sunday. It is a hell-of-a hard ride—hot and lots of hills. I figured if I could get Ears through that, we could do Tevis. Roger's mule got a suspensory injury doing two hard back to back rides and he was out of Tevis. The good thing about having Ears at my house was I could feed and train as I thought best. I also did conditioning rides that were part of Tevis because I didn't know the terrain or route. Really good quality, short rides and then give him two weeks off before Tevis and let him plump up was my plan.

All was going swell until something spooked Ears and Tux and they went through my fence. Double dang. I couldn't put him on antibiotics this close to Tevis because of drug testing, so I had to wrap and ice *three* of his legs twice a day. The day before I was to head up to Robie, where the race starts, he was still swollen in one leg; I iced him, crossed my fingers and loaded up. Fortunately by the time I got to Robie, his leg was OK.

We had done so well in our other races, I put in for "pen one" and we got it. I had a few people say, "Are you sure you want to be in that pen? It is for the fast horses—top ten finishers. And it is really aggressive on a single-track path in the dark." I thought about it for a second and then said, "Think about it as being on a freeway. Everyone else is in a Mini Cooper and I am in a Suburban." And off we went.

I can tell you there was something about those first six miles before we hit the bottom of Squaw that just told me, "We are going to make this." He just had this purpose like I have never felt, like this was it. In the dark with all the other horses around he remained steady. He didn't speed up or slow down or get flustered. I knew that Ears was going to take me to the finish, all I had to do is hang on!

I ran into Mark Montgomery who rescues and trains mustangs. He has a darn fast mustang that he was riding. We chatted a bit while we watched other riders blowing by on the climb back up Squaw, and we shook our heads. Maybe they were going too fast for the good of their animals. We started riding out together. I knew Cougar Rock was coming up and I told him I wanted to do it.

Mark said, "Okay, I will help you." So we followed his mustang and at the start of the climb up Cougar Rock, his mustang stopped and spun around right in front of Ear's head. Oh my God! Ears was like, "What the hell?" And decided to turn around too. I said, "I don't think so, Bud" and pushed him forward. To get back at me he said, "The heck with following the arrows—that will take too long. I can *jump* this! And he did; it was over in a second. Thank God I used to ride mountain bikes tandem and that is exactly what it felt like. Oops, I am not in the saddle anymore and my right leg came out of the stirrup, but no worries, we got this!

Cougar Rock is not actually as scary as it looks, but the pictures taken while you go up it are magnificent. It is a big mound with nice granite rock in the middle. As you head up you see arrows that point you in the direction of the best footing. Where the arrow veered to the left, Ears just jumped and landed on the top. I knew he was a good jumper from our past rides, but this was so powerful it threw me up off the saddle.

Ears and I came into our first crew and vet check six minutes ahead of the time I wanted. Ears was doing great and did not give one hesitation; not once in the ride did I doubt we would make it to the finish. Because he pulsed down faster than Mark's mustang, we left without them.

For me this next section of the ride would be crucial. It had two very hard canyons and we hit them in the peak of the heat. Because a few places are so steep and stony, some riders get off and run down, leading their horses. There was no way in Hell *I* was going to get off my mule that has way better footing than I do. Actually, I had run with Ears several times before, and each one ended up with me on the ground in front of him. The first time I crossed in front of him and hit his legs and went down, another time he stepped on my spurs and I tripped. But he must have known that I was going down because he never stepped on me.

Eve and Ears at Cougar Rock

At the bottom of the first canyon was The Swinging Bridge—and my second oops moment. This is a story. Because I had been doing conditioning rides on Ears at parts of Tevis, we discovered that bridge before the actual race. You are supposed to get off and lead your mount across. Well, let me tell you, that mother really swings! Ears almost ran me over getting to the other side. I knew the bridge might be an issue for the race.

I was also told that if it was hot in the canyons, like 110 degrees, I better get him to stand in the water and cool off or he will blow coming out of the canyon and won't make it. Also, to make sure you follow someone into the water and if they are not going into the water, get off and tie him to a tree and wait until someone will take their horse to the water.

Oh, the best part at the ride meeting was, we were actually told *not to cross the river*, there is no trail out and NO spotters. I was riding with this gal from back East and I asked her if she was going to get her horse wet in the water, since that would be the only place to cool him off before the climb up Devil's Thumb.

It is a bit tricky entering the river as it is a sharp left kind of one-way traffic. If you stay straight you head over the bridge. She took the turn and her horse slipped due to another horse coming back out of the water, and fell, and she came off. She was OK, but we looked at her horse's legs and I said to get him in the water so we can see how bad it is. While I am looking at her horse's legs Ears goes, "Oh hey, there is that damn bridge again, and I think I will just cross the river instead." Well, shit, once he makes up his mind, you can't stop him.

He plunged in and we went down deep; he came up and he jumped out, but we got hit by a tree branch and came back into the water. I told him to find another spot, he did and jumped up and out, and off we went up to Devil's Thumb. Later the photographer who was on spot for pictures told me that my water shots were great, but my river exit had her heart in her throat.

After crossing the river, we started our trek up a series of switchbacks to Devil's Thumb. Funny, I never saw Devil's Thumb before and couldn't figure out why they called it that until my girlfriend pointed it out. But if you ask me it looks like a certain body part I will not mention.

It was great to get to the top as I knew the couple that was running the aid station, Pat and Steve Hallmark. I don't know who was happier to see who. I have to say you feel like the Queen of Sheba when you come into an aid station. People run up and offer you fruit or a platter of sandwiches, refill your water, and a few times I never got off Ears.

About a hundred feet or so before the Deadwood vet check there is a table and someone hands you your check-in and check-out card, takes your number down and what time you arrived. Well, Ears took it upon himself to head straight for the food area which I guess he could see or smell off in the distance. As we blew by the timers, I yelled, "I will be right back!" When I could get him turned around, we picked up our card with the gals laughing at me.

After Tevis, I did another ride at Camp Far West. As I was walking back to my trailer this lady stops me and says, "Is that Ears?" I said that it was, and she blurts out, "Oh my God, you two were so funny. I was at the table when you and your mule blew by. I was so happy to hear you finished." That just brought a smile to my face.

We did great at the Deadwood vet check, got great scores, and I stayed longer than I needed because Ears wanted to eat more. El Dorado Canyon was next and a lot of people don't like it because it plunges off to the right, but I thought the footing and the trail were just fine. When we got to the bottom there were a couple large water troughs for the animals before the climb back up to Michigan Bluff.

There were some riders down there, and I did not want to follow them as I knew Ears would try to keep up. I asked one guy who looked pretty strong if he would hold Ears while I sponged him off and let the other riders get out of eyesight. *Wrong* move! Not only did Ears want to go with the other horses, he dragged the poor guy through the mud with me running after him trying to jump on before we hit the hill—as I was yelling, "I am sorry!"

When we got to Michigan Bluff there were many tubs of water and lots of people to help you cool down your equine, and I saw a few people that I knew, which is nice. In just a mile or so was the next vet check: Chicken Hawk. But the one I really wanted to get to was Foresthill as my crew was there. Let me tell you those were the longest four or so miles. But once hitting the road, the excitement was great: shower and clean clothes, here I come.

The Forrest Hill stop never looked so good when I got there. I took a shower, ate, and again, Ears was ready to go. Next stop Auburn and the finish line—I hoped. When it got dark, I was like, dang, this guy is hauling ass, no pun intended, and I can't see shit. I knew those trails and there is a drop to the river, and he was making the turns so fast, I was just hanging on. There was a woman in front of me, and I asked her if she would slow down a second so I could get off and slow him down a bit, and she said, "Ride your own ride." Or something like that.

I went to jump off and a stirrup went flying off, and I ended up hanging onto Ear's neck and pulled a groin muscle on the way down. I broke my fall on my left knee on a *rock*. But oh my gosh, Ears came to a complete stop like, "What was that all about?" And just then I heard a voice say, "Is that the crazy Eve on a mule? What are you doing out here by yourself?"

And I said, "The same thing you are, Mark Montgomery!" I was never so happy to see him, well, I couldn't actually *see* him—it was so dark. He said he would not leave me, and he had never finished Tevis before. I said, "Well, neither have I, but I plan on finishing this thing." I was getting motion sick and had to use Mark as a bumper for Ears. I would yell, "Move to the left, wait, move to the right." I think Ears finally got the point I did not want him to pass Mustang Cody.

We had two more vet checks: Francisco and Quarry. At both I fell off Ears when I was trying to dismount because my leg was toast. At Francisco people ran and got me a chair and Advil, stuffed my face with food, and trotted out Ears. Then when we were ready to go, I barely made it to the mounting block, and off we went. Leaving the Quarry, Mark said he was going to turn off his light as the moon had finally made its way up. Crossing No Hands Bridge was breathtaking in the moonlight and being out there doing Tevis just gave me the shivers. Also, I knew exactly where we were and that we were almost at the finish line.

As we made it to the finish my girlfriend was up there yelling and cheering at Mark and me. We were so toast she had to lead us to the stadium to cross under the banner. Mark had said, "Let's hold hands as we go under" and we did. Thank God or I would have fallen off my mule. I was an hour and a half off the time I wanted to come in, but ever so proud of me and Ears. I still smile every time I think of all the things that went on…

I am going to really miss that darn mule. But here comes the twist. JoDe told Roger that I am in good standings for AERC points, and also they have a new 2016 Mule Award, and if I can finish off the season I might place well. So I get a call from JoDe and she says Roger says I can finish the season on Ears. I can never thank Roger Downey enough for allowing me the experience of a lifetime with the great, amazing, and endearing mule, Ears Looking At You!

Eve and Ears did win the new award. Here is an outline from the AERC: "New in 2016! The American Mule Association is sponsoring an award to the mule with the highest endurance mileage in one season. This award is in remembrance of Marirose Six, a Mountain region member who ran Marirose's Mule School (and Horses Too) and competed on many mules, most notably Lucky Six Nellie. The recipient will be the mule and rider team with the highest endurance (50- or more mile rides) mileage for the season. In case of a tie the award will go to the team with the most 100-mile completions in the season. This award is open to any mule and rider team. An engraved plaque will be given at the AERC convention national awards."

For 2018, Eve plans on riding Tevis with Tux. She says, "It will be so emotional as he is my very first horse, and he is who he is because of me. We shall see if all the conditioning I have done pays off. I don't really know if he is a 100-mile horse or not, but it is all about the journey to get there and we will go as far as he can or wants. They say 'To finish is to win' but I say, 'To start the journey with your forever horse is to win.' The bond you have with your horse is as good as gold. Oh, and Tux told me I need to get in shape as I will have to get off him in the canyons to tail him up.

***

Eve rode Tevis with Tux in 2018 and finished, getting both the coveted Cougar Rock photo and the awesome Tevis buckle, and in July, 2019, Roger decided to give Ears to Eve, so that will be the beginning of another chapter in this quirky mule and equally determined lady, Eve's, lives.

Kimberly Henson
And
Saddle Your Cattle!

I met Kimberly, who lived in California, through Eve who rode Ears in the 2016 Tevis Cup ride. It was all long distance via email and phone conversations, but Eve was correct: Kimberly did have a story to share. The first and most obvious question had to be: Why cattle?

"I have always been hardwired for cattle for some reason. The first animal I remember drawing was a cow; I didn't even know what it was, and I was in love with it. I was four or five and was just so fascinated with that shape. From then on, I was always looking for cattle in the landscape. I wasn't bit by the horse bug. My mom was, and she had a really nice horse boarding stable, later my sister took it over and she was a horse lover. You are hardwired for what you are hardwired for, aren't ya?

"In the economic downturn of 2005, my husband thought there might be a crash imminent so we sold our home and moved to the country, got some milk goats, a Dexter cow we could breed, some chickens, and started a garden. The cow had a little bull calf that was going to be for meat. When we lived in Texas, we raised beef cattle for the table, so I was OK with that idea—but there was something about this little guy that was so endearing that I had second thoughts. My husband was standoffish toward the calf, he was fond of saying, 'Oh, you are going to taste so good.' But I am like, oh Lord, what are we going to do?

"Finally, I told my husband, 'We have to have *the* conversation.' He said, 'What's that?' I said, 'We can't eat this little calf. We are going to find a way for him to contribute to our little homestead. If we end up off the grid, we are going to need something to haul us into town."

I said, "Tell me about Dexter cattle. Aren't they small?"

"Well, yes, but they can pull. I wasn't thinking about riding any at this point. I named the calf Dozer and after my husband and I had '*the* conversation,' he called Dozer over to him and said, 'I love you, we aren't going to eat you.' That calf had always been very distant with my husband because he hadn't opened his heart to the calf."

"Right, he was going to *eat* him," I said.

"Yes, and he was going to taste darn good! So after my husband did that Dozer came right up to him and has been in love with my husband ever since. It is amazing when we open our hearts to our animals what responses we can get from them. My mom had her retired Tennessee Walking mare at our place and she was a very alpha mare. We kept the cows and the horse in separate pastures because we were afraid the mare might hurt them, or try to 'own' the calf. We have the most darling picture of the cow bringing the baby up to the gate so Sissy, the horse, could meet him. After a while we put them together in the same pasture. Sissy had a free standing 12 x 12 stall where we put her hay. One day when Dozer was about five months old, he went in and decided he would eat her hay. Sissy came into her stall and started stomping the ground; she wanted him to go. I have seen her pick up the goats by the neck and gently toss them out of her stall. She was very frustrated—he should go.

"Dozer backed up very slowly perpendicular to her, put his head down and butted her in the stomach. You knew he was saying, 'Don't rush me.' Then he slowly walked outside. Sissy and Dozer had this little game they played. He wanted to lick her back leg; she wasn't sure about that and picked up her leg like she was going to kick him. He'd back off, think about it, and then come back up to her leg. Eventually he got close enough to lick it. Sissy was a mixture of, 'I like this' to 'How can he get away with this?'"

"Why do you think he wanted to lick her *leg*?"

"Licking is the way cows show their affection to one another and her leg was all he could reach. I remember another time when they were in separate pastures and Sissy walked up to the pipe gate and sidestepped close so Dozer could stick his little head through and lick her leg, but first they had to do the 'game' of threat-kick. Dozer was so fascinating that I just decided I had to do something special with him. I was also discovering that being around the cattle, especially Dozer, calmed me

216

down, and I found it very therapeutic. I did massage therapy out of my home, so I had time to work with Dozer. I took him down to our little town (in a trailer) and led him down the sidewalk to socialize him. It was so funny; he would see himself in a store window and stop and moo at it. The folks at the local English riding store loved to see him come by and gave me little tidbits about riding. I also took him around to a lot of different events so he would be used to things, and then I decided to enter him in the parade. Now he was eight months old. "By that time, I had decided I was going to teach him to be a riding steer. I had seen pictures of third world people riding their cows and thought that was neat. For the parade I had a banner made: *Riding Steer in Training* and I led him down the street. I had no idea how to do it, I just had a goal. When he was about two years old, I started to get on him. He is a big boy, and I am a small woman. People cannot believe he is a Dexter because he is so big—he looks more like an Angus.

Kimberly and Dozer

His sire and dam were only 45 inches at the shoulder!

"I started working with Dozer on the ground. My mom tried to give me tips she used with her horses. I used a bareback pad and sat on him, but I was slipping off and he was rubbing me off on the gates. He didn't know what I wanted because I had no idea how to teach him. I started to Google 'Riding cows,' and found Dee Dee Stauss, *Premier Riding Longhorns.* I couldn't even ride Dozer, but I thought, 'I have to ride a longhorn!' My motto was: 'If you can conceive it, you can achieve it!' Others were doing it, I could too—I was driven. I got hold of Dee Dee and said that I really would love to have a Texas Longhorn. She asked me what my experience was, I said that I didn't have any, but I wanted a full size one. She said that I needed to start with a young one where we could 'grow with the horns.'

"Dee Dee had a small herd of longhorns and each year she would save out a steer or two to be riding steer prospects or pasture pets. She had lots of horse experience, showed all over the country for years, really knew horses, and she used that to help her train the riding steers. I was having a hard time with Dozer because I was trying to use a hackamore and also he didn't have the right ground handling that I learned to do later with Jazzy. Dozer was just too strong headed. This is when I found the nose bit. The nose bit is about a one-and-a-half-inch bolt that goes through the nose septum with rings on each end. There have been people who thought that was just harsh, but like using a bit in a horse's mouth, it is all in how you use it. If you teach your steer leg and seat aids, you seldom have to even use the nose bit. We train them to be very responsive to the bit, just like horse trainers want the horses to be 'light in the bit.'

"My husband isn't a real dyed-in-the-wool animal lover, but since I wanted a Longhorn and had contacted Dee Dee to get one, we drove out there in my mom's old, but well kept, truck, that my husband wasn't even sure was 'sound' but it got us there and back."

"What year would this have been?"

"2010. We got to Dee Dee's ranch and saw Jazzy—Premier Longhorn's All That Jazz. She showed me what she had been teaching him, but she hadn't had time to expose him to all the things Dozer had seen, like himself in a story window. We had brought a chicken in a cage along to keep him company on the way home. It was a hen who was laying eggs so my husband would put the raw eggs in his protein drink every day. We got to stay and visit with Dee Dee and learned how she bred for conformation and color—black and white being an unusual color, and temperament. Not every Longhorn could be a riding steer. Jazzy wasn't socialized with people as much as Dozer because Dee Dee didn't have the time I did. Nor had he ever been in a stock trailer, so he was madder than hell the whole way across the country. He had about four-inch horns and we worried that he might use them on us, but soon we saw that he was not going to do that. Dee Dee had said that we would grow 'with the horns' meaning that as the horns got longer, our training and bonding and his learning that I was alpha, and my learning to communicate with him as a herd animal, would have grown also.

"We were so nervous hauling him that we drove thirty-three hours straight. We were 'driving under the influence' by the time we got home. But we got home, and put the hen back in the chicken coop. The chickens *never* went across the road to where the pasture was. Never, *ever.* They didn't even look down the driveway, but the next morning this hen took the whole flock down the driveway, across the street."

"To meet her steer friend? Oh my gosh!"

"I couldn't believe it. We had to keep them locked up for a week so she could get Jazzy out of her mind! He hasn't had a chance to see the chickens since because I don't want to take a chance one might get hurt.

"Getting back to growing with the horns, this was part of the training: I would stand at his left shoulder, face forward, and taught him to move *off* of pressure, not into it and throw his head back (into me). When I placed my hand on the back of his horn, standing next to his neck, that was his cue to not move the broad side of his horn toward me and he learned to be 'light'; it didn't take a lot of pressure."

I said, "That is pretty amazing because I have grown up with cows and that is just kinda different because cows don't think like horses."

"Right, they are more 'whoa' than 'go!' But what we found was that they *did respond* like horses do. The only thing he doesn't like to do, and I don't do it, is lunging (having a horse, for instance, run in circles around you attached to a long rope to get the 'kinks' out, or exercise). They got more whoa than go, so they think 'what in heck are you trying to do?' I did soon realize that I needed some professional help in training the steers. Now I had two, and couldn't ride one. The first horse trainer I tried was a very well-known gal around here—Rachael Chao. I met her at a local fund raiser that I had taken the boys to. I remember that I had them tied too close together and they were kind of arguing with each other, misbehaving like teenagers and I was trying to handle them. They were both young, Jazzy was maybe close to two, and Dozer was three. She was very interested in them, and I said that I was trying to teach them to ride and having a hard time of it. She said, 'Maybe I can help you.' I was doing massage out of my home, so I traded massages for cow training.

"I asked her if she would come over to our place. At that time, I had Dozer and Jazzy. When she arrived, Jazzy was behind a big bush, but Dozer saw us and started walking down the cow path toward us. He turned around and mooed for Jazzy. Next I hear a strange sound coming from behind the bush, like Jazzy is saying, 'No, not coming out.' Dozer didn't usually moo at other cows and only seldom to us, but now he escalated his mooing to Jazzy, and started pawing at the ground, making dust fly. Again, that strange sound from Jazzy behind the bush—it sounded a little like a goat. But Jazzy finally came out and sauntered down to Dozer and they both walked up to us. Rachael never got on him because she was pregnant, but she applied the basic Natural Horsemanship method to steer training. She was so amazed at how quickly they learned and how responsive they were.

"What I have learned when I started treating these guys not only as pets, but as part of the herd—our herd, was seeing their personalities develop. Next I started entering them in various parades, the 'Loomis before Thanksgiving parade' is a favorite, taught them how to pull a wagon, bow, step up on a pedestal—Dozer can't get all four feet on one because his legs are too short. I taught Jazzy by using a clicker, and I still don't know what in heck I am doing with a clicker, but he picked it up so quick. Now it is just a hand signal." As we developed that partnership, they, genuinely seem to enjoy spending time with me and are willing to learn new things."

"Did you use treats at all with your clicker training?"

"Yeah, but because Jazzy was young, had horns and all the energy of a young one, he would sometimes try to mug me a little bit, so I thought, you know what, he loves his belly scratched, why take a chance at getting broadsided by an ever-growing horn? They do get their cookies afterwards which are just alfalfa and oat hay cubes. Another thing I have to do is be sure and fly spray Jazzy very well before I work with him. Longhorns use their horns like hands. They can lift a calf out of a pond, scratch their backs and nail a fly on their rump. I don't want to be in the way of an instinctual move like that. So, I make sure flies aren't an issue when we work together."

"Oh my gosh, *yes* to the fly spray, and I wondered about using treats because I use them, but every animal can get pushy, and I was trying to envision having that happen with a Longhorn. I agree, belly scratches are much better. Tell me about riding. Do you just walk?"

"No, actually the first video on my website: Texaslonghornexperience.com is a video we did on a trail of Jazzy and me loping. Now you have to understand, I had probably only been on a horse about twelve times, but I had loped so I knew the feeling. I had ridden Jazzy probably more than 50 times, but I had never loped him; I didn't know how he would respond. I had a plan. There was a nice trail with some cattle in a field at the end, and he liked to go visit them. So, I thought I would point him in that direction. Prior to that, I had taken him to another friend's arena and asked a very well-known trainer to get on Jazzy and put him into a lope—I wanted to see what it looked like. He had never been on a cow before, but with all the skill and confidence that he had, he quickly had Jazzy in a lope around the arena. He looked like a rocking horse. The trainer said, 'This feels like a gaited horse.' I thought that didn't look dangerous at all, I was sure *I* could do it.

"I got my friend to video us, pointed Jazzy toward the cows, encouraged him to trot, and then lope. With all the ground work and 'in the saddle' time I had put in, he loped away from the cows just as easily. It was fun. That ride is on my website (I have since learned to lower my hands when I ride)."

"Hey," I said, "can I ask you a question that you don't have to answer, but how old were you when started all this saddle cattle work?"

"57 and I'm 66 now."

"Oh my gosh, lady! I love you. You truly are an inspiration!"

"Oh, thanks, but I've learned green on green does create black and blue. I *have* injured myself and ended up in the hospital twice, but by no fault of Jazzy's."

"Well, we horse people fall off and go to the hospital too. OK, so you are loping down towards the cows—now here is a question. You know when cows are loose, they buck and jump and have a grand time. You aren't afraid Jazzy will take off and do that while you are running towards the other cows out of the sheer joy of running?"

"Well, I worked with him so much, and again, his head is under control with the nose bit. He did that once in the arena when he was much younger. He saw Dozer at the other end and thought he'd run down there and meet him, and bounced me off. I wasn't as good a rider then as I am now. We loped down to the cows in the field, stopped and waited about ten minutes and then came back. I could tell he was getting tired. Cows are more whoa than go, remember.

"On the website is a video of us in an arena calf sorting. That is the kind of area work he *loves*. At first the calves didn't take him seriously—they were like, 'Oh you are one of us.' My trainer told me to make a lot of noise on top of him, because the calves were not taking us seriously. He got a little too close and hooked one in the butt and the calf scurried off with the rest following, so I learned not to get that close, just close enough to make them move.

"The only thing he was ever afraid of was a llama. That is one time I got hurt. It was New Year's Day and a friend and I were riding. She was on Dozer and we went a different way that took us by someone's home that had a llama. He saw that llama and went, 'Holy cow, *what* is that?' He was nervous and a few doors down we got back to my friend's house where he had been before and was just fine. But today he was nervous and when we got to the house, her three dogs jumped off the couch, ran to the storm door, jumped up on it and started barking. I was in the process of getting out of the saddle when this happened and Jazzy jumped and twisted in place. I remember flying off saying, 'Oh for God's sakes.' I ended up with three pins in my femur, a broken toe, and a fractured ankle. I was on the ground, I couldn't get up—and you know a horse might run off, but when Jazzy saw that I fell, he turned full around and put his head down to the ground and just stared at me.

"My friend walked Jazzy back to the horse trailer, but the whole time he had his head cocked back looking at me, I could just sense that he had feelings about what happened. He looked very concerned. Later when I came back from the hospital, he was up in the pasture chewing his cud; he saw the truck and I stuck my arm out of the window and shook it like a cow would shake its horn. Immediately he did the same thing. It took me two months to get back down to the pasture to see him. When I did, he arched his back and ducked his head and made strange gurgling noises. So I know he has a real connection with me.

"The second time I got hurt I was knocked unconscious by an altercation that Jazzy got into with Dozer. The boys were now a little older and I was starting to see that if I did something with Dozer first like put on a halter or harness him to hook to a wagon, Jazzy would get all excited."

"Do you think he was jealous?"

"No, more like Dozer was incapacitated and this was his chance to get the upper hand. Every now and then I would see Jazzy challenge Dozer in the pasture."

I chuckled. "Mercy, that would be no challenge to me, what was Dozer thinking? I would suggest he run the other way."

"Dozer has a low center of gravity, so he could push Jazzy half way across the pasture, and I have video of that, and Jazzy turns around and runs away."

"Jazzy never used his horns on Dozer?"

"Well, he may have because Dozer is lame now; I will get to that later. I began to realize that if I wanted to get Dozer, I had to get Jazzy first. But that was after I got knocked unconscious. What happened was that I decided I was going to do a lesson on the pedestal with Jazzy and I was going to tie Dozer up, thankfully with a quick release snap. I had Jazzy up on the pedestal, dropped the lead rope to teach him to 'stand/stay' while I walked around him. Well, he saw Dozer tied up and he decided to get right off that pedestal and go after him. I grabbed the long lead rope and tried to pull him back, and the next thing I remember is that I am waking up on the ground; I had hit my head on the pedestal.

"Dozer had been able to pull loose because of the quick release and they must have taken the fight out to the pasture. The road is right next to the fence line, and from the ground I saw a brown truck slowing down and I thought that someone was going to come and help me, but he just drove off. I think he slowed down to see them fight and never even saw me lying in the dirt. The occasional times they would do that again, Dozer always won. A year ago, I noticed that Dozer had a little limp and I took him to our teaching hospital where they did some ultrasounds, x-rays, and a complete exam, but couldn't find anything. They decided it must be a soft tissue trauma; well the only thing that I can think of that might have done that was if he slipped when they were going at it. Now Jazzy was challenging Dozer more. He may have gotten him down and used his horns. He can't really use the tips because they are so long, but he could have hit his head into Dozer's hip for instance. From then on I have had to separate them because I cannot take that risk again. Now they have to take turns in the pasture. It is sad, but much safer.

"Now when we ride on the trails, I always have the person riding Dozer to be very aware of the fact that these guys want to behave badly. Particularly when Dozer is out of the pasture and you could just see the gleam in Jazzy's eye. It became less and less fun. Also, I use Jazzy's halter and his nose bit when I take him anywhere for that extra safety. I don't have much time to ride anymore with my new job, but when I do ride with anyone, it is just my friends Debby and Lacy, and they both have donkeys that get along well with Jazzy."

I laughed and said, "I can see that. I have been thinking that how cows think is a lot like my mules, so a donkey would be a lot the same. So you don't go loping off into the sunset anymore on Jazzy?"

"Well, I do in the summer. We don't go very far or stay out very long, and I almost always ride with my friends because that is safer. There are a lot of horses in this area and when we first started riding the boys and would come across horse riders, we always stopped and hollered letting them know there was a cow ahead. Usually the girls riding the horses are talking and not really paying good attention. Everybody stops and we ask the horse riders if they want us to get off the trail, or just stand still and let them go around. Every horse's response can be different. It is usually the 'cow horses' that are the most spooked. The cows are out of context here, it doesn't make sense to them!

"But one thing I have noticed, Rose, is really interesting. We always keep it safe, cows like to stand still—and the donkeys too, I guess, but the more we go out and run into horses that get used to us, more and more horses who have *never* seen someone riding a cow, have *no* reaction to it."

I said, "Right, they somehow pick it out of the universe. It is like the 100th Monkey effect. The idea basically is that when a certain critical number achieves awareness, it may be communicated from mind to mind. I love that story. It is an amazing concept."

"We invite horse riders to follow us if they want to condition their horses, and some do. We have a good rapport with the horse community. The only problem came from a 'dressage queen.' We had gotten permission to ride in an area for a lesson when Jazzy was younger, as long as I was willing to share it with someone else. I was walking Jazzy up to the area where there was only this dressage rider. She took one look at Jazzy and said dramatically, 'You are *not* going to bring *that thing* in here, are you?'

"We have taken both of them to events; the most memorable is going to senior events at churches or senior care facilities. I have had several very senior seniors tell me with tears in their eyes how wonderful it was to see a cow again. One remembered milking a cow before school, and then *riding* it to school and back home and milk it again. It was just delightful to hear some of these cattle stories."

"How old are the boys now and what are you currently doing with them?"

"Jazzy is eight and Dozer nine and a half. I had to teach them that I could take one out of the pasture and leave the other one. Thankfully, no one ever figured out how to jump the fence. There was a horse in the pasture for company. Now that Dozer is lame, I am just doing a lot of ground work, therapeutic bodywork, petting, loving on him, and walking with him; he can step up on the pedestal with his front feet, and bow. Dozer isn't as well broke as Jazzy, so he is a little more stubborn; I have ridden Jazzy more because he is kind of a star, and he was more responsive to the training. That being said, horse people friends love to ride Dozer, he is more like an old trail horse, following Jazzy.

"One day my friend Lacy and I were riding the boys. She had a helmet camera on. We were at the Taylor Ranch bird sanctuary and we stopped at one of the water troughs—and this was about five years ago— I turned Jazzy's head to the left to keep him in the stopped position. What that did was make it so Jazzy could see Dozer straight on. Jazzy just sort of cocked his head like a challenge, Dozer's ears flipped and the next thing we knew they were in a head fight with both of us on their backs! We were able to quickly pull them away from each other because we had the nose bits. We didn't really understand what happened until we saw the video and saw their body language, and then we realized we had to keep them more away from each other. We started back down the trail with Dozer mad as hell, following Jazzy. Then he speeds up and butts Jazzy in the rear end. Jazzy jumps in place, and trots off a few steps. So, we learned something that day—keep them more apart. Even in the parades we were careful to keep them a certain distance from each other."

I said, "Now *that is* different from horses and mules. We had been commenting on how cows, donkeys and mules were similar in many aspects, but this *is* definitely unusual."

"They are headstrong. That is the way they see life. When we take them out, we let them know they are working, but we hadn't realized they would act out like that on the trail, but we learned. We learned to be aware and watch their body language."

I said, "You are great now because you can read them. Many

horse people never really learn to read their horses, mules or donkeys and it can cause many problems for which the animal is always blamed, and many times it isn't their fault. And when it comes to 'the pain thing' riders and owners need to be very vigilant to read small problems before they become big one. For instance, if a horse or mule has a sore back issue, it can escalate to bucking, running off or some other evasion to being ridden. Or many do not like the girth being tightened, so you should do it in stages, not all at once. My mule, Susie, hates that. Turned out when the chiropractor came, she had a rib out of place. What is it like girthing up a steer?"

"The biggest problem was finding the right size, one big enough, but they never seemed to mind it being tightened, but I forgot to tell you more about putting in the nose bit and that early training. We had the vet come out when they were about eighteen months old; she numbed the nose with a paste, then an injection of anesthetic, then when they were perfectly numb, she surgically opened up the septum and inserted the nose bit. It is good to have the nose bit with the rings inside the nostrils so they don't get caught on anything. Then it heals for six weeks, and then we hook up the long lines and drive them. We have someone lead them with their halter to show them what we want. Later we get on and ride."

I told Kimberly that I absolutely loved her story, and loved her steers, especially that big boy with those awesome horns. Kimberly had some hints for anyone who might want to do it: Imprint at birth, do basic ground handling when they are babies and keep doing it as they get older (especially if it is a longhorn!), and if you know how to train a horse, or know someone who can, you can train any willing bovine.

"See you on the trails!" she said.

JANE KERR

Jane is the lovely person on our cover. I met her through Bev Pettit, the photographer. When I gave Bev an idea of what I wanted for the cover picture, she sent me several to look at. I fell in love with "Jane." The book wouldn't be complete without her story, so Nadine and I again went south to Wickenburg, Arizona.

Jane said, "I am from North Dakota originally and moved to the Scottsdale area to work for my aunt who had horses when I was eighteen. My family were not horse people, and I think they thought this was 'just a stage' I was going through, and I would grow out of it—but I never really did. I worked for a couple of other people after my aunt, and I met my husband, Gibb, while working for a different ranch. He was just starting his own trail riding business at that time. His first memory of life was riding a pony—horses are in his blood—that is for sure.

"He got a trail riding contract up in Park City, Utah, and asked me to go along with him. That was just a summer deal and we came back south to Arizona for the winter. In this business you have to follow the seasons and keep your horses fed and working, otherwise they become a huge expense."

"They are the same horses and you take them back and forth with you? How many of them?"

"Yes. We started out with fifteen or twenty, I think we have around one hundred right now."

"Oh my. You don't haul them all back and forth, do you?"

"Yes, pretty close."

"Now that should be a good story. How in heck do you do that, and do you own the place in Utah and here?"

"You do it in stages, and you try to be organized as much as you can, but it basically works out that where there is an empty space in a trailer, you put a horse—and its equipment. Our business is a contract business; we contract horses for different places, so we don't own the land. We had worked for Ande at the Flying E for a couple of years—Gibb leased horses out to the Flying E. Then he started getting more lease opportunities, and our business grew. We can lease out a horse to a person for a season or for instance, forty horses to the Flying E.

"Roughly sixty will go out on lease and we keep about thirty-five for us to use. In Utah, I don't do a lot of the rides, I am more the manager. Down here I get to do more rides."

I asked her if she had any funny, scary, or human-interest stories to share.

"We are a very safe outfit; we have few scary things, but when you deal with animals you never quite know what might happen. I remember when my husband and I first started he had twenty horses and he leased them out to a friend of ours in Sedona and then we went to work for him. We stayed in a bunk house and I was the only girl. It was tough, but you do what you have to, like wait in line for the bathroom.

"It is hard getting started in any business, but I remember we did a few rides in Park City and we didn't get paid right away. We were broke—we took our last ten dollars to get white paint to make a 'If you liked your ride, hug your horse and tip your guide' sign. I did two rides and didn't get any tips. That is kinda the thing with this business—you work for tips. Back then I did it all, and my husband shod the horses. Now we have someone who does all of our shoeing."

I said, "Tell me a little about your horses because they have to be special. Do you raise your horses?"

"They are. Without our horses we would have no business. We have just started raising a few horses. It has become harder and harder to find the right horses for our business because the market has really changed in the last ten years. We used to be able to find a nice trail gelding for about $1500.00, now we can't. I think in part it is because there are not as many cowboys making good horses anymore. Horses need a job to be good, and the cowboys out riding every day, made great horses, and they might have eight horses in their string. When the horses got past a certain age, they would 'retire' them to a more easy life like what we do. And cowboys like to trade horses. If one doesn't exactly suit him, he will sell and get another one, but there is nothing really wrong with that horse. But the horses have to have a work ethic, and be trustworthy. We still go to some sales back East; some are Amish horses because they use their horses for everything. They are starting to ride their horses more because they will bring more at the sales."

228

"Do you have horses that don't make it and you have to rehome?"

"Sure. Some horses love this and will do it forever, some get tired of it, and you want to tell before it goes past the horse's expression that they are unhappy. We are good at reading our horses, and that is where the experience of being around *a lot* of different horses come in."

"How would you explain reading a horse?"

"For instance, you might notice that the horse's eyes get a wide, worried look; he might move around a lot. Some of these horses are well trained and with a rider who is moving all around and jiggling the reins, he cannot figure out what he is supposed to do. We can sell these horses and make pretty good money because many people want a horse that has 'seen the country' but is more sensitive. There is usually a place for a horse even if not with us. We had a horse who was a bad cribber (wood chewer/air sucker, a *nasty* habit). Not only is it a bad habit, but all the other horses can pick it up. I told the guy who came to see this horse that he was *perfect* and he was beautiful, except he was a cribber. I wanted to be sure the man understood what cribbing was, and that this horse did it. The man said, 'Oh yes, I have one at home that cribs—they can crib together!' So that horse found the perfect home."

"So, tell me about moving one hundred or so horses."

"We have two trailers, and a friend of ours has a big semi-trailer that can haul about twenty-five to thirty, so he will usually take two loads and we juggle the rest of the horses between contract rides at both places. The trip takes about ten hours and we drive straight through. We always try to leave early in case of problems, such as flat tires."

I said, "I showed horses for nearly thirty years, and I had some 'incidents.' Surely you have too."

"I do. My husband and I usually haul our rigs together. We might leave half an hour apart, but we are on the road at the same time, so we can help each other. The first time that I took a load by myself was this fall coming down to Wickenburg. It was the last group of horses; I think there were eight, head to tail in the stock trailer. One horse is tied one way and the other so its rear was at the other horse's head. There are fewer squabbles, you can get more in, and it isn't uncomfortable for the horses this way. The horses are happy to go to Arizona; they don't want to stay in Utah for the winter!

"I was headed south, the horses were fussing a little more than usual—I had mares, geldings and some younger horses that weren't used

229

to each other. As I was coming through St. George, Utah, I looked in my mirror and my trailer fender is hanging off to the side. A tire had blown."

"You didn't feel it blow?"

"No, I think because that load was moving around anyway, I didn't notice. Later I found out that it had just blown because I had a guy behind me tell me that. I put my hazards on and since I was just coming into St. George I wanted to get to the exit and then pull off. As I was hobbling along, I noticed that that guy was still behind me in a tool truck. He pulled in front of me when I stopped, he was just a young kid, and he got out of his truck, got a jack and started going to work on the trailer."

"How would you jack it up with all those horses in there? We had one of those 'jiffy jack tandem axel ramp' things that you pulled your good tire up on, and you could leave all the horses in the trailer. We never went anywhere without it."

"We always have a 'trailer aid' which is what we call them, in every single truck. But for some reason, there was *no* trailer aid in that truck. We have water, emergency food, everything you might need if you were stranded, in the trucks, but this time, no trailer aid. This kid got the jack out of my truck because it was a bigger one, but we couldn't get it up. He said he would escort me in and that there was a trailer place right next door to where he worked, and should be able to help me. I drove slowly, limping in. Because the trailer had two axels and two wheels, I could do that. I didn't grow up driving trucks and trailers, I just learned in the last couple of years, so just going in and out and backing up trying to find someone to fix the tire was stressful. I stopped at the Dodge dealership—I was driving a Dodge—but he said they didn't have time. Then I went into the RV place and they said they were kinda busy, next I went over to the Mitsubishi place and he said 'Oh yes, we will help you.' He was so nice; he took pictures of the horses, and gave me the key to their little service truck and told me to drive across the road to the tire store and get a spare tire. I had a spare which was put on the trailer, but I couldn't do it because I couldn't get the trailer jacked up. He didn't want me to go down the road without a spare. They get me all squared away and I asked what I owed them, and he said, 'Don't worry about it.' I tipped him, but they were just super."

"Mitsubishi, huh? We must remember them!"

"Yeah, and the kid who stopped was just like an angel. I didn't even have time to panic about anything. When I called my husband later, he was really mad that he couldn't help me; he was already here in

Wickenburg. And then the trailer lights went out and because of the tire situation, I was two hours late, so drove the last way with no lights, and it was dark. Every time I saw someone come up behind me, I turned my flashers on—they worked. My husband said that for my peace of mind, anytime a tire needs changing at the ranch, *I* am going to do it. I am fine with that because I need to.

"The trailer was brand new too because my husband wants good stuff so we don't have breakdowns, however, sometimes things just happen anyway. But we made it home. The broken trailer fender stuck out like those metal spikes you see on chariot wheels; we must have looked pretty funny going down the road. He said he isn't going to let me travel by myself again, but I said, 'It's fine, I handled it.' He actually got two flats on his way down, and they were brand new tires. He was mad because he was charged $800.00 for a Chinese tire and I got mine for $400.00 and it was a much better tire."

"What is it like living with a hundred horses?"

"For one thing, you never get any time off, they have to be fed and cared for and you never know what will happen. I have to take a horse in to have his eye removed tomorrow. We got him a month ago, super nice horse, but he somehow banged his eye really bad, and it wouldn't heal. We think he will do just fine for us after he adjusts to having one eye. When we first got started, we had a big draft cross named Buckeye that was an excellent horse. One day we were out feeding and he just reared up, fell over backwards and died. We think it was a heart attack. Our horses mean a lot to us, but you also have to look at it financially. With the one who is having the eye removed, we thought about it, but he is a young horse, so we will do the surgery. We will mate him with a driving partner since he is broke to drive and he doesn't need to see to the inside to do that job.

"We feed alfalfa grass mix hay, once a day in big tractor tires. They eat the alfalfa first and then graze on the grass until it is gone. We feed them all in one large group. We have about one hundred horses, but they are seldom all in one place as we have the different horse leases. We don't keep that many here at this ranch because we worry about the well. For instance, when they get here, thirty-five horses go right over to the Flying E."

"How many do you have here right now?"

"You don't really count, because then you start doing the math and realize how much hay you are feeding, but we have about fifty.

Right out here by us are some mares that are pregnant. We keep them separate from the others. We have gotten some of our geldings out of Mexico, and they don't have a vet castrate them, they just do it themselves, so many are 'proud cut' meaning not all the testicle has been removed and they still act like stallions. It actually isn't a big deal unless you have mares in the herd. All of our leases want geldings anyway."

"And you don't have attitude problems?"

"No. I do think there are different variations of being proud cut because I have seen one that you wouldn't put a person on, and another that is a great kid's horse. When we first got him, my husband rode him and he bucked hard every morning. After about two years he stopped, then I rode him, the guides rode him and finally we thought he was suitable to be in the 'string.' He was a horse we bought when we were just getting started. We didn't have a lot of money, we knew he wasn't the perfect dude horse, but we thought we could train him. Then too, when you are young you like a challenge—now we don't like as many challenges! The people he liked the best were those who were scared to death and just hung onto the saddle horn. He realized those folks were no threat to him. If he had a more aggressive rider, he would show you attitude: 'Bring it.' And that is part of your job of matching your horses to your rider. That horse could have been a bad horse that somebody probably would have done away with."

I said, "I have read stories of other animals—dogs, horses, mules—realizing that a person 'knows nothing, and is not a threat to me.'"

"Yes. And it is funny because that horse is probably twenty-seven years old now and I guarantee you that if my husband would saddle him, he'd buck. But now he is a top kid horse. He is kind—I have had a kid fall off and he just stood there. He is a good horse.

"Sometimes we will get a horse that needs a special diet, a stall or a blanket, and we sell those, and people are happy to have them to coddle and ride. We cannot do that. We like Quarter horse crosses, or draft crosses. Temperament-wise, they are very good. The bred mares back there have just enough draft to make them a little larger, but not really big and we are breeding them to a Quarter horse stud. We will see how it goes. Right now we have some three-year-olds under saddle and I might be biased, but I like them. They might be just a little bit too gentle. With some gentle horses we buy, they do one ride, and then later when we ask them to go out on another they are like: Are you serious? They don't have a good work ethic, and the people can't/won't kick them. We don't ask *that* much of them! A horse that has a bit more spunk, spirit to them, those are the ones who will keep going. We also were getting some horses out of Mexico."

"Why would you do that?"

"Yeah, it seems odd—because they are a 'tool' down there. They still need the horse to do a job. They are not pets. They are more like the Amish horses. I think the breeding is Quarter horse and maybe some Andalusian. The dude ranches like the Andalusian blood because they have a good lope, and the dudes can ride it. We have some out there that you can hardly get to trot. They go from a walk to a lope. The horses are not always very pretty, but they are tough."

"But you sort of need pretty, don't you? Your people wouldn't want to ride an ugly 'jug head' would they?"

"Absolutely, but it is funny. We have a buckskin horse that is the ugliest horse you have ever seen. He has a huge head, no hip, but he is a buckskin and everybody thinks he is the most beautiful horse we have."

We laughed. I said, "We horse people say, 'you can't ride color,' but dudes *can*!"

Jane said, "We did our wedding pictures out here and he was the only darn horse that would get in the picture. I was so mad because all the other horses stood back but he kept getting in all the pictures.

"One of the hardest things with a hundred or so horses is keeping the coggins papers organized. Each horse has a blood test every year, which is required by law. Every now and then the driver of the semi will get pulled over and asked for them, so each horse has to have his correct papers. Sometimes when you get ready to load for a lease job, a horse will come up lame, and then you have to replace it and get the correct coggins papers. Another thing which is just part of the job is picking the right horse for the right rider on these trail rides. For instance, if you get a rider who is scared, and will end up just hanging onto the saddle horn, you can't pick a laid-back horse that needs to be kicked to keep up, because they will never do that.

"What people like in horses is different. My husband will like a horse and when I ride it, I don't know why, and at times he gets on one that I love and he doesn't. One of my pet peeves is someone asking if this is a good horse because they are all good, they just fit people differently."

"Do you have a weight limit?"

"That is always a hard subject. Roughly it is 250, but if you get a super athletic person who is more, a horse can carry that weight better than someone who is out of shape. It is more physical ability. We say that you have to be able to mount your horse unassisted. We help them get on here, but if something happens on the trail, it is a safety issue that they have to be able to get back on."

"Have you ever had anything to do with mules? They have become my new equine love."

"I have met a few really good mules, also a few really bad ones."

"Well, tell. Tell your bad mule stories."

"We had a big draft mule called Teton. My husband went to shoe him one day and the mule jerked his front foot away. My husband kinda poked him in the belly and said, 'Knock it off.' When he bent down to pick that foot up again, Teton kicked him in the face. He waited until he knew he could get him. That is a mule for you, they wait until they can deliver their 'justice.'"

I said, "That is absolutely correct. He never should have hit him; you cannot treat a mule like you do a horse. They will take correction and punishment, but it has to be fair. The horses are more forgiving, I think."

"Exactly. Nope, that is very true. We had a palomino mule that I loved, but the thing with mules with this business is some people don't like it, they say, you are on a donkey, or an ass. And then there are people who specifically ask for a mule, so you can never win. I do like the mules for back country trips. We don't have any right now. I do remember one time I was trail riding a mule and she stopped and took her hind foot and scratched behind her ear while I was on her! Now that is balance and talent."

"Are you happy with your life and what you are doing? Any thoughts to share?"

"I didn't know I would be doing this, I kinda fell into it, got a little lucky, and worked hard."

"You enjoy working with people as well as the animals?"

"I do, but probably more the animals. The hardest part about this business is finding people to work for us that are good with both. A lot of good horse people are good with horses because they are not good with people—they prefer horses. Another thing that is very frustrating to me is that people think we don't have compassion for our horses because we make them go on trail rides and work. I think it is just the opposite.

These horses like their job, if they don't, like I said earlier, we find them another home."

"Do you have any older horses? What happens to them when they are no longer useful?"

"It is hard. My husband just lost his really good horse to cancer last year, and we have Rooster, an old horse, that has been with us for years. When his time comes, we will put him down and bury him. When they have paid your rent and worked for you, you have to do the right thing."

I said, "That is the sentiment that the ranch women have who raise cattle for the table. They love them and want their lives to be good, and for them to have a 'good end.' But they still are a business. You gals all appreciate what the animals do for you, and you are good stewards."

I said that I knew, after chatting with my ranch ladies, that this kind of life was hard, but rewarding and they would never change it.

Jane shared a quote to end her story: *This is the worst way to make a living, but it is the best way of life.*

And that says it all.

ABOUT THE AUTHOR

Rose retired from showing and breeding nationally recognized Tennessee Walking Horses and managing the New Acre Farm boarding facility in 2012, and moved with Hal and Bob to a small horse friendly ranch-subdivision in Prescott, Arizona. She continues to support diverse animal welfare groups and write about her continuing escapades. She is an artist and now enjoys the West as inspiration. Moving with the human family were the horses: Praise Hallelujah, and Sunday Praise (*The Horse That Wouldn't Trot*), the mules: Susie Q, Ruth Ann and Magic (*Mules, Mules and More Mules*), Cagney and Lacy the geese, Hershey, Lady Blue, Arizona and Maggie, the dogs and Charm, Molly and Possum, the cats.

Rose's favorite relaxation comes from riding Susie Q on the cow paths and exploring the Prescott National Forest.

All profits from Rose's books are donated to small "Mom and Pop" animal support groups. She can be contacted through her website: www.rosemiller...